Ernest Hemingway

Thought in Action

Mark Cirino

THE UNIVERSITY OF WISCONSIN PRESS

The University of Wisconsin Press
1930 Monroe Street, 3rd Floor
Madison, Wisconsin 53711-2059
uwpress.wisc.edu

3 Henrietta Street
London WC2E 8LU, England
eurospanbookstore.com

Printed in the United States of America

Library of Congress Cataloging-in-Publication Data
Cirino, Mark, 1971–
Ernest Hemingway : thought in action / Mark Cirino.
p.   cm.—(Studies in American thought and culture)
Includes bibliographical references and index.
ISBN 978-0-299-28654-5 (pbk.: alk. paper)
ISBN 978-0-299-28653-8 (e-book)
1. Hemingway, Ernest, 1899–1961—Criticism and interpretation.
2. Consciousness in literature.
I. Title.   II. Series: Studies in American thought and culture.
PS3515.E37Z584615   2012
813′.52—dc23
2011041962

A version of chapter 1 was published in *Papers on Language and Literature* 47, no. 2 (Spring 2011),
copyright © 2011 by the Board of Trustees, Southern Illinois University Edwardsville; reproduced
by permission. A version of chapter 3 was published in *Ernest Hemingway and the Geography of Memory*,
edited by Mark Cirino and Mark P. Ott (Kent, OH: Kent State University Press, 2010), copyright
© 2009 by the Kent State University Press; reprinted with permission. A version of chapter 5 was
published in *The Hemingway Review* 30, no. 1 (Fall 2010), copyright © 2010 the Ernest Hemingway
Foundation; all rights reserved.

for
Kristen

and for our two sons
Luca *and* **Noah**

Contents

Acknowledgments

I am indebted to so many people for their kindness to me during the writing of this book. I am proud to acknowledge some of them here.

This book could not have been written without generous grants from the Hemingway Society, the John F. Kennedy Museum and Library, the Graduate Center of the City University of New York, and the University of Evansville.

André Aciman, Mario DiGangi, Marc Dolan, Edmund L. Epstein, John Freccero, and George Guida for their expertise, encouragement, and generosity during my graduate studies.

Morris Dickstein for graciously reading so much of my work and for all the enjoyable, valuable discussions — I'm so grateful.

Larry Kritzman and John Paul Russo.

Susan F. Beegel, Kirk Curnutt, Carl P. Eby, Robert Paul Lamb, Erik Nakjavani, and Mark P. Ott from the Hemingway Society for their support, suggestions, candor, and curiosity.

Matt Blank, Matthew J. Bolton, Anton Borst, David Davis, and Caroline Hellman for their friendship and counsel and understanding. Thanks, guys.

My colleagues at the University of Evansville: Arthur Brown, Dan Byrne, Larry Caldwell, Bill Hemminger, Kristie Hochwender, and Lesley Pleasant. Thanks to Kevin Kay and Laura Summers for their many contributions and outsized patience.

Gwen Walker, Paul S. Boyer, Adam Mehring, and the entire team at the University of Wisconsin Press.

To Antonio and Linda D. Cirino (1941–2007). For everything.

Abbreviations of Hemingway Texts

ARIT   *Across the River and into the Trees*
BL   *By-line: Ernest Hemingway: Selected Articles and Dispatches of Four Decades*
CSS   *The Complete Short Stories of Ernest Hemingway: The Finca Vigía Edition*
DIA   *Death in the Afternoon*
FTA   *A Farewell to Arms*
FWBT   *For Whom the Bell Tolls*
GOE   *The Garden of Eden*
IIS   *Islands in the Stream*
MF   *A Moveable Feast*
MF-RE   *A Moveable Feast: The Restored Edition*
NAS   *The Nick Adams Stories*
OMS   *The Old Man and the Sea*
Poems   *Complete Poems*
SL   *Ernest Hemingway: Selected Letters, 1917–1961*
SS   *The Short Stories of Ernest Hemingway*
SAR   *The Sun Also Rises*
Facsimile *The Sun Also Rises: A Facsimile Edition*
UK   *Under Kilimanjaro*

Ernest Hemingway

Introduction

Ernest Hemingway and
the Life of the Mind

This is what I enjoy. This is the best part of life. The life of the mind. This is
not killing kudu.

Green Hills of Africa

Live the full life of the mind, exhilarated by new ideas, intoxicated by the
Romance of the unusual.

"Banal Story"

*I*n 1921, Ernest Hemingway wrote a frivolous epistolary fragment entitled
"Because I Think Deeper."[1] The 1,800-word narrative is remarkable for its
explanation of the source of the narrator's own woes: he is burdened with the
artist's hypersensitivity, an impulse to intellectualize, an excess of consciousness.
The narrator, Ralph Spencer Williams, writes to his fiancée's sister and suggests
what might be the source of the constant tension that divides the two of them:

> Through 23 years of my life I have, through some unknown reason, reverenced
> an ideal peculiar to mankind, an ideal which has grown in magnitude to such a
> high estate of thought that even the slightest reference to it causes a feeling of

resentment to show in me from within, and I cannot help it showing. . . . I have always thought, and thought, and thought perhaps too much so, but always placing myself in the other person's position and thinking what I would do under the circumstances in their position, then continuing in the path of what I think is just. (qtd. in Griffin 162)

Ralph's letter continues, explaining that his sometimes-prickly personality can be attributed to his cerebral, introspective nature, which is difficult for other people to understand:

I know that I do not enter into a lot of jests and humorous pastimes, bringing forth amusement, and I have seen that it has been noticed at different times before this. I have regretted it always. . . . I have often tried to overcome these feelings so that they might not show on the surface, but I see I have not been successful and that they are still noticed.

I do not like to see things which do not add charm or grace to a woman because of the nature of my living and the formation of my ideal, because I think deeper and have a higher standard for such things than the average man has. (163)

As inane as this prose might be, Ralph's self-analysis anticipates the problem of the Hemingway hero in all the writing that would follow. The writer mocks his own lofty ideals; he admits to a strong impulse to contemplate or to intellectualize things, particularly the examination of other psychological and moral perspectives; and, perhaps most important, he alludes to feelings that "might not show on the surface," prefiguring Hemingway's iceberg principle of writing, in which objective facts appear for the reader to see and emotion, memory, abstractions, and vulnerability are implied but hidden from view.

Literary criticism has accused Hemingway of many things since the 1920s, but thinking too deeply is not one of them. Hemingway himself was complicit in promoting the stereotype of his life and his work as fiercely anti-intellectual. Even within the Hemingway text, characters who do think deeply tend to be lampooned as ineffectual navel-gazers or scorned as feeble and effeminate. The recurring putdown from the lunkheaded assassins in "The Killers" is "bright boy" (SS 280, et passim), an insult that sets up the story's last line, the advice that the inquisitive, sensitive, idealistic hero should snuff out his imagination, that although he has an idea, he had "better not think about it" (289).[2] The title of the story, then, refers not just to those who sanction murder, those who commit it, or those who are apathetic in the face of it but also to the killers of the imagination and the innocence and sensibilities of impressionable protagonists like Nick.

The pattern of Hemingway's characterization of "deep thinking" and those who spend their time in thought can be discerned by a brief survey, each example substantiating the surface disdain for such activity. In *The Sun Also Rises*, Jake Barnes and the alcoholic novelist Harvey Stone converse about the most famous American intellectual of the age, H. L. Mencken. A pause occurs, during which the men supposedly succumb to profound contemplation:

> "Oh, nobody reads him now," Harvey said, "except the people that used to read the Alexander Hamilton Institute."
> "Well," I said. "That was a good thing, too."
> "Sure," said Harvey. So we sat and thought deeply for a while.
> "Have another port?"
> "All right," said Harvey. (50)

What is the content of this moment of rumination? Hemingway is conveying the emptiness, the lack of substance, the awkward silence. The suggestion of more wine to fill the void is quickly accepted—alcohol as a grateful alternative to serious thought, or perhaps the depressing realization of the absence of such thoughts.

In "The Three-Day Blow," from *In Our Time*, Nick Adams and his friend Bill drunkenly engage in a conversation that nominally passes for deep thoughts, as they compare the relative benefits of Nick's abstemious father to Bill's father, who may be an alcoholic. Bill refers to his father's "tough time" with drinking, to which Nick responds lamely, "It all evens up." The narrator, adopting a tone of deadpan judgment, then sums up the scene: "They sat looking into the fire and thinking of this profound truth" (SS 120). Later, the narrator wryly notes: "They were conducting the conversation on a high plane" (121), needling the two boys who fancy themselves capable of subtle abstractions, when they are merely losing control of their usual restraint under the new effects of alcohol.

Likewise, in typically lively banter between Frederic Henry and Rinaldi in *A Farewell to Arms*, the phenomenon of such deep thinking is called into question. Rinaldi begins the exchange by positioning himself as the embodiment of rational thought:

> "I am the snake. I am the snake of reason."
> "You're getting it mixed. The apple was reason."
> "No, it was the snake." He was more cheerful.

"You are better when you don't think so deeply," I said.

"I love you, baby," he said. "You puncture me when I become a great Italian thinker. But I know many things I can't say. I know more than you." (170)

Like all Hemingway heroes and narrators, including the author himself, Frederic "punctures" those who would dare to think deeply—just as Jake and the narrator of "The Three-Day Blow" mock it—deflating the characters' hot air or pretentiousness. However, Ralph Spencer Williams has already indicated why this characterization might provoke a red flag. The act of thinking deeply strikes the Hemingway hero as a sacred, painfully personal activity, to the extent that witnessing it in someone else recalls the vulnerability that such hyperconsciousness entails.

The same sort of unease with cognition exists in the final pages of Hemingway's posthumously published African novel, *Under Kilimanjaro*, which concludes with Hemingway—the fictional protagonist—examining the behavior of dung beetles and speculating on their role in his proposed religion. "I had always liked to see the dung beetles work and since I had learned that they were the sacred scarabs of Egypt . . . I thought we might find some place for them in the religion. . . . Watching them I thought of the words for a dung beetle hymn." This preposterous scenario is then examined from two outside perspectives: "Ngui and Mthuka were watching me because they knew I was in a moment of profound thought" (439). As a moment of self-parody, the description is at the same time instructive. During this lengthy (August 1953–January 1954) and important safari in Hemingway's life, the moment that he chooses to isolate explicitly as being one of serious contemplation is an instance that is obviously idiotic.

This treatment of thought echoes an earlier moment in *Under Kilimanjaro*, in which three dead baboons are positioned in a way that causes the narrator to remark, "One of the heads was tipped back in contemplation. The other two were sunk forward in the appearance of deep thought" (174). Michael Reynolds, Hemingway's preeminent biographer, characterizes the entire narrative of the African novel as being "an ironic, self-deprecating, and humorous account of the contemplative life of the writer juxtaposed against the active life of a temporary game ranger protecting the village of the Wakamba natives" (*Final Years* 285). Hemingway's fiction depended on the same juxtaposition.

Hemingway's consistent stance was to diminish—at least superficially—the profundity of his genuinely deep thoughts and to mock others and even himself when they regarded their own thoughts as being particularly valuable. However, the very act of writing begins with the premise that one considers one's own thoughts to be worth sharing; when Hemingway highlights his insipid thoughts rather than his truly intelligent or even ingenious ideas, he creates the anticerebral smokescreen behind which he operated during his entire career.

This struggle with the notion of deep thinking outlines the paradox that marks the central tension in Hemingway's fiction: on one hand, there is an excess of thought on the part of the intelligent, introspective, creative man; on the other hand, there is the burden with which such cognition saddles the protagonist. In varying inflections, the Hemingway hero must face an internal battle of managing consciousness as he attempts to negotiate through past traumas, future urgencies, and present complications.

Previous critics who have discerned a psychological depth to the Hemingway text have tended to focus on unconscious motives, engaging largely in psychoanalytic readings. Gertrude Stein's early review of Hemingway's *Three Stories and Ten Poems* pointed to Hemingway's intelligence as its strongest trait. She also advised that Hemingway "should stick to poetry and intelligence," two aspects of Hemingway's career that tend not to be celebrated. In 1924, Edmund Wilson found "profound emotions and complex states of mind" hidden beneath a deceptively simple surface of prose ("Dry Points" 340). Malcolm Cowley's influential introduction to *The Portable Hemingway* in 1944 located Hemingway's fiction in the hallowed American tradition of Poe, Melville, and Hawthorne, alluding to a dark layer lurking beneath a restrained prose style. In 1952, Philip Young revolutionized Hemingway studies with his "wound theory" that owed much to psychoanalysis, suggesting that Hemingway spent his entire career trying to exorcise traumatic memories from being blown up as a young man during World War I. Young's premise was the progenitor of various subsequent psychological investigations into Hemingway's works, most notably Kenneth S. Lynn's incendiary 1987 psychobiography, which imputed great significance into Hemingway's relationship with his mother, including the apparently scarring stigma of having been dressed up in girl's clothing as a young boy. Other critics, such as Gerry Brenner, Richard B. Hovey, Carl P. Eby, Mark Spilka, Thomas Strychacz, Richard Fantina, Erik Nakjavani, and Debra Moddelmog, along with the collaboration of Nancy Comley and Robert Scholes, have offered provocative gender and psychoanalytic readings of the man and his work.

Although these critics have made valuable contributions in identifying the psychological layer to Hemingway's work, in many ways they have skipped consciousness and headed straight for the unconscious. Hemingway is never accepted as a member of Leon Edel's pantheon of "psychological novelists," writers using the art form defined by Henry James as dramatizing "what a man thinks and what he feels" (*Art of the Novel* 66). Michael Reynolds repeats the definition that modernism as an art form chronicles the "mental reaction to things,"[3] which, Reynolds concludes, Hemingway "indeed focused on" (*Young Hemingway* 159). Contrary to high Modernists such as Ezra Pound, James Joyce, and T. S. Eliot, Hemingway's depiction of the "mental reaction" of his characters is as fascinating for its effacements and restraint as for its effusion or flamboyance.

Hemingway's characters struggled with their thoughts and feelings, because their thoughts and feelings are either unpleasant or wholly incompatible with the present moment, in which action is required. Thoughts and feelings interfere, although Hemingway's main characters are people who always do think deeply and feel intensely. When Nick Adams observes, "Thinking was no good. It started and went on so" (CSS 497), it is tempting to read the first sentence and ignore the explanation. Thought is feared because of its power and distrusted because of its unpredictability, not scorned because of its unimportance. Nick is keenly aware of thought's capacity to overwhelm his performance and to paralyze him for any activity or responsibility. The Hemingway hero is introspective enough to know his own impulse to think about things, which often leads to overthinking things; this tendency becomes the constant struggle that dominates the Hemingway text.

A celebrated example of this tension offers a useful illustration. The history behind F. Scott Fitzgerald's suggested revisions of Hemingway's 1927 short story "Fifty Grand" has been well chronicled. However, this incident pertains to the present discussion not as a salacious biographical anecdote or to provide retrospective textual minutiae. Instead, this conflict's enduring controversy is itself the issue.

"Fifty Grand," included in Hemingway's second volume of short stories, *Men Without Women*, was inspired by the anecdote with which the typescript draft begins:

> Up at the gym over the Garden one time somebody says to Jack, "Say Jack how did you happen to beat Leonard anyway?" And Jack says, "Well, you see Benny's an awful smart boxer. All the time he's in there he's thinking and all the time he's thinking I was hitting him."[4] (qtd. in Beegel, *Craft of Omission* 15)

Fitzgerald's objection was similar to his misgivings about the original beginning of *The Sun Also Rises*, what he perceived to be Hemingway's "tendency to envelope or . . . to *embalm* in mere wordiness an anecdote or joke" (*Life in Letters* 142, emphasis in original). As Susan Beegel notes in her discussion of Hemingway's impulse to include the anecdote, "Thinking takes time, and boxing is a sport in which speed is of the essence" (15).[5] Beegel's point must be extended: life, at times, is a sport in which speed is of the essence. Hemingway's characters find themselves (or place themselves) in situations in which a quick, strategic, pragmatic response is more appropriate than contemplation and conceptualization, despite the characters' natural tendencies to indulge their memories, imaginative speculation, and ruminations.

Hemingway's remorse over his acquiescence to Fitzgerald's edits of "Fifty Grand" festered literally for the rest of his life. In his 1959 essay, "The Art of the Short Story," Hemingway recounts his version of the circumstances behind the editorial change and his regret over excising "that lovely revelation of the metaphysics of boxing." Hemingway's essay taunts Fitzgerald for not appreciating that Hemingway was "trying to explain to him how a truly great boxer like Jack Britton functioned" (89). Hemingway considered Fitzgerald's change a "mutilation," and he harbored resentment until his death. One reason for this enduring grudge might be that Hemingway rued disobeying his instincts as a writer, ironically behaving in the same way as the excerpt negatively portrays Benny Leonard. Although Fitzgerald and others might not have understood it, for Hemingway, the central thrust to his literary project was to dramatize the compromised functioning of thought as the modern consciousness is incorporated into the activities of the twentieth-century man of action.

Hemingway's portrayal of thinking during war examined this compromise at its most extreme. In Hemingway's introduction to *Men at War*, the anthology of war writing he edited, he writes, "Cowardice, as distinguished from panic, is almost always simply a lack of ability to suspend the functioning of the imagination. Learning to suspend your imagination and live completely in the very second of the present minute with no before and no after is the greatest gift a soldier can acquire. It, naturally, is the opposite of all those gifts a writer should have" (xxiv). Hemingway elsewhere confirms that imagination "is the one thing beside honesty that a good writer must have" (BL 215). Hemingway's articulation of this conflict is a revelation: he is here disclosing the tension that defines his work, the internal struggle between a man of action and a man of thought. This dichotomy is always in play and sometimes baldly explicit. Robert Jordan initially coaxes himself, "Turn off the thinking now. . . . You're a bridge-blower now. Not a thinker" (FWBT 17), just as he later disingenuously asserts, "My mind is in suspension until we win the war" (245). David Bourne, also a writer, recalls his similar attitude during the war: "I suspended thinking about it while it was happening. I only felt and saw and acted and thought tactically" (GOE 184). In a 1938 letter to Maxwell Perkins, Hemingway blames his depressed mood on the rigors of living in a war zone while simultaneously trying to write his stories of the Spanish Civil War: "If I sound bitter or gloomy throw it out. It's that it takes one kind of training and frame of mind to do what I've been doing and another to write prose" (Bruccoli, *Only Thing* 253). In *Across the River and into the Trees*, Hemingway's blustering Colonel Cantwell offers Shakespeare the highest possible praise: "The winner and still the undisputed champion. . . . He writes like a soldier himself" (159), the ultimate artist who marries the full scope of the imagination with the harsh realities of the real world, including the dangers of war.

Even beyond the men of action who must negotiate the streams of their thoughts in boxing and war, Hemingway located writing itself as an active performance, often better served by instinct, intuition, or mysteriously unconscious inspiration than by intellectualizing the artistic process. In one of Hemingway's earliest efforts, the burgeoning fiction writer Nick Adams explains, "Then there were times when you had to write. Not conscience. Just peristaltic action" (NAS 238).[6] Although Hemingway enjoyed portraying himself as a gritty laborer in contrast to those he perceived as effortless natural talents like Joyce or Fitzgerald, Hemingway's description early in *A Moveable Feast* describes the kind of creation that transcends the intellect: "The story was writing itself and I was having a hard time keeping up with it" (6). This depth of inspiration equates to the epigraph that precedes Hemingway's "Scott Fitzgerald" chapter in *A Moveable Feast*, in which he describes a pristine talent that Fitzgerald himself does not even understand, whose downfall is that he "learned to think" (147).[7] As Marc Dolan phrases it, "Hemingway implies that their difference was the difference between art and craft" (65). Art, then, is motivated by unconscious inspiration; craft is produced through arduous effort, a conscious and even conscientious sense of duty.

In Hemingway, the burden of consciousness oppresses not just the art of imaginative writing but also the art of bullfighting.[8] A parallel in Hemingway between bullfighting and writing is always active; in *The Sun Also Rises*, the bullfighting prodigy Pedro Romero serves as an artistic exemplar for Hemingway just as he serves as a chivalric or masculine ideal for Jake Barnes. In *Death in the Afternoon*, speaking pejoratively of Cayetano Ordóñez, Hemingway writes, "What had happened was that the horn wound, the first real goring, had taken all his valor. He never got it back. He had too much imagination" (90).[9] Hemingway later dismisses a bullfighter because of "his wound that made him think" (274–75), the same self-consciousness that he perceived to be Fitzgerald's downfall and harmful to a writer. The aim of a good bullfighter, as with Antonio Ordóñez in Hemingway's late study, *The Dangerous Summer*, is to try to achieve "the state of nothing that he always had before the gate opened" (182).

Hemingway's bullfighting short story "The Undefeated" features a brilliant explication of the matador's stream of consciousness as he fights a bull. Ultimately, consciousness becomes an obstacle in the arena of action: "his brain worked slowly and in words. He knew all about bulls.[10] He did not have to think about them. He just did the right thing" (SS 260). A character like Ralph Spencer Williams, prone to think deeper than the rest of us, would not have lasted long as a bullfighter, however keen his abstract thoughts might be.

In each of these activities, Hemingway sides with the French philosopher Henri Bergson's distinction between intuition and intellect, in which intuition "goes in the very direction of life" and is "almost completely sacrificed to intellect" (*Creative Evolution* 267). Bergson's point, as Hemingway demonstrates repeatedly, is that while there are rare moments where intellectual consideration is appropriate, ultimately, according to Bergson, "speculation is a luxury, while action is a necessity" (44). Hemingway's soldiers and bullfighters and hunters and boxers and even writers are capable of thought, but readers are encountering them at that moment when such cognition is unnecessary, unhelpful, or unwelcome. In some cases, Hemingway protagonists intentionally place themselves in situations that will distract from thought and memory.

In Hemingway criticism, the most astute observation of this phenomenon belongs to Dewey Ganzel, well worth quoting in full:

> the suspension of the imagination, while it protects a soldier from cowardice, necessarily thwarts his full awareness of life—a value which is, at least implicitly, as important to Hemingway as courage. The countervailing attractions of these antithetical views of life create the characteristic tension in Hemingway's treatment of men at war: on the one hand there is the necessity for courage under fire which demands that one "live completely in the very second of the present minute with no before and no after"; on the other, the pull of memory and desire which forces the present into a sequence of past and future emotions and appetites. (578)

Ganzel might have broadened his point: it is not just war that must be negotiated with thought but any physical human activity whatsoever, including writing. The action of life—not only warfare—must be reconciled with the life of the mind.

For Hemingway, regulated activities like hunting, bullfighting, fishing, and boxing approximated the same decision-making necessities as war, a gesture toward danger, albeit formalized or even ritualized, where a man's conduct, expertise, courage, honor, and intelligence could be determined. Hemingway was always alert to the balance of thought and action that a man possessed. Throughout his work, we see the tragedy that befalls ruminative old fishermen, contemplative bullfighters, and analytical boxers.

Such characterizations are easily misconstrued, as they have been by critics for decades. James Wood refers to Hemingway's "literary hostility to Mind" (90), an encapsulation not just reductive but careless in its sweeping misjudgment. His bravado to the contrary, Hemingway finally acknowledged, in a 1953 letter: "You must truly know that no matter how stupid people act, in order not to argue with fools, any writer that you respect at all, or that has given you pleasure, can think a little bit" (SL 808). Critics who have equated the Hemingway hero's reluctance to ruminate with the writer's wish systematically to renounce or minimize thought neglect the context. When Robert Jordan and Nick in "Big Two-Hearted River" hope to stem the tide of their own surging streams of consciousness, this quest is not a sign that they believe that thinking is unimportant but rather, paradoxically, it reflects their knowledge of just how mighty their own thoughts are. As Nick says ruefully in "A Way You'll Never Be," "Let's not talk about how I am . . . It's a subject I know too much about to want to think about it any more" (SS 407). If thought were an inessential part of a man's existence, then there would be no need for him to structure his behavior in avoidance of it. Nick is terrified to allow memory to exercise its power, but readers must not draw the conclusion that, as the prototypical Hemingway hero, he is incapable of such cognition or inherently uninclined to think.

The Hemingway protagonist is a reluctant intellectual, a sensitive, pensive man with an impulse toward introspection, though the demands of his current situation prohibit such a luxury. Some critics found this tension to be artificial and resented the façade that Hemingway constructed. William Carlos Williams wrote that Hemingway "assumes a cloak of vulgarity to protect a Jamesian sensitivity to detail" (273). Carl Van Doren's reading of *Green Hills of Africa* gauges Hemingway "a very sensitive man, subtle and articulate beneath his swaggering surfaces" (qtd. in Reynolds, *The 1930s* 214). Philip Young also cautions the reader against being distracted by Hemingway's surface appearance: "The rather thin shell of the 'callous' Hemingway hero was painfully drawn over a deep wound as a defense against reopening it," Young writes. "When the man could retrench himself, and stop thinking, and hold tight, and win a code to live by, he could get along" (202). These critical evaluations point to Hemingway's opposition to intellectual thought in order either to stifle traumatic memory or to engage in complicated or dangerous activity. None of these judgments argues that Hemingway is incapable of intellectual thought, a false conclusion that too many readers have accepted.

Hemingway creates only men of thought: Nick Adams, David Bourne, and Harry from "The Snows of Kilimanjaro" are writers of fiction; Jake Barnes is a journalist; Frederic Henry is a student of architecture; Robert Jordan is a writer and teacher; Thomas Hudson is a painter of seascapes. These occupations are all creative and cerebral. Of course, in the works in which Hemingway is his own protagonist, such as *Death in the Afternoon, The Dangerous Summer, Green Hills of Africa,* and *Under Kilimanjaro,* the narratives also deal with an imaginative writer who is immersed in active and sometimes dangerous pursuits.[11] The tension in a Hemingway text emerges when these thoughtful characters find themselves in urgent crises—situations of violence and danger or fiascos of love—and/or coping with the fallout from such events of the past. In *A Farewell to Arms,* Frederic Henry has experienced the trauma of action and the tragedy of love, and the novel revisits them through the power of his memory. Bergson writes, "The characteristic of the man of action is the promptitude with which he summons to the help of a given situation all the memories which have reference to it; yet it is also the insurmountable barrier which encounters, when they present themselves on the threshold of his consciousness, memories that are useless or indifferent" (*Matter and Memory* 153). To Bergson's two neutral adjectives, "useless" and "indifferent," we might add a more negative series: "traumatic," "unpleasant," and "distracting." While explicating his "iceberg theory" in *Death in the Afternoon,* Hemingway adds his own inflection to Bergson's point, arguing, "A great enough writer seems to be born with knowledge. But he really is not; he has only been born with the ability to learn in a quicker ratio to the passage of time than other men and without conscious application, and with an intelligence to accept or reject what is already presented as knowledge" (191–92). The fascinating aspect of Hemingway's observation is his positing of the writer as a man of action; Bergson's point might very well deal with being a soldier or a firefighter, whereas Hemingway, writing in the context of a disquisition on bullfighting, includes writers among those whose instincts must be refined for rapid response.

In a scene in *Islands in the Stream* that echoes Santiago's struggle in *The Old Man and the Sea,* Thomas Hudson's son David has a long, ultimately unsuccessful battle with an enormous fish and, like Santiago, is described as an automaton: "David was lifting and reeling as he lowered, lifting and reeling as he lowered, as regularly as a machine" (112); "The boy was working like a machine again" (124); "David went to work like a machine, or like a very tired boy performing as a machine" (136). In the account of El Sordo's last stand in *For Whom the Bell Tolls,* too, the young Republican Joaquín digs dirt "in a steady, almost machine-like desperation" (308). This adaptation of robotism is not the natural state of man in the Hemingway universe but its antithesis. That his characters must automate themselves bespeaks the massivity of urgency in the present situation.

Hemingway's life and writing career coincided with literary modernism and the ascent of the modern psychological novel, which focused inward on the thoughts and feelings of the characters as opposed to narratives of external, objective events. Throughout the critical response to this literary movement, Hemingway is minimized, ignored, or even lampooned as a straw man, a comic figure demonstrating only the brutish, behaviorist tendencies of men in action. In *The Psychological Novel, 1900–1950*, Leon Edel's essential treatment of the form, Hemingway is not mentioned a single time. Edel devotes his attention to Faulkner, Proust, Woolf, Joyce, Dorothy Richardson, and Henry James. In subsequent treatments of the genre, such as those by Shiv K. Kumar, Melvin J. Friedman, and Robert Humphrey, Hemingway is deemed similarly irrelevant to a discussion of consciousness in fiction, as those studies strictly adhere to the modern psychological novelists Edel selected.

Critics have overlooked the importance of thought to Hemingway's work because they regarded his work as inadequate in the tradition dominated by Proust, Joyce, Woolf, and James. Perhaps any bit of activity and virility— particularly given Hemingway's boisterous public exaggerations—would have distracted from the thoughtful content of his prose. Alberto Moravia's obituary of Hemingway links him to writers who were famously linked to active, physical experiences, such as D'Annunzio, Lawrence, Malraux, Theodore Roosevelt, and Byron;[12] however, Moravia sees "nothing in common" between Hemingway and Proust (438). John Wain's perceptive reading of Hemingway finds "heroic simplicities that are not simple, of unreflective action that is yet more action of the mind than of the body. His vision of life embodied itself in fables concerning physical activity and the outdoor world, but there is never any doubt that for Hemingway, as for all sensitive men, the real battleground is inward . . . this does not mean that he exalted the external matter over the inward essence" (21). To this end, Charles Scribner Jr.'s brief Preface to *The Garden of Eden* contains one of the most lucid critical comments ever written about Hemingway's merit as a psychological novelist:

> the conception of Hemingway as a writer primarily absorbed with external action fails to take into account his profound interest in character. On the surface, many of his stories may seem to deal with exciting physical events, but, like Conrad, he was always primarily interested in the effect such events had in the minds of the individuals concerned . . . one can always find the interplay of character under the surface of the action. (viii)

Scribner's comments seem so obvious as to be unremarkable, but the over-whelming critical response to Hemingway has ignored and even contradicted this fundamental observation.

In Dorrit Cohn's *Transparent Minds*, her narratological examination of consciousness in fiction, Hemingway is emblematic of writers whose work does not measure up to the techniques of psychological novelists such as Joyce, Woolf, and Proust. "If Hemingway's men monologize more frankly," Cohn writes, "this frankness reflects the altered norms of his society and the enlarged social compass of modern fiction rather than an altered conception of internal language itself. Interior monologue is interesting only to the degree that it departs from the colloquial model and attempts the mimesis of an unheard language" (90). However, Cohn's judgment that, for instance, Nick's obsessive metacognition in "Big Two-Hearted River" is uninteresting discounts Hemingway's innovation, which is the translation of the unwieldy web of consciousness into an accessible form, forcing the acutely sensitive mind to respond to heightened physical action—unseen in Dorothy Richardson, Henry James, or Proust—and the devastating trauma of the past. Although Hemingway would occasionally—most conspicuously with the italicized flashbacks in "The Snows of Kilimanjaro" and the soliloquies in *To Have and Have Not*—attempt to convey Cohn's notion of "an unheard language" (or at least a language previously heard only in *The Sound and the Fury* and *Ulysses*), Hemingway was at his most innovative when he avoided subscribing to narratologists' rules for what was interesting.

The omission or castigation of Hemingway in these studies may ultimately be less fascinating than his characterization by those who would hold him up as presenting the dark side of consciousness, the opposite of the writers being discussed. Cohn regards Hemingway as presiding over the "behaviorism of the Hemingway school" of fiction (9), almost an ominous, shadowy headmaster who rejects thinking and spurns intelligence among his students. Cohn is not alone in her judgment. Philip Rahv wrote in 1937 that Hemingway's "method of inarticulate virility is no substitute for consciousness" (64). D. S. Savage refers to Hemingway's approach as "the adaptation of the technical artistic conscience to the subaverage human consciousness" (31), savage criticism indeed.

But this critical savagery, however, does not even approach the apotheosis of all Hemingway detractors, Wyndham Lewis in his essay "The Dumb Ox: A Study of Ernest Hemingway." This legendary evisceration, worth reading for the sheer entertainment value and the hysteria of the putdowns, may be discredited, but the essence of the charge has stuck. The central accusation is that Hemingway is artless, presenting reality in its most unrefined, unstylized mode. According to Lewis, Hemingway's characters have no free will, no consciousness, no political thoughts, no introspection. He refers to Hemingway as "the simple American man," presenting "almost purely an art of action" (188). The Hemingway hero, Lewis continues, "is a dull-witted, bovine, monosyllabic simpleton," a "lethargic and stuttering dummy" (196). Although an essay this vitriolic is more extremely stated than the prevailing view, even in the mid-1930s—following the publication of virtually all of his major short stories, as well as *The Sun Also Rises* and *A Farewell to Arms*—Hemingway's characters were still routinely referred to in terms of animals, savages, subhumans, primitives, illiterates, or idiots.

Hemingway's exclusion from any study that surveys the first half of twentieth-century American literature is a serious charge, a perpetuation of a stereotype that persists to the present day. In fact, Hemingway saw himself very much in the tradition of the psychological novel; his literary heroes and major influences were all members of Edel's pantheon, including Joyce, Proust, Henry James, and Faulkner. Michael Reynolds compiled "Hemingway's Recommended Reading List" (*Hemingway's Reading* 72), culled from Hemingway's numerous writings, statements, and letters about literature. Reynolds's list is formed almost entirely by the writers that Edel and the others discuss: of the twenty-five titles, twenty are by novelists whose psychological credentials are unanimously extolled: Joyce, James, Tolstoy, Fielding, Turgenev, Flaubert, Stendhal, Proust, D. H. Lawrence, Dostoevsky, Twain, and Thomas Mann.[13] As careful as Hemingway was to promote his active, masculine image, this reading list resembles that of a literary egghead, a lover of literature for whom the inward journey was of paramount interest. If emotion was often the portion of the iceberg beneath the surface of his fiction, so too was intellectual cogitation.

Hemingway's brand of the modern psychological novel is, as with Bergson's *élan vital* and William James's pragmatism, thought with an eye toward action. His soldiers, lovers, brawlers, hunters, fishers, drinkers, and even writers have difficult balances to strike between the incessant streams of their consciousness and the demands of the situation in which they find themselves. Even when these streams do not flow at the chaotic pace and unpredictable and exhilarating patterns of the Joyce, Proust, Woolf, or Faulkner text, its value in presenting consciousness in action is not diminished. In most cases, the Hemingway hero must actively prevent his thoughts from such an uncontrollable pace. Although William James introduced the metaphor of a "stream" of thought, the fictional novelist in the manuscript of *To Have and Have Not* does him one better. "My damned head races like a mill race. I make up the whole thing conversations and all. Can't stop it" (JFK 204).[14] James posits a stream of consciousness; however, to most Hemingway heroes, a stream equates to a millrace, a swift, overwhelming current. Instead, one finds that Hemingway's characters wish that consciousness were a faucet, by which the flow can be controlled, made more or less intense, hotter or colder, and, ultimately, turned off entirely.

Reviewing *A Farewell to Arms*, Henry Hazlitt intended to be snide, writing, "Imagine what would happen if a character from Henry James or Proust were to stray by accident into a Hemingway novel!" (38). A serious reader of Hemingway must not laugh along but instead embrace that hypothetical as entirely plausible, and quite intriguing besides. It just might allow a deeper appreciation of all three writers. A reasonable start would be to take Hemingway at his word. Hemingway announced in 1950 that his goal for the then forthcoming *Across the River and into the Trees* was to be "better than Proust if Proust had been to the wars and liked to fuck and was in love" (SL 691). Hemingway also mused, "I wonder what Henry James would have done with the materials of our time" (qtd. in Baker, *Writer as Artist* 193),[15] suggesting that, although his work was not a replication of Proust or James's style, it might have attempted to apply a similar approach to the beleaguered, traumatized post–World War I consciousness. Speaking facetiously about his writing strategy in a 1954 letter, Hemingway wrote, "It's like this. You sit down to write like Flaubert, H. James (not Jesse) etc. and two characters with spears come and stand easy outside the tent" (SL 826). The remark is a joke, but a revealing one. Hemingway is describing an attitude in which he would love to be the meticulously introspective novelist he is inclined to be, except that real life gets in the way.

Hemingway read the novelists who have been canonized as psychologically astute and also immersed himself in psychology texts. As part of his voracious reading, Hemingway's library included several volumes of Havelock Ellis, the icon of the psychology of sex (Reynolds, *Hemingway's Reading* 121); Descartes (Brasch and Sigman 124); Sigmund Freud and Ernest Jones (152, 205); Santayana (317); Susanne Langer (218); and—presumably at the behest of Gertrude Stein—William James's *Psychology* (Reynolds, *Hemingway's Reading* 141), as well as another volume of James's writings (Brasch and Sigman 202). Hemingway also owned the work of a progenitor of studies of the psychological novel, Joseph Collins's 1923 book *The Doctor Looks at Literature* (Reynolds, *Hemingway's Reading* 111). In addition to literature, Hemingway also studied the psychological approach to art, war, animals, crime, government, medicine, and ethics, as well as the methodology of psychoanalysis itself. Hemingway once decried the practitioners of Freudian psychoanalytic criticism as "Junior F.B.I.-men" (SL 751), and—legend has it—told Ava Gardner that the only analyst he ever relied on was his "Portable Corona number three" (Hotchner 139), his trusty typewriter. As Robert Jordan acknowledges of his own limitations in his desire to examine the motives of other people, "he was no psychiatrist" (FWBT 137).

Jordan is a writer and soldier who must analyze the behavior of other people, but his interest is pragmatic and not psychoanalytic.

David Lodge, a writer sympathetic to Hemingway, acknowledges that Hemingway was influenced by the masters of modernism but then claims that he "wrote a very different kind of fiction . . . he stays scrupulously on the surface." Lodge finds that Hemingway "omitted from his stories . . . all the psychological analysis and introspection that one finds in James or Joyce or Woolf" (70). Lodge's point parrots a stereotype about Hemingway that is superficially true but still misreads or at least misrepresents Hemingway's work. For instance, in "The Killers," Nick responds to being gagged and bound by thugs with an apparently anti-introspective, unanalytical remark. The narrator reports of Nick: "He had never had a towel in his mouth before" (SS 286). This sensory, objective detail replaces an introspective analysis of the incident, one that would be utterly laughable. The narrator could have stated the obvious: "Nick had never known evil before. Nick was frightened. Nick thought he was going to die," and so on. By acknowledging the sensation of the towel, the astute reader is receptive to the unstated attendant emotions. Hemingway's style is not antithetical to introspection, but, in restraining self-analysis, his characters pay deference to the situation in which they find themselves. A hostage cannot assess the metaphysical implications of his abduction at the moment of his release. In Hemingway narratives that afford the protagonist snatches of leisure time—for example, *The Old Man and the Sea*, *For Whom the Bell Tolls*, *Islands in the Stream*, and *The Sun Also Rises*—the protagonists certainly do take the opportunity to reflect and gaze within.

Each chapter of this book examines an aspect of the way consciousness functions in a different Hemingway text. Although Hemingway has been the subject of countless psychoanalytic readings, the intent of this book is to discuss his fiction for its focus on the cognition of Hemingway's characters and the role that those thoughts play in contributing to the drama and richness of the narrative. In the next two chapters, "Big Two-Hearted River" and *The Old Man and the Sea* are discussed as twin dramas of metacognition, an internal struggle, rather than as parables or paradigmatic examples of man versus nature in literature. In chapter 3, *A Farewell to Arms* is examined as a study of a soldier's conflicted memory, evoking structural and dimensional complexities that Hemingway always strove to achieve. Chapter 4 synthesizes the discussion of the thought-action dichotomy in his fiction by focusing on one of his less-celebrated works, the posthumous Gulf Stream novel *Islands in the Stream* as an inferior articulation of the balance struck more successfully in *For Whom the Bell Tolls*. Chapters 5 and 6 explore what is perhaps Hemingway's most important theme: the phenomenology and metaphysics of the dying, both the aesthetic and the moral necessity to witness violence, as well as the vision and consciousness of the dying individual. The study concludes by focusing on Hemingway's understanding of the self and his use of voids in consciousness to denote secular conversion or permanent extinction.

Unlike studies of artists such as Picasso, Henry James, Dostoevsky, Langston Hughes, or Bob Dylan, it is decidedly unproductive to attempt a linear study of Hemingway's progression as an artist, positing a simple trajectory to his writing. Instead, Hemingway worked cyclically, revisiting the same themes, situations, and settings after World War II that he had depicted as a young writer.[16] However, a compelling narrative of Hemingway's career-long concern with consciousness emerges: we have the protagonist in isolation (chapters 1 and 2) and negotiating the trauma of the past (chapter 3), which he then incorporates into the demands of the present (chapter 4). This treatment of consciousness is then applied to Hemingway's notorious preoccupation with violence and death (chapters 5 and 6), until finally the conclusion addresses Hemingway as a storyteller and his focus on the development of a protagonist, the consciousness converted to a more refined form.

In focusing on this specific example of Hemingway's work, I am hoping merely to open up avenues of discussion and future critical conversations that have previously been missing. Although it sometimes denies it, literary criticism asks more questions than it answers. Literary criticism should never posture as being definitive; much has been written about Hemingway in the past ninety years, and reaction to his work will surely continue as long as people are alive to read it. The ultimate purpose of a literary critic is to provoke thought and to impart knowledge so that when the general reader returns to Hemingway's text, he or she will more fully appreciate and enjoy the work itself.

That is absolutely my goal with this book.

1

The Solitary Consciousness I

Metacognition and Mental Control in "Big Two-Hearted River"

> Thinks I, this is what comes of my not thinking.
> Mark Twain, *Adventures of Huckleberry Finn*

> To determine not to think it was to think of it still, to suffer from it still.
> Marcel Proust, *Swann's Way*

At this point in Hemingway studies, it is well understood that in "Big Two-Hearted River," Nick Adams seeks a return to simplicity after his harrowing experience in World War I and that Hemingway's prose replicates the veteran's internal quest for manageable simplicity. At story's end, Nick avoids the physical swamp at the edge of the stream and, by doing so, fends off the metaphorical swamp of his own psyche. But as we approach the ninetieth year of "Big Two-Hearted River" exegesis—a practice pioneered by Gertrude Stein, F. Scott Fitzgerald, and Hemingway himself—a crucial question remains unasked: Is Nick's strategy—to return to the Michigan woods of his youth, by himself, systematically replacing the thoughts of the war with immediate, pleasant stimulation from nature and camping—benign and productive or self-defeating and doomed from the start?

Just as with former New York Giants football star Lawrence Taylor's notoriously dubious scheme of battling drug addiction by playing innumerable hours of golf in order to occupy himself, a program of self-treatment which he asserts "literally saved his life" (Newport 3), Nick's strategy of rehabilitation depends upon focused self-distraction—to consider a more agreeable topic instead of confronting the source of his unpleasant memories. "Big Two-Hearted River" is a silent drama of metacognition; in his solitude, Nick's thoughts are occupied by his own thoughts. Therefore, the condition of Nick's consciousness becomes the narrative's primary concern. In ways unsurpassed in all of Hemingway, the text presents extended external metaphors to illuminate psychological corollaries.

Mental control, a slippery concept in the philosophy of mind, is exercised when people "suppress a thought, concentrate on a sensation, inhibit an emotion, maintain a mood, stir up a desire, squelch a craving, or otherwise exert influence on their own mental states" (Wegner and Pennebaker 1). Inherent in this definition is an implicit anxiety about the way a person feels, has felt, or soon might feel. If a person knew he would remain permanently and unalterably content, he would not exert energy trying to maintain positive feelings or alter negative ones. Likewise, in the unconscious thought avoidance that Freud addressed, he found that "the motive and purpose of repression was nothing else than the avoidance of unpleasure" (*Psychological Works* 153). Therefore, in their endeavors to control their mental states, Hemingway's heroes possess a level of introspection and self-awareness not always granted them. "Big Two-Hearted River" demonstrates the subtlety and complexity with which Hemingway understood mental control, in the sense that Nick wishes to adjust his cognitive activity as neatly as one might manipulate sound levels on the equalizer of a stereo. In his metacognitive grappling, Nick is forced to ask: Am I satisfied with my thoughts? Are they pleasant? Are they productive? If so, how can I sustain them? Or, are they painful and harmful? If so, how might I eliminate them?

Once Nick disembarks the train in Seney, he is able not just to access the actual stream that is full of trout but also to monitor better the internal stream of his thoughts. Other than the helpful baggage man who is referred to but unseen, and his old friend Hopkins, who appears only in the story's single extended reminiscence, Nick is alone. The only other characters spring from nature, and Nick relates to each one differently: grasshoppers, trout, a mosquito, a mink, a kingfisher. These creatures elicit telling reactions from Nick, but he has made the crucial decision to fish and camp alone. In an early draft of the story, which more closely adheres to its autobiographical inspiration, Nick is accompanied by a group of friends. By changing the narrative to one man's solo journey,

Hemingway allows Nick to focus more meticulously upon his stated objective: escaping "the need for thinking, the need to write, other needs" (SS 210). His quest to control his surroundings and to satisfy his preference for solitude is clear: "Nick did not like to fish with other men on the river. Unless they were of your party, they spoiled it" (225). And, in this extreme setting, even if they were members of his party, they would be not a welcome distraction but instead an unpredictable variable to which he was not willing to expose his vulnerable state of mind.

In a note to himself during the 1924 drafting of "Big Two-Hearted River," Hemingway sketched the story, tracing the protagonist's crisis: "He thinks [. . .] gets uncomfortable, restless, tries to stop thinking, more uncomfortable and restless, the thinking goes on, speeds up, can't shake it—comes home to camp—hot before storm—storm—in morning creek flooded, hikes to the railroad" (qtd. in Reynolds, *Paris Years* 209). As Hemingway's outline makes apparent and as the published narrative bears out, the story's concern was never the setting, the contrived antagonists of the trout, the chores of hiking and cooking, or conformance to any kind of behavioral code for constructing a proper camp. There is hardly a narrative to speak of. Hemingway confessed to Gertrude Stein and Alice B. Toklas that "nothing happens" (SL 122).[1] The issue that does justify the narrative is Nick's tortured consciousness, his struggle to control it— Nick "*tries* to stop thinking"—and the depiction of his failure, when he "can't shake it." This outline describes a psyche out of control.

In the published story, Nick feels his mind begin to activate, but he "knew he could choke it" (SS 218), having sufficiently exhausted himself. Although Nick is comforted to know he can ultimately dominate his thoughts, it is nevertheless revealing for a man to view his own mind so antagonistically and in such violent terms. Healthy individuals do not need to choke their thoughts to control them. "One of the most compelling occasions for mental control is in the face of mental turmoil," explain Daniel M. Wegner and James W. Pennebaker, pioneers on the topic. "When the mind is reeling in response to some traumatic event . . . it is natural to attempt to quell the storm by dimming sensation, stopping thought, or blocking the emotion" (5–6). To appreciate the ominous use of "choking" in Hemingway, one need only recall *A Farewell to Arms*, in which choking causes the stillbirth of Frederic Henry and Catherine Barkley's son and is also the verb that describes the bombing death of Passini, as well as Frederic's succumbing to general anesthesia (327, 55, 107).[2]

In "Big Two-Hearted River," Nick Adams's journey to the woods and the river is a retreat to a setting filled with happy distractions, a quest for familiar simplicity and manageable complexity. Nick's hope is that if the external world can be managed, it will grant a period of stability to the chaotic thoughts and traumatic memories that persistently plague his mind. Nick's project should not be imputed to reflect Hemingway's philosophy of life, a systematic renunciation of thought, or devaluation of consciousness. Nick, after all, is in an emotionally extreme situation in his life, which makes him such a compelling character to explore in fiction. Philip Young speaks forcefully to this point, describing Nick's compulsive routine as suggesting "much less that he is the mindless primitive the Hemingway hero was so often thought to be than that he is desperately protecting his mind against whatever it is that he is escaping" (45). Sheldon Norman Grebstein seconds this view of "Big Two-Hearted River," confirming that the style "has sometimes been interpreted or misconstrued by hostile critics as the writer's incapacity for complex thought and his distrust of intellection" (83). To extend Grebstein's point, the prevailing premise that a protagonist who avoids thought is therefore uninterested in thought is utterly illogical. If Nick Adams were not predisposed to think, then the narrative would have no tension and no point. If a nonthinker chooses to abandon thought, it is a nonstory. Nick, however, has a fiction writer's curiosity and sensitivity to experience. The simmering conflict in "Big Two-Hearted River," as in many other Hemingway texts, stems from Nick's powerful impulse to think and from his determination to restrain himself.

Tony Tanner's chapter on Hemingway in his study of American literature refers to the description that Nick "did not want to rush his sensations any" (SS 227) as "one of the most important in the whole of Hemingway." Tanner elaborates: "It explains the conduct of his main characters, it explains the structure of his prose, it even hints at his total philosophy." Tanner concludes that Hemingway's prose is "essentially outward-looking" (*Reign of Wonder* 255), citing moments when he "sheds all complexity of thought and follows the naive, wondering eye as it enters into a reverent communion with the earth that abideth forever" (257). Of course, this elimination of complexity is necessary, given Nick's particular circumstance. Tanner somewhat recklessly invites a reading of these extreme moments to characterize the entirety of Hemingway and all his characters. Failing to recognize the specific emotional urgency of Nick's situation leads to the attribution of an ethos to Hemingway that misrepresents and even undervalues his intent. If Nick's decision to calm his sensations were not a struggle, then the reading of Hemingway's characters as intellectual primitives could be granted. However, nothing is more inherently complex than a metacognitive civil war raging beneath the surface of the Hemingway protagonist. As William James writes in his description of such an internal struggle, "The whole drama is a mental drama. The whole difficulty is a mental difficulty, a difficulty with an object of our thought" (*Principles*, II: 564). Tanner's point fails to appreciate the edict from James as well as from Bergson that the complexity of thought—as Hemingway always showed—can never be completely shed, except through the abandonment of consciousness that precedes or coincides with death.

When Nick prepares his tent before dinner, Hemingway's language eerily mimics his protagonist's consciousness.

> Now things were done. There had been this to do. Now it was done. It had been a hard trip. He was very tired. That was done. He had made his camp. He was settled. Nothing could touch him. It was a good place to camp. He was there, in the good place. He was in his home where he had made it. Now he was hungry. (215)

In this extraordinarily crafted passage, sixty-three of the sixty-seven words (94 percent) are monosyllabic. Twelve of the thirteen sentences (92 percent) have no punctuation marks other than a period at the end, and the other has but one comma. The first twenty-two words of the excerpt are monosyllabic; before the "hungry" that ends the excerpt is another stretch of thirty. The four disyllabic words are themselves far from complex: "very," "settled," "nothing," and "hungry."[3] Matthew Stewart comments on this passage, concluding similarly: "Here style is in absolute service to content, the short declarative sentences echoing both Nick's methodical construction of the camp and his continued need for simplicity and controlled action. By keeping things simple, the repetitions drive home Nick's self-created domestic ease" (91).

The omission of advanced vocabulary gestures toward the central omission of the story, which Hemingway would explain later in his career. In *A Moveable Feast*, Hemingway refers to "Big Two-Hearted River" as a story "about coming back from the war but there was no mention of the war in it" (76). Even this sentence summarizing "Big Two-Hearted River" contains the word "war" two times, which is twice more than it appears in the story. In "Soldier's Home," a story one-third the length of "Big Two-Hearted River," the word "war" is mentioned nine times, including in the first sentence.[4]

Although William Faulkner would later charge that Hemingway "never used a word where the reader might check his usage by a dictionary" (qtd. in Blotner II: 1233),[5] a story like "Big Two-Hearted River" demonstrates the purpose behind such a rigid, apparently simple style. Readers can imagine the absurdity of a narrative about a quest for simplicity if it were rendered in the vocabulary of Faulkner's Quentin Compson (or his father), or Joyce's

Stephen Dedalus. In "Big Two-Hearted River," with its unwavering thematic focus on mental control, a similar control had to be mimicked by the vocabulary, syntax, and grammar of the writer. The avoidance of even a single exclamation point suggests that the vulnerable mind of the protagonist could not withstand such excitement.

Nick's fishing expedition as an exercise in mental control begins the moment he steps off the train. All his activities and sensations become modulated, measured, and assessed as being not enough, too much, or just right. Mostly, Nick is guarding against excess, against any unwieldy stimulation that will overwhelm the makeshift defenses erected to guard his fragile psyche. Readers are prepared for this cautious behavior at the beginning of Part Two of the narrative, when Nick finds "plenty of good grasshoppers" that will serve as bait. From all those grasshoppers, his selection is telling: "Nick picked them up, taking only the medium-sized brown ones, and put them into the bottle" (221). After Nick lifts a log and sees several hundred more grasshoppers, he repeats the behavior: "Nick put about fifty of the medium browns into the bottle" (221). Virtually every activity on the camping trip follows this approach, a hypersensitivity to the necessity of his tentativeness. Nick controls his excitement and eagerness to fish immediately by not skipping breakfast; he decides against the more flamboyant technique of "flopping" flapjacks; although he makes two big flapjacks and a third small one, he eats only a big and a small, saving the second big one until later; he is content to secure one trout as opposed to many; and most significant—and this may be the central insight that Nick gleans from the camping trip—Nick concludes that it would be reckless to enter the swamp.

Whenever Nick acts contrary to this compulsively controlled, carefully modulated behavior, he gets a harsh reminder of his current limitations. When he ventures into the Big Two-Hearted itself, the description is unambiguous: "He stepped into the stream. It was a shock. . . . The water was a rising cold shock" (224). Surely, the word "shock" is not used—much less repeated—to describe Nick without the added, wholly accurate psychological connotation attached to the physical sensation. Furthermore, the specificity in narration is telling, that the *water* is responsible for the shock and not anything more abstract or internal. After catching and releasing a too-small trout, Nick leaves the shallows, knowing he could catch no big ones there. Predictably, when Nick leaves the sure terrain of the shallows, he is at the mercy of the rude stream and, hence, the anarchic rapids of his own stream of consciousness. Nick hooks the biggest trout he has ever seen, which ends up breaking his leader and escaping. As the too-cold water provides too-heightened emotions, so does this battle that was unwise and anathema to Nick's prior (and subsequent) self-control during the camping trip: "Nick's hand was shaky. He reeled in slowly. The thrill had been too much. He felt, vaguely, a little sick, as though it would be better to sit down. . . . He went over and sat on the logs. He did not want to rush his sensations any" (226–27), leading to the line central to Tanner's reading. A "reeling" Nick's corrective behavior is to traverse the logs "where it was not too deep" (227). Avoiding deep waters will prevent the "deep thinking" to which Hemingway heroes always know they might succumb.

The obsessive discourse of measurement and excess is made evident by Nick's acute awareness of the several similar occasions when things are too much. Readers are told when Nick's backpack is "too heavy . . . much too heavy" (210); of the inefficacy of looking "too steadily" at hills in the distance (211); of the river running "too fast and smooth" to make a sound (213); of the beans and spaghetti being "too hot" and, even after ketchup, "still too hot" (216); Nick knows when the coffee is "too hot to pour" (217); in the morning he is "really too hurried" for breakfast (221); with the big trout, the line rushes out "[t]oo fast" (226); battling the trout, Nick feels when "the strain was too great; the hardness too tight," and sums up the ill-advised encounter: "The thrill had been too much" (226). The solution to this entire adventure, during which he must guard against too much of everything and too much of anything, soon emerges: to carry on fishing in waters that were "not too deep" (227). The story enacts the aphorism from Blake's "Proverbs of Hell," that "you never know what is enough unless you know what is more than enough" (37). By the end of the narrative, Nick knows his limits and will not risk ceding mental control to the Big Two-Hearted River or to the similarly unpredictable stream of his consciousness.

Nick's incessant gauging of the volume of his sensory intake and emotional reactions is extended to the gauging of mental activity, of the psychological exertion of his brain, an act of self-monitoring that calls for intense introspection, self-scrutiny, and keen self-knowledge. When Nick notices the "sooty black" grasshoppers (211), he identifies with their traumatized state, the grasshoppers having "turned black from living in the burned-over land" (212). Despite this grim realization, Nick must maintain the objective of his mission, to avoid thoughts of war and the "need for thinking" entirely (210). Nick is focused on mental control so intensely, however, that he finds a way to process his observation about the grasshoppers: "Nick had wondered about them as he walked, without really thinking about them" (211). He continues, comprehending their state and the cause but never brooding over it or responding in an overly emotional way: "He wondered how long they would stay that way" (212). For Nick, to "wonder" equals thinking diminished. It skims the surface of a perception, taking notice of it with innocent, superficial speculation and quickly processing it, without allowing it the full depth of exploration that the topic might ordinarily merit.[6]

In the long chapter devoted to "Will" in *The Principles of Psychology*, William James describes the concept of thought avoidance. He outlines a behavioral phenomenon that is consistent with Nick's central struggle in the story. James argues that, for a man who is in a dominant frame of mind, it takes an over- whelming "effort of attention" to undo the body's tendency to sustain the pre- vailing mood (II: 562). "When any strong emotional state whatever is upon us," James writes, "the tendency is for no images but such as are congruous with it to come up. If others by chance offer themselves, they are instantly smothered and crowded out" (563). In this sense, the story treats the challenge posed to Nick's will, his determination to break out of the mental condition that has suf- focated him since his return from the war. A central difference between "Sol- dier's Home" and "Big Two-Hearted River" is that Krebs becomes victorious when he ultimately decides to move to Kansas City, a change in environment that will afford him the opportunity to recuperate on his own terms; in "Big Two-Hearted River," Nick arrives in the temporary sanctuary of his choosing, and the compromised capacities of his mental willpower play themselves out.

The confrontation between focusing on external or internal objects emerges in Bergson's analysis in *Creative Evolution* of the idea of "nothing." Although Nick's temporary ideal would be to think about nothing—to be completely beyond "the need for thinking" and literally to have it "all back of him" (SS 210), a com- plete annihilation of thought, memory, sensation, and perception is impossible. Bergson describes an experiment where he tries to reduce his thoughts to nothing, to eliminate his sensations and his recollections, and to reduce the consciousness of his body to zero. Ultimately, Bergson realizes the project's futility:

> But no! At the very instant that my consciousness is extinguished, another
> consciousness lights up—or rather, it was already alight: it had arisen the
> instant before, in order to witness the extinction of the first; for the first could
> disappear only for another and in the presence of another. I see myself annihilated
> only if I have already resuscitated myself by an act which is positive, however
> involuntary and unconscious. So, do what I will, I am always perceiving
> something, either from without or from within. . . . I can by turns imagine a
> nought of external perception or a nought of internal perception, but not both
> at once, for the absence of one consists, at bottom, in the exclusive presence of
> the other. (278–79)

Bergson is affirming William James's first fundamental rule of consciousness, which is that thought is constant and unavoidable. Although seemingly intuitive, establishing consciousness as a perpetual feature of a sentient being is a foundational law. Bergson has described a volatile competition between internal and external stimuli that perhaps is not foreign to any of us, but this interplay is not typically a centerpiece for an entire narrative. Hemingway's assertion that nothing happens in "Big Two-Hearted River" is self-deprecatory and misleading, because something does happen; the arena of activity has merely turned inward, from the Italian front to the consciousness of a shell-shocked veteran.

James also imagines a situation similar to Bergson's, of the complete eradication of thought. "It is difficult not to suppose," James writes, "something like this scattered condition of mind to be the usual state of brutes when not actively engaged in some pursuit. Fatigue, monotonous mechanical occupations that end by being automatically carried on, tend to produce it in men" (I: 404). James's image is precisely the accusation that has been incorrectly applied to Hemingway's characters. Hemingway is not concerned with unthinking brutes, but his sensitive, introspective characters often perversely envy and emulate the limited mental state of brutes, because they feel that their own excessively cognitive inclinations distract and impede them from completing a task or maintaining a pleasant existence. They are unable to reconcile the competing demands of the internal and external worlds. In the reductive, false dichotomy between the "man of thought" and the "man of action," which is discussed in greater detail in chapter 4, Hemingway posits the unhappy compromise that the man of action can act effectively only by pretending that he is not a man of thought. The man of thought can protect himself only by immersing himself in action that will occupy his attention.

The concept of "nothing" introduces two integral aspects of Hemingway's writing: his "iceberg principle" of writing, in which whatever the writer knows is omitted in order to provide the unseen tension of the story, and also the theme of "*nada*," the depressed, nihilistic state that haunts the characters in "A Clean Well-Lighted Place," among other narratives. Bergson argues that the concept of nothing "is, at bottom, the idea of Everything, together with a movement of the mind that keeps jumping from one thing to another, refuses to stand still, and concentrates all its attention on this refusal by never determining its actual position except by relation to that which it has just left" (*Creative Evolution* 296).[7] Bergson's point introduces an entirely new slant to the old waiter's "*nada*" prayer in "A Clean Well-Lighted Place": if the old waiter is commenting on nothing and giving it a name, can he, by definition, be living in the state of nothing to which critics have always consigned him, and he has consigned himself?

Although the word "war" does not appear in "Big Two-Hearted River," the text was preceded by the intentional authorial decision to excise the word, which means it first entered the consciousness of the writer who chose not to write it. By preventing the word from appearing, he ensured that the word would become pervasive despite its absence and that it would exist as the text's unspoken obsession. This obsession becomes more powerful by lurking beneath the surface of the text, the subterranean part of the iceberg that provides the dignity of the story's movement. In the same way, Nick Adams chose to take the trip to the woods for a specific reason: to avoid thinking about the war. But within the motivation itself exists the very thought Nick was determined to avoid in the first place. Thus, just as Hemingway made war more present by omitting its mention, by erasing the unpleasant memories, paradoxically, Nick has potentially made those memories the axis around which his life revolves. By trying to reduce his thoughts and memories to nothing, he risks having them become everything and all consuming.

One of Daniel M. Wegner's central contributions to the psychology of mental control has been his claim that suppressing a thought often leads to its "hyperaccessibility," an ironic effect whereby, for example, the pleasant distraction of the Big Two-Hearted River might in the future remind Nick that it had served as a distraction for the war, making it instead an unhappy place. Nick might begin to consider the woods not as an Edenic paradise but as a secret refuge where he can avoid thoughts of the war. The distracter creates, Wegner writes, "associations between the unwanted thought and all the various distracters" ("You Can't Always Think" 214). Might a round of golf for Lawrence Taylor now carry new associative baggage, and have lost its original purity? As Bergson points out, "To represent 'Nothing,' we must either imagine it or conceive it" (*Creative Evolution* 278). It is impossible to suppress a thought without first planning to suppress it (although it can be buried by an unconscious Freudian repression); therefore, to plan to avoid thinking about a topic must inherently involve thinking of that topic on some level of cognition.

However, Nick's strategy involves more than turning himself off and entirely eliminating his consciousness. He attempts not simply to banish the thoughts of war from his mind but, more sensibly, to *replace* these unpleasant thoughts. While on the surface "concentration" and "distraction" seem antonymous, the relationship between those words is actually more nuanced. If "concentration" means "to pay attention to one thing," we might usefully define "distraction" as "to pay attention to something else," T. S. Eliot's notion in

"Burnt Norton" of being "Distracted from distraction by distraction" (120). When Nick is paying attention to making coffee, he is in essence tricking himself into paying attention to not paying attention about his war memories. As Wegner phrases it in his study, *White Bears and Other Unwanted Thoughts*, "We cannot concentrate well without suppressing, and we cannot suppress well without concentrating" (12). Therefore, when Nick suggests that he stop the need for *thinking*, the word serves as shorthand for "unpleasant thinking" or "thinking about the war." Consciousness is not a faucet to be turned off any more than the current of a stream can be stopped. Both can, however, with much effort, be redirected.[8] To extend the metaphor of the stereo equalizer, consciousness is like a stereo where the individual can adjust sound levels on the equalizer but is forbidden to turn the power off.

Wegner describes psychological experiments that support Nick's project of distraction, of suppressing one thought and concentrating on a more favorable one, devoting a chapter to the importance of choosing surroundings that are conducive to thought control. Nick's deliberate trip into the woods confirms Wegner's argument: "we must go to places that will allow us to see and hear what we want to hold in consciousness; we must retain those objects that remind us of what we truly wish to think" (98). Once Nick (like Krebs and Jake Barnes) carries out Wegner's first stage—removal—he fastidiously engages in what Wegner considers to be the best strategy for defending oneself against unwanted thoughts: focused distraction. Since we cannot entirely avoid thought, we must redirect our attention. The title of Wegner's book refers to a famous psychological experiment in which the subject is instructed not to think of a white bear, which becomes impossible once the idea is introduced. "If we wish to suppress a thought," Wegner writes, "it is necessary to become absorbed in another thought. The distracter we seek should be something intrinsically interesting and engaging to us. . . . The things that interest people most are the things that provide good exercise for their abilities" (70). Nick's engagement in the rudimentary mechanics of camping suggests he has chosen well.

A literary counterpoint might well be the fourth chapter of James Joyce's *Ulysses*, a veritable textbook for the representation of consciousness in fiction and a novel to which Nick Adams refers explicitly in "On Writing," the excised ending to "Big Two-Hearted River." The Calypso episode of *Ulysses* depicts Leopold Bloom engaged in a mundane activity—preparing breakfast in bed for his wife, Molly. The benefit of habitual behavior is that it frees one's mind to ruminate. Bloom, therefore, is able to brood about his wife's infidelity, his daughter's emerging sexuality, and his son's untimely death. By performing the routine action, he is able to attend to the thoughts that are troubling him. Nick does precisely the opposite. He, too, is executing a routine that he has done countless times, yet, unlike Bloom, he does not want to ruminate, so his concentration unnecessarily adheres to the tasks that he performs. He is occupying his consciousness with a challenge he might ordinarily accomplish unconsciously, thus defeating the economizing function of habit, producing the unsettling effect that his behavior is unmistakably compulsive.

William James, explaining habit, writes, "The more of the details of our daily life we can hand over to the effortless custody of automatism, the more our higher powers of mind will be set free for their own proper work" (I: 122). Later, James writes of the automaton: "A low brain does few things, and in doing them perfectly forfeits all other use" (I: 140). Indeed, in discussing "Big Two-Hearted River," the critic Larry Andrews picks up on James's term: "it is through assuming the role of the automaton," he writes, "that Nick hopes to recover" (3). Nick understands the function of habit and the function of mind, and yet it would be his greatest nightmare to allow the higher powers of his mind to be, in James's phrase, "set free." His goal is to choke, not to release. Although consciousness does not exert effort on that which is habitual, Nick luxuriates in the familiar details of the present moment and is able to engage in behavior that is not at all risky, as well as to contemplate habitual stimuli that are also comparatively safe. When Bloom makes tea, for instance, it is hardly the elaborate process that Nick considers his own task to be. Bloom's summation of the tea-making process is: "Cup of tea soon. Good. Mouth dry" (4.14). While he would appreciate Bloom's monosyllabic description, Nick's act of brewing a pot of coffee becomes a rare—actually singular—moment of reverie and retrospection.

James calls living creatures "bundles of habits" (I: 104) and explains that *"habit simplifies the movements required to achieve a given result, makes them more accurate and diminishes fatigue"* (I: 112, emphasis in original). In "Big Two-Hearted River," however, Nick is not interested in diminishing fatigue. Quite the opposite. Nick intentionally avoids striking the river early in his hike, instead carrying his heavy pack deeper into the woods. As Nick settles down at the end of Part One, we learn, "He could have made camp hours before if he had wanted to" (SS 216); later, he feels his mind "starting to work. He knew he could choke it because he was tired enough" (218). Nick does not want to consign all his activity to habit, the better to keep his mind alert and refreshed. He intentionally exhausts himself, increases rather than diminishes fatigue, which he knows will allow him to sleep. James quotes Henry Maudsley[9] on this very point. If habit did not exist to simplify a man's behavior, Maudsley writes, "the washing of his hands or the fastening of a button would be as difficult to him on each occasion as to the child on its first trial; and he would, furthermore, *be completely exhausted by his exertions . . . the conscious effort of the will soon produces exhaustion"* (qtd. in James, *Principles*, I: 114, emphasis added). For Nick Adams, this scenario does not carry the negative cast that Maudsley intends. By exercising his "effort of attention" in James's words or "effort of will" in Maudsley's, Nick expends all of his cognitive powers on simple, safe, or irrelevant things so that he will have no mental energy left for rumination, retrospection, or introspection.

If Leopold Bloom can reduce his tea-making to monosyllabic grunts, for Nick the task is more complex. In the superficial puzzle of the narrative, the central question becomes: How does one prepare a pot of coffee in the proper manner? Every other activity has been done precisely and expertly, and Nick wants to make sure the coffee will be handled with the same deliberation. At the minimum, Nick invests exaggerated importance in this issue, preferring to engage in an internal debate over coffee preparation rather than face the struggle of coming to terms with his war experience. Furthermore, Hemingway's presentation of Nick's organization of his external surroundings as a metaphor for the desire to replicate that order internally would become a hallmark of his fiction. For this reason, Hemingway's classic story is called "A Clean, Well-Lighted Place" and not "A Clean Well-Lighted Café." When a Hemingway character immerses himself in external sensory details, it often signals a desire to avoid the messy and arduous business of introspection. In *The Sun Also Rises*, for example, rather than disclose what Jake Barnes sees in the mirror when he looks at his injured bare body and how he feels about it, he interrupts his thoughts by musing inanely about the French-ness of his room's interior decoration.

The brief coffee-making episode in "Big Two-Hearted River" has attracted significant critical curiosity because it stands as the only reverie in the story. Nick's recollection of Hopkins serves the same narrative function as Santiago's recollection of his arm-wrestling exploits against "the great negro from Cienfuegos" in *The Old Man and the Sea* (69), a brief remembered episode that shows, as Richard Michael O'Brien posits, "the continuity of a consciousness in time . . . and the transcendence of isolation in space and time that the very holding of these values entails" (266). The memories in both narratives are rare gems of nostalgia that sneak through carefully controlled censors to provide glimpses of a mind not constrained by the urgent assignment, be it Nick's focus on the mechanics of his fishing trip or Santiago's task of capturing the marlin. As memories go, Nick's reminiscence of Hopkins is fairly unrevealing when compared with the gravity of the thoughts he is attempting to avoid. The very inclusion of this memory, though, is telling. Directly leading up to the coffee episode, Nick on three separate occasions forgets something with respect to dinner: to eat bread with his first plateful, to get water for the coffee, and the proper procedure to make coffee. "He could remember an argument about it with Hopkins," we are told, "but not which side he had taken" (SS 216–17). This episode that may seem extraneous in fact contains a key to reading Hemingway's career-long obsession with detailing the types of drinks his characters order, how the drinks are made, how his drinkers like them, what food the drinks accompany, how much it costs, and who pays for it all. By investigating the external detail, the character is relieved of performing a similar, more imperative, more painful inventory of the mind. The brief Hopkins passage reveals Nick's glee in trying to recall inconsequential nostalgia, as opposed to the struggle of trying to forget a tremendously important traumatic memory.

Robert Gibb, who refers to the memory of Hopkins as "pleasant but insufficient," aptly points out that "nostalgia for the middle past is no match for the horrors of the immediate past" (256). As Gibb suggests, Nick is defusing the power of memory by training it onto a comparatively harmless topic. The psychologist James W. Pennebaker observes a similar phenomenon in his interviews with traumatized subjects, noting: "the interviewee either changes the topic to something superficial or focuses on minutiae surrounding the topic." He points out that, "when under stress, the person focuses more narrowly or superficially on the stressful topic and/or is concerned with superficial issues unrelated to it" (90–91). Therefore, the overemphasis in some interpretations on the unpleasantness of the memory of Hopkins ignores the context; although a marginally unhappy incident in Nick's life, compared to the emotions of being blown up in Italy, it is, in Pennebaker's words, "moving to a *lower level of analysis*" (91, emphasis in original). Hemingway's intuitive grasp of this phenomenon of human consciousness makes the memory of Hopkins in "Big Two-Hearted River" so crucial precisely because of its relative triviality.

The analysis of the proper way to make coffee eventually wanes, and, as the coffee boils, Nick eats, introducing the following moment:

> While he waited for the coffee to boil, he opened a small can of apricots. He liked to open cans. He emptied the can of apricots out into a tin cup. While he watched the coffee on the fire, he drank the juice syrup of the apricots, carefully at first to keep from spilling, then *meditatively*, sucking the apricots down. (SS 217, emphasis added)

Hemingway has given Nick Adams his madeleine episode. If what makes Marcel's madeleine moment so quintessentially Proustian is its lavish exploration of involuntary memory triggered by the little cake, then what makes Nick's apricot juice moment so quintessentially Hemingwayesque is its language of omission, the iceberg theory manifest. Assigning the description "meditatively" to the act of drinking is a stunning adverbial choice in this context. Paired with the prior adverb "carefully," they represent the psychological extremes of the camping trip. For the vast majority of the story, Nick is careful not to meditate; when Nick eats the apricots, though, he surrenders to careful meditation. As in Proust, when the combination of food and beverage provokes an associative memory, Nick is transported to wartime, when consuming canned fruit was a necessity. However, unlike Proust, Hemingway does not expose the content of the meditation and refuses to pursue its source.[10] Since Marcel's memory is a warm and wonderful sensation, Proust has no qualms about exploring its source in detail. The involuntary memory in *Swann's Way* is an "exquisite pleasure" and an "all-powerful joy" (60). Too many of Nick Adams's memories, of course, are dreadful. All Hemingway reveals, therefore, is the mysterious evocative quality of the fruit, as with Proust's madeleine. The writer's aesthetic restraint matches the protagonist's mental control by withholding the information from the reader, which mimics the way the character does not verbalize it and instead seeks to refuse its entry into consciousness. Hemingway gives only Nick's judgment of the strictly sensory detail of this drinking: "They were better than fresh apricots" (217). The comment is insipid, a wholly inadequate replacement of the content of the memory, which serves the story's thematic purpose.

Nick's attempt to control his cognitive functioning, his endeavor to manage his sensory intake, ultimately determines how "Big Two-Hearted River" is interpreted. In the excised ending posthumously published as "On Writing," Nick's fragile victory is more explicitly stated. The conclusion of the "mental conversation" that Hemingway (and Stein) deemed extraneous reads: "He was holding something in his head" (NAS 241). This final line echoes another from earlier: "He climbed the bank of the stream, reeling up his line and started through the brush. He ate a sandwich. He was in a hurry and the rod bothered him. He was not thinking. He was holding something in his head. He wanted to get back to camp and get to work" (240). The phrase "holding something in his head" is an apt poetic rendering of mental control; Nick has gained mastery of an idea, harnessed a thunderbolt of inspiration, and he is holding it, rather than being held by it. He is controlling it, rather than being hostage to it. Furthermore, the significance of Nick "holding" something in his head rather than having to "choke it" demonstrates a less antagonistic relationship with his own mind. The verb "hold" signals the holding pattern and demonstrates Nick's confidence that he will eventually have a more stable relationship with his memory, that the "plenty of days coming when he could fish the swamp" promises a period of difficult self-searching and reconciliation with the horrors of war (SS 232). "Big Two-Hearted River" is certainly progress, a first step, no matter how tentative. "Big Two-Hearted River" must not be seen as a gloomy example of a young man who has surrendered. Nick's decision to "quell the storm" swirling in his psyche—perhaps the same storm Hemingway drew up in his manuscript sketch of the story's movement—is the equivalent of a surgeon who waits until his patient's swelling subsides before performing the necessary operation.

For Nick to be "not thinking" while also "holding something in his head" in consecutive sentences appears paradoxical. However, it is apparent that, at this moment, Nick equates "thinking" to tortured rumination upon the past, while "holding something" is the Bergsonian idea of acting upon inspiration, of thought as action. The "work" Nick is eager to begin is the effort to compose immortal fiction. If "On Writing" might be considered as a conclusion to *In Our Time*, the accepted reading of the collection as a Bildungsroman must be modified to consider the volume a Künstlerroman, the narrative of an artist's maturation. This artistic exorcism gestures toward a more clinical way to avoid painful cognition over a traumatic event. Daniel Gold and Wegner explain that "ruminations often occur following traumatic events. We think and stew, trying to make sense of the unsensible. Based on a cathartic view of expression, until we talk about and release those thoughts, they will continue. Like a pressure cooker that needs to let off steam, it is beneficial, if not necessary, to express our thoughts" (1251).[11] This human need, after all, brought forth psychotherapy and, probably, the ritual of confession.[12]

The last line of "Big Two-Hearted River"—"There were plenty of days coming when he could fish the swamp" (232)—signals knowing discipline. Nick understands he has a future, one that promises more than his current capabilities permit. The last line is not naive and a signal of the futility of the journey to the river. The acknowledgment of the "plenty of days coming" is something Nick could not have asserted during the war. His present belief that in the future he will be capable of more adventurous, unpredictable activity is the most self-aware, mature moment any Hemingway protagonist ever experiences. The camping trip serves as a gauge to test Nick's limits, the capacity of his sensations, emotions, and thought. It may be a disappointment, but it is not a defeat to find that his limitations are more constricting than they were when he was a boy or will be in the future. "Big Two-Hearted River" represents progress toward the final destination, not an easy answer that solves all Nick's problems.

As a first step, however, Nick is on dangerous ground even as he walks his familiar paths. He has unwittingly created toxic associations between his beloved childhood sanctuary and World War I. Furthermore, by suppressing his thoughts, he risks exacerbating them. Psychologists studying mental control show that subjects derive an initial excitement by suppressing "exciting thoughts" and then receive a more powerful effect by those thoughts when they eventually resurface (Wegner et al. 409). The phenomenon of sexual suppression leading to flamboyant and unexpected articulations of these submerged emotions has become accepted, even in Hemingway's work; the same phenomenon is produced by the suppression of trauma. The cautionary tale of this story, then, is that Nick has left plenty of unfinished business and has not left this business in the most secure position. Just as Lawrence Taylor's problem requires professional help rather than self-diagnosis, Nick cannot fish his way out of his shock. Nick knows that there are plenty of days coming when he will be able to fish the swamp, and he needs to remember that there are plenty of days coming when he must.

2

The Solitary Consciousness II

Metacognition and Mental Control
in *The Old Man and the Sea*

> The voice of the sea is seductive; never ceasing, whispering, clamoring,
> murmuring, inviting the soul to wander for a spell in abysses of solitude; to
> lose itself in mazes of inward contemplation.
>
> Kate Chopin, The Awakening

> Yes, as every one knows, meditation and water are wedded for ever.
>
> Herman Melville, Moby-Dick

*A*s we have seen in Hemingway's early masterpiece "Big Two-Hearted
River," Shakespearean soliloquies, and Thoreau's *Walden,* the activity of
consciousness is never more imbued with depth and complexity than when a
protagonist is alone. The two most poignant moments of *The Sun Also Rises,* for
example, show Jake Barnes alone: in chapter 4, when he exposes his wound as
he undresses in front of a mirror, and in chapter 14, as he puts down Turgenev's
Sportsman's Sketches and struggles to fall asleep in the heady Pamplona night.
During these moments, Jake is not distracted by the activities of Paris and the
fiesta or by his cadre of drinkers and fishermen; his inhibitions overwhelmed by
alcohol, Jake's true introspective nature emerges, and, during those revealing

moments of solitude, readers are given access to what he calls the "oversensitized state" of his mind (SAR 153). These moments of metacognition elevate to a moving narrative what might otherwise have been a frivolous collection of drinking anecdotes. In Nick Adams stories like "Now I Lay Me" and "A Way You'll Never Be," the interiority of the Hemingway hero is revealed most vividly in moments of solitude. Nick's camping trip in "Big Two-Hearted River," which was examined in the previous chapter, and Santiago in *The Old Man and the Sea* provide unmediated views of the protagonists' consciousness in ways unparalleled in any other Hemingway narrative. Hemingway's solitary men reveal their complex mental states more freely when unencumbered by the complexity of human interaction and thus are not forced into an unconvincing persona, a transparent façade of stoicism.

Chapter 1's discussion of "Big Two-Hearted River" begins the discussion of the solitary consciousness at the apex of Hemingway's achievement. Hemingway's early story is often regarded as his masterpiece by Hemingway scholars and is generally considered the exceptional text to those who may ordinarily marginalize Hemingway. *The Old Man and the Sea*, on the other hand, is considered antithetical to the virtuosity of "Big Two-Hearted River." The novella is generally seen as Hemingway's most simple tale, a poorly disguised fable, or a one-dimensional metaphor for the aging writer's last grasp at greatness or even relevance. As William E. Cain has remarked, the novella holds "only a marginal place in Hemingway studies" (113). In Susan F. Beegel's recap of the historical development of Hemingway criticism, she points to the lack of interest in *The Old Man and the Sea*, a result of what she terms "its simplistic approach to courage and endurance in the face of adversity" ("Conclusion" 281). A representative early review of *The Old Man and the Sea* asserts, "His novels have more power than depth, more action than thought. There is no introspection, there is only outer action. . . . There is no inwardness; only things being done; nothing is being deeply contemplated" (Freehof 47). Those who would diminish any Hemingway text because of its simplicity ignore Hemingway's own warning from his Nobel Prize acceptance speech, just two years after *The Old Man and the Sea*: "Things may not be immediately discernible in what a man writes . . . but eventually they are quite clear" (qtd. in Bruccoli, *Mechanism* 134). In 1958, Hemingway similarly cautioned an interviewer against reflexive reactions to his work: "You can be sure that there is much more than will be read at any first reading" (Plimpton 29–30). Hemingway's reputation is based largely on his principle of omission, his iceberg theory that is tempting to misconstrue as simplism or absence of depth.

As he did so often during the second half of his career, Hemingway's project with *The Old Man and the Sea* was to revisit an earlier narrative; in its meticulous focus on the solitary consciousness, *The Old Man and the Sea* becomes an improbable sequel to "Big Two-Hearted River." Critics have previously linked *The Old Man and the Sea* with "Big Two-Hearted River," although usually to discredit the novella. In Kenji Nakajima's monograph devoted to "Big Two-Hearted River," he finds a parallel between the story and *The Old Man and the Sea* but considers the latter narrative vastly inferior, claiming that Hemingway's "vain attempt to return" to "Big Two-Hearted River" ended in a "miserable parody" (1, 78). Robert Brainard Pearsall also links the two texts, suggesting that Nick's trout "would reappear as a giant marlin" (65). Thomas Strychacz devotes a chapter in his *Hemingway's Theaters of Masculinity* to readings of "Big Two-Hearted River" and *The Old Man and the Sea*, viewing them as voices of the "self offstage" (221) and focusing keenly on the evocation of manhood and performance in the two narratives.

The psychological layer to *The Old Man and the Sea* can be fully excavated only if it is read with "Big Two-Hearted River" in mind and even treated as a restatement and reevaluation of the early story. The narratives are so superficially opposed that each becomes an inverted mirror image of the other, forming memorable bookends to Hemingway's career. Nick Adams is Hemingway's youngest protagonist and Santiago his oldest. Nick is a young man returning to simplicity after his harrowing experience in World War I; the old man is in his final days, desperately plunging into a situation that is dangerous from its inception. In "Big Two-Hearted River," solitude is central to Nick's goal; Santiago, although also alone, often wishes the boy Manolin had accompanied him. Nick avoids the physical swamp at the edge of the stream and, by doing so, avoids the harrowing unknown of his psyche. Santiago, however, is forced into the far reaches of the gulf, past where all other fishermen work, and thus into the darker regions of his mind. Nick seeks to avoid the "tragic adventure" of the swamp (SS 231), but Santiago has no such luxury; *The Old Man and the Sea* becomes exactly the tragedy that "Big Two-Hearted River" could have been had Nick not possessed the self-awareness and restraint to limit his activity. In an ironic touch, the young man must behave with safety and caution, while the old man rages against the dying of the light, recklessly heeding the call to adventure.[1] Nick's strategy of rehabilitation hinges on self-distraction—to consider anything except his one unpleasant memory—while Santiago's goal is concentration, to focus only on the task at hand, regardless of the difficulty of maintaining such mental discipline.

Although these narratives are opposites in all of these respects, both dramatize metacognition; in their solitude and through their travails, each character's thoughts are occupied by his own thoughts. Therefore, the management of each man's consciousness becomes the primary concern of the narrative. In "Big Two-Hearted River," the ritual of camping matches the order that Nick seeks in his mind; in *The Old Man and the Sea*, Santiago's quest is related not to the physical act of fishing but rather to the internal sustenance of mental solvency, mental control, sanity, the mastery of consciousness.

The swamp Nick prudently avoids in "Big Two-Hearted River" out of respect for his fragile psyche becomes the arena of activity in *The Old Man and the Sea*. From the inception of the journey, the old man's mission will be not one of psychological recuperation but instead a trial of superhuman physical exertion. The Cuban coastline contains no swamp like Nick's in Michigan; however, as a vague well of dread and a metaphor representing risk, chance, and the unknown, the far reaches of the sea serve a similar function. Santiago must sail headlong into the most unpredictable, uncontrollable area of the gulf waters. The old man compares his own heroic abandon with the marlin's: "His [the fish's] choice had been to stay in the deep dark water far out beyond all snares and traps and treacheries. My choice was to go there to find him beyond all people. Beyond all people in the world" (50). Nick's solitary excursion also takes him to a point of seclusion, but because other people are the snares and traps and treacheries, variables too complicated and disruptive for his process of recuperation. The plight of Nick's counterpart, Harold Krebs, in "Soldier's Home" demonstrates what might have befallen Nick had he not carefully monitored his association with other people. The end of "Soldier's Home" shows Krebs resolving to leave home and set off by himself, a victory no matter where he ends up.

Just as Nick equates the swamp with tragic adventure, Santiago's notion of entering the terrain of the "deep dark water" openly invites such tragedy. Therefore, it is no surprise when Santiago's journey ends disastrously, least of all to Santiago, who always understood the magnitude of his gamble. After the marlin has been attacked by sharks, Santiago apologizes directly to the fish, saying, "I shouldn't have gone out so far, fish" (110) and, again, "I am sorry that I went too far out" (115); he then reprimands himself: "You violated your luck when you went too far outside" (116). He explicitly admits the cause of his downfall: "And what beat you, he thought. 'Nothing,' he said aloud. 'I went out too far'" (120). Nick's goal is to revisit the terrain with which he is most familiar; Santiago must break free from his usual fishing spots, since they have been decidedly unlucky over the previous eighty-four days. The novel's final image is of Santiago "dreaming about the lions" of his youth (127), which puts him—in his unconscious—into the comfortable and familiar grounds that Nick enjoys, even though he did not have that luxury during his final adventure.

If *The Old Man and the Sea* is read as a narrative of metacognition in the tradition of "Big Two-Hearted River," Hemingway's own statements regarding its creation carry profound resonance. Hemingway reveals that his true intent is to track the trajectory of Santiago's interiority, not to measure the size and weight of the fish or to fixate on any external encounters and activities.

Although the psychological aspect of *The Old Man and the Sea* is not nearly as celebrated as that of "Big Two-Hearted River," the cognition of the protagonist serves a virtually identical role in the narrative and was equally essential to Hemingway's project. Hemingway's journalistic work for *Esquire* in the 1930s hints at the psychological dimension to *The Old Man and the Sea*. In "Out in the Stream: A Cuban Letter," published in August 1934, Hemingway describes fishing for marlin off the north coast of Cuba. "You have a lot of time to think out in the gulf," Hemingway writes, describing how one is able to fish more casually and "still have time to speculate on higher and lower things" (BL 172). Hemingway, realizing that he was, like Ishmael in this chapter's epigraph, linking meditation and water and perhaps subverting his carefully manufactured man-of-action self-image, then mocks himself: "You may be bored blind with the whole thing and be waiting for the action to begin or the conversation to start. Gentlemen, I'd like to oblige you but this is one of those instructive ones. This is one of those contemplative pieces of the sort that Izaak Walton[2] used to write" (173). Later in the article, Hemingway writes that, when fishing, "while you wait there is plenty of time to think" (174); he allows that catching marlin "is a fairly full time job although it allows plenty of time for thinking" (177). Such an insistence on the meditative value of fishing informs the later description of Santiago's struggle.

Two years later, Hemingway pinned down more specifically the story of the old fisherman he wanted to include in his never-realized Land, Sea, and Air epic, which was to include *The Old Man and the Sea* as an epilogue. In a 1936 article for *Esquire* called "On the Blue Water: A Gulf Stream Letter," Hemingway recounts:

> an old man fishing alone in a skiff out of Cabañas hooked a great marlin that, on the heavy sashcord handline, pulled the skiff far out to sea. Two days later the old man was picked up by fishermen sixty miles to the eastward, the head and forward part of the marlin lashed alongside. What was left of the fish, less than half, weighed eight hundred pounds. The old man had stayed with him a

day, a night, a day and another night while the fish swam deep and pulled the boat. When he had come up the old man had pulled the boat up on him and harpooned him. Lashed alongside the sharks had hit him and the old man had fought them out alone in the Gulf Stream in a skiff, clubbing them, stabbing at them, lunging at them with an oar until he was exhausted and the sharks had eaten all that they could hold. He was crying in the boat when the fishermen picked him up, *half crazy from his loss,* and the sharks were still circling the boat. (BL 239–40, emphasis added).

This actual event that inspired Hemingway and provided him with the trajectory of the novella's plot is crucial because Hemingway remarks on the old man's mental state, the loss or lapse of his sanity. The physical fatigue is understandable, but the old man's potential descent into madness adds a layer of psychological gravity to the simple fishing adventure. The battle with the marlin and the sharks, after all, is relevant only for its impact on Santiago's internal confrontation with his pride, endurance, and the difficult feat of mental control, a battle that Santiago eventually loses.

In a letter to Scribner's editor Maxwell Perkins on 7 February 1939 — roughly the midpoint between the publication dates of *In Our Time* and *The Old Man and the Sea* — Hemingway reveals ideas for forthcoming projects, one of which would become *The Old Man and the Sea*:

> And three very long ones I want to write now. . . . One about the old commercial fisherman who fought the swordfish all alone in his skiff for 4 days and four nights and the sharks finally eating it after he had it alongside and could not get it into the boat. That's a wonderful story of the Cuban coast. . . . *Everything he does and everything he thinks* in all that long fight with the boat out of sight of all the other boats all alone on the sea. (SL 479, emphasis added)

Even at this nascent stage of *The Old Man and the Sea*, Hemingway's focus rests on the cognition of the old man in equal measure to the physical battle with the fish. Santiago's action and Santiago's thoughts are of equivalent importance in Hemingway's schema of the narrative. Since the publication of *The Old Man and the Sea*, critics have generally overlooked this carefully crafted equilibrium.

Just as Nick Adams's life story is a battle to stave off insanity — reaching its terrifying zenith in "A Way You'll Never Be" — Santiago's struggle is also psychological. For Hemingway, the physical and psychological aspects to fiction were never a simple either/or proposition. A story did not need to be taxonomized as either a mindless action-adventure or a static meditation; Hemingway's goal was to portray Santiago's strained thoughts during moments of action and compromised actions during moments of contemplation.

The night before Santiago embarks upon his epic fishing expedition, his young friend Manolin realizes that he has failed to bring the old man toiletries, linen, and other comforts. He excoriates himself, asking, "Why am I so thoughtless?" (21). Moments earlier, the old man had praised Martin, the owner of the Terrace bar, for providing victuals and utensils, saying, "He is very thoughtful for us" (20). These adjectives—"thoughtless" and "thoughtful"—are obviously meant to be synonyms for, respectively, "inconsiderate" and "considerate" and are based on how each person has treated Santiago. However, by framing the discourse in terms of thought-quantity, the characters introduce a thematic notion that informs the rest of the novella, as well as forcefully recalling "Big Two-Hearted River." Manolin's criticism of thought-lessness directly following Santiago's praise of thought-fulness assumes tremendous significance when Santiago becomes physically imperiled and psychologically unstable.

Just as from the beginning of "Big Two-Hearted River" it is evident that Nick is alone in the woods, the same solitude is firmly established in the first sentence of *The Old Man and the Sea*: "He was an old man who fished alone in a skiff in the Gulf Stream and he had gone eighty-four days now without taking a fish" (9). When Manolin praises Santiago's singular skill as a fisherman, he simultaneously alludes to the isolation necessary to the old man's ultimate task: "But there is only you" (23). Santiago's characterization as a man of nature is vivid as with Nick's treatment of the birds, insects, and fish as kin (even those he kills); the old man "looked ahead and saw a flight of wild ducks etching themselves against the sky . . . and he knew no man was ever alone on the sea" (60–61). Santiago constantly refers to the marlin as his friend and the porpoises, marlin, and stars as his brothers. He also wishes several times that Manolin were with him to help him land the marlin; however, after the sharks massacre his prize catch, his fantasy is revealing: "I wish it had been a dream now and that I had never hooked the fish and was alone in bed on the newspapers" (103). The old man's desire for solitude is ultimately stronger than his desire to be reunited with his dead wife, or to spend time with the boy, or to relax over a cold beer with the men of the village at the Terrace.

Ultimately, Santiago's external adventure is an elaborate metaphor for the internal struggle that occurs, which is the old man's tenacious determination to retain mental control during his pain, fatigue, and solitude. The physical death implied at the end of the narrative is precipitated only after Santiago has surrendered control of his own consciousness. The most devastating sequence in *The Old Man and the Sea* occurs in a concentrated three-paragraph span.

Santiago spits discharge into the ocean and admits to the sharks that he has been killed, and those actions are followed by the description of a vacant psyche, a void in consciousness that marks the tragedy of the story.

> The old man could hardly breathe now and he felt a strange taste in his mouth. It was coppery and sweet and he was afraid of it for a moment. But there was not much of it.
>
> He spat into the ocean and said, "Eat that, *galanos*. And make a dream you've killed a man."
>
> He knew he was beaten now finally and without remedy . . . He settled the sack around his shoulders and put the skiff on her course. He sailed lightly now and he had no thoughts nor any feelings of any kind. He was past everything now and he sailed the skiff to make his home port as well and as intelligently as he could. (119)

The state of thought-lessness and feeling-lessness into which Santiago has descended, the state of being "past everything," recalls the purported void of safety Nick savors at the beginning of "Big Two-Hearted River," in which he feels shielded from "the need for thinking, the need to write, other needs" (SS 210). However, the difference in context is crucial. For Santiago, the loss of thought and feeling and the detachment from "everything" signal his tragic loss of consciousness, an inescapable doom that has suddenly inverted the triumph of securing the great fish.[3] Hemingway, whose interest in writing *The Old Man and the Sea* focused on chronicling the old man's thoughts during the struggle, portrays Santiago at the end of the struggle as having those thoughts entirely drained out of him.

The theme of mental control emerges when Santiago recognizes that he is in for a colossal battle with the marlin. A small bird distracts Santiago, whose concentration is taken away from the marlin on his hook, and the fish lurches, cutting the old man's hand. The old man vows that he will not allow himself to be so careless again:

> How did I let the fish cut me with that one quick pull he made? I must be getting very stupid. Or perhaps I was looking at the small bird and thinking of him. Now I will pay attention to my work and then I must eat the tuna so that I will not have a failure of strength. (56)

This moment is Santiago's wake-up call. At once, he steels himself with nutrients for physical strength and then commands himself to maintain mental clarity to focus on the task. The moment establishes the twin challenges of the journey, ideas that compete throughout the narrative: the sanity and saliency of the old man's thoughts on one hand and the physical health of his weakening body on the other. The excerpt that signals Santiago's demise, too, fuses these two defeats: the extinguishing of consciousness ("no thoughts nor any feelings of any kind" [119]) and the spitting of bile from his diseased body, admitting impending death to the sharks. Hemingway represents the death of the old man through an explicit investigation of Santiago's consciousness and mental state, with the physical consequences of the frailty of his thought left ominously implicit.

By investing such thematic significance into the moment in which the small bird appears, Hemingway echoes William James, who uses a similar metaphor for the stream of thought. "Like a bird's life," James writes of consciousness, "it seems to be made of an alternation of flights and perchings" (*Principles*, I: 243), where the resting places represent unchanging, stable thoughts and the moments of flight are occupied by thoughts relating those more static observations and perceptions. To James, the resting points are "substantive parts" of the stream of consciousness, and flight connotes "transitive parts." As demonstrated by Santiago, the perching of a bird lulls the old man into a mental resting point, causing a lapse in his attention towards the more urgent, dangerous task at hand.

The Old Man and the Sea continues as Hemingway's most evocative extended portrait of metacognition since "Big Two-Hearted River."[4] Even before Santiago hooks the marlin, he interrupts one of his ruminations about rich fishermen listening to baseball on the radio. "Now is no time to think of baseball, he thought. Now is the time to think of only one thing. That which I was born for" (40). Just as "Big Two-Hearted River" is metacognitive in that Nick wishes to distract himself, *The Old Man and the Sea* is equally metacognitive in that Santiago must concentrate. The difficulty is that, because of the nature of the rigors of the expedition, Santiago is perpetually distracted from his central task: by baseball, by memories of hand wrestling, by wishing the boy were with him, by his physical ailments, by other animals on the sea, and so on. James makes an eloquent point on the nature of attention, writing, "Effort is felt only when there is a conflict of interests in the mind. The idea A may be intrinsically exciting to us. The idea Z may derive its interest from association with some remoter good" (I: 451). If pleasant memories and thoughts are Category A thoughts, the business at hand requires sustaining thoughts in Category Z. Even early in the journey, Santiago knows "now is no time" (40) for distracting thoughts. James, in elucidating distraction, illuminates the inner conflict that makes *The Old Man and the Sea* worth serious examination: "As concentrated attention accelerates perception, so, conversely perception of a stimulus is *retarded by anything which either baffles or distracts the attention* with which we await it" (I: 429, emphasis in original). Echoing this point a century later, the philosopher Daniel Dennett writes:

> Simple or overlearned tasks without serious competition can be routinely executed without the enlistment of extra forces, and hence unconsciously, but when a task is difficult or unpleasant, it requires "concentration," something "we" accomplish with the help of much self-admonition and various other mnemonic tricks, rehearsals, and other self-manipulations. Often we find it helps to talk out loud, a throwback to the crude but effective strategies of which our private thoughts are sleek descendants. (277)

Unlike Nick, Santiago needs his perceptive powers to be at their maximum level in order for him to land the marlin. Dennett's phrases resonate in *The Old Man and the Sea*, which is filled with both Santiago's "self-admonitions" and his speaking out loud.

This reality—the practical benefit of concentration versus the temptation of more pleasant, easier thoughts—will haunt Santiago for the three days and two nights of his struggle. After the initial challenge of hooking and trying to control the fish, Santiago settles himself and comprehends the magnitude of the battle he will have. The description even at the beginning of the struggle is of a futile challenge: "He rested sitting on the un-stepped mast and sail and tried not to think but only to endure" (46). A struggle though it may be, physical endurance is more feasible for Santiago to sustain than is not-thinking. Moments later, the issue becomes less the complete erasure of thoughts than the matter of controlling them properly. After another thought about baseball and listening to games as pleasant distraction, Santiago gives himself a self-admonition of the kind Dennett describes: "Then he thought, think of it always. Think of what you are doing. You must do nothing stupid" (48). The balance—among not thinking at all versus unhelpful thoughts versus disciplined concentration on the task at hand—oscillates for the rest of the novella. To determine whether *The Old Man and the Sea* is a tragedy or a triumph, it must be understood which of these three possible mental states ultimately predominates.

At times, Santiago is tempted to eradicate entirely his stream of consciousness, knowing that he would perform his task better as an automaton. He interrupts a pleasant meditation about his recurring dreams of lions on the beach: "Don't think, old man, he said to himself" (66), which quickly becomes "He felt very tired now . . . and he tried to think of other things. He thought of the Big Leagues" (67). After the shark attacks the prize marlin, Santiago articulates his most memorable philosophy—"man is not made for defeat. . . . A man can be destroyed but not defeated"—and then immediately excoriates himself: "Don't think, old man," and then finally responds, defending his own consciousness: "But I must think, he thought. Because it is all I have left" (103). He then coaches himself, "Think about something, cheerful, old man" (104). Erik Nakjavani's article on this phenomenon in Hemingway's work shrewdly underscores this moment, pointing out that "the attenuation of the hyperactivity of the mind by *redirecting its focus* replaces the activity of non-thinking as the easier of the two tasks to be achieved" ("Nonthinking" 184, emphasis in original). With Santiago's enactment of this scheme—"Think about something cheerful"—Nakjavani's observation validates Daniel M. Wegner's thesis that the stream of consciousness can be redirected to avoid dangerous targets far more easily than the brakes can be slammed on. A more general view comes from Linda W. Wagner, who finds this moment in *The Old Man and the Sea* notable because "new in this novel is the explicit injunction to think. Contrary to the earlier admonitions of Barnes, Henry, Morgan, Jordan, Thomas Hudson, and Cantwell that they not think—because, we suppose, Hamlet-like, they would be too fearful to act" (526), Santiago coaches himself to think.

Although Santiago knows that self-distraction is the better option, the old man lapses into the snares and traps and treacheries of the mind that are dogging him, remorseful over the massacre of the beautiful fish, an act he considers sinful, thus producing a decidedly unwelcome emotion. While Wagner's observation frames the Hemingway corpus in a valuable way, her observation about the novella is at times contradicted forcefully: "Do not think about sin, he thought. . . . Do not think about sin. It is much too late for that and there are people who are paid to do it. Let them think about it" (105). Then, the novella's dialectic is outlined between helpful and unhelpful thinking, as is Santiago's impulse to meditation: "But he liked to think about all things that he was involved in and since there was nothing to read and he did not have a radio, he thought much and he kept on thinking about sin" (105). Predictably, as he continues contemplating the events of the fishing journey, he interrupts himself with his familiar self-admonition: "You think too much, old man" (105). Even given these frequent repetitions, estimations of *The Old Man and the Sea* have tended to underestimate the old man's cognitive hyperactivity. To regard Santiago as a simple Cuban fisherman is an overly provincial response to the narrative; perhaps those views ultimately reveal more about the critic than about the character himself. It is true that the narrator says of Santiago, "He was too simple to wonder when he had attained humility" (13), but, after tracking his consciousness for three days, we must conclude that either Santiago is far from simple or that all human beings, scrutinized sufficiently, are far from simple. Santiago may be unassuming, modest, and humble, but his thoughts under stress are conflicted and complex. Santiago, too, has powers that are not immediately discernible.

After Santiago tells himself once again that he thinks too much, the balance of the novel is composed of this internal competition over the utility of his thoughts. Recalling the beginning of the expedition where he vows to concentrate by saying, "Now is the time to think of only one thing" (40), he repeats the idea toward its end: "Now is no time to think of what you do not have. Think of what you can do with what there is" (110). Following this self-reflexive "good counsel" (110), offered in twenty-two monosyllabic words, an intense episode of confused metacognition ensues: "He did not want to think of the mutilated under-side of the fish. . . . He was a fish to keep a man all winter, he thought. Don't think of that. . . . What can I think of now? he thought. Nothing. I must think of nothing and wait for the next ones" (111). Santiago must replace thinking with doing, enacting Bergson's tenet that "we think only in order to act. Our intellect has been cast in the mold of action" (*Creative Evolution* 44). Carlos Baker also links the Hemingway hero to pragmatism, arguing that the function of the Hemingway hero's thought "is, in the end, to serve as a guide for action. The abstraction has little meaning for him until it is particularized in a specific situation" (*Writer as Artist* 155). Baker's point may suggest the reason why "The Snows of Kilimanjaro" is such a conspicuous text in Hemingway's career, the exception where surrendering to death elicits abstractions and fantasy and ultimately legitimizes them.

Although Santiago understands and would agree with those who argue for the practical utility of thought, this concept is easier to aphorize than to enact. In one of the few critical pieces associating Hemingway with Bergson, Green D. Wyrick negates his ingenious linking of the two writers with a catastrophic misreading of *The Old Man and the Sea*. "The *élan vital*," Wyrick writes, "or Hemingway's 'real thing,' is superbly captured for our time in *The Old Man and the Sea*. The world may break, crucify, and destroy, but that is the way of the world. The fact that Santiago survives, is happy and ready to fish again, proves for the first time that Hemingway will allow this twentieth century to sustain such men" (19). Wyrick's contentions that Santiago (a) survives (b) is happy, and (c) is ready to fish again are three swings and misses. *The Old Man and the Sea* demonstrates the spiritual sustenance of the old man despite his physical and psychological destruction. There is no textual indication that Santiago is "ready to fish again." Had he more days to fish, the old man would not have sailed so desperately into the dangerous waters. This journey has killed Santiago.

As the late afternoon comes, Santiago tells himself, "You're tired, old man. . . . You're tired inside" (112). The variation is telling, a distinction between general physical exhaustion and mental fatigue. Santiago wants to address the fish as he has for most of the narrative, but he does not feel he can speak to a mutilated corpse. Despite his pervasive fatigue, he is struck by an idea, worded in an important way: "Then something came into his head" (115). That "something" is the idea to speak to the marlin as "Half fish," which he does, apologizing for straying too far from the more conservative fishing routine. However, the characterization that an idea "came into his head" must be contrasted to the end of "On Writing," the excised conclusion to "Big Two-Hearted River," when Nick is the one with enough control over his thoughts to be "holding something in his head" (NAS 241). The distinction between these two instances is the difference between a sudden intrusion and the fortuitous control of that intrusion. Unlike the necessary recklessness of the old man, Nick's cautious behavior in "Big Two-Hearted River" enables such mental control.

The paragraph describing the tragic outcome of the old man's battle is unambiguous: "He knew he was beaten now finally and without remedy . . . He sailed lightly now and he had no thoughts nor any feelings of any kind. He was past everything now" (119). The end of *The Old Man and the Sea*, with its depiction of the permanent loss of mental control and an individual's authority over his own consciousness, echoes the beginning of "Big Two-Hearted River," which dramatizes a temporary suspension of introspection in order to gain stability. Nick speaks of days ahead where the swamp might be fished on his terms; Santiago's eighty-four day drought has thrust him into the position where he must plunge into the trickiest waters, which yield the most valuable rewards but also the greatest danger. The loss of the fish is only metaphorical to the losses that go along with it: the loss of thought, the loss of sensation, the loss of memory, and the loss of his powers of attention. "The old man," he is described, "paid no attention to them [the sharks] and did not pay attention to anything except steering" (119). In this sense, Santiago has been reduced to the shell-shocked Nick Adams, concentrating on a mundane task that might otherwise be performed habitually, in order to distract himself from the sharks, his illness and fatigue, and the misery of his current situation.

Narratologically, Hemingway's technique for representing Santiago's consciousness utilizes more elaborate stylistic devices than does "Big Two-Hearted River," mimicking the various techniques Santiago himself must use. Faced with the challenge of conveying the old man's thoughts in solitude, Hemingway uses an array of methods, both to break up monotony and to include the reader more intimately in Santiago's cognitive processes. C. P. Heaton's mathematical breakdown of *The Old Man and the Sea* discloses that of the 1,735 sentences in the novella, "261 (15 percent) are found in dialogue between the old man and the boy, 226 (13 percent) are spoken aloud by the old man and are in quotation marks, and 503 (29 percent) are thoughts of the old man. Of these thoughts, 501 are not enclosed in quotes" (14). It would take some straining and an unshakeable faith in Hemingway's attention to detail to find a skeleton key to Hemingway's technique, as if a certain strategy for reporting the old man's thoughts or speech were used in each instance for a logical reason. However, the mere presence of the myriad styles adds to the narrative's complexity and highlights the focus on Santiago's consciousness.

Dorrit Cohn's *Transparent Minds* provides narratological tools to taxonomize the various ways Hemingway conveys the solitary consciousness. In *The Old Man and the Sea*, Hemingway employs what Cohn calls "psycho-narration," what is more traditionally referred to as "omniscient description," a tool that allows the narrator to report authoritatively the private thoughts of the old man (e.g., the closing line: "The old man was dreaming about the lions" [127]). Cohn also refers to "quoted monologue," which she defines as "a character's mental discourse" (14). As Heaton observes, Hemingway spends most of *The Old Man and the Sea* in this mode, with Santiago's thoughts emerging through things he says aloud to himself or to other creatures or objects, his thoughts quoted directly or described by the narrator. A third category Cohn discusses in her section on third-person narratives is "narrated monologue," which occurs when the narrator adopts the consciousness of the narrator when describing that consciousness. Hemingway adopts this technique in the sixty-seven word excerpt of "Big Two-Hearted River" mentioned in the previous chapter, in which sixty-three of the words are monosyllables, the precision of the narration suggesting Nick's meticulous thought processes, to convey consciousness not only through information imparted but also stylistically. Between "Big Two-Hearted River" and *The Old Man and the Sea*, there is only one exclamation point, at the moment when Santiago screams "Now!" upon striking the hooked marlin (OMS 44).[5] "Big Two-Hearted River" contains none. In these two narratives, with mental control always of paramount importance, a similar control had to be mimicked by the vocabulary, syntax, and grammar of the writer.

Santiago's tendency to speak aloud while he is alone is one conspicuously artificial conceit of the novella. Although he knows it is "considered a virtue not to talk unnecessarily at sea," the old man in this circumstance "said his thoughts" when he is alone "since there was no one that they could annoy" (39). Santiago speaks to himself, to his hands, to no one in general, to the fish he has landed, and to other animals he encounters. A more striking use of the bifurcation between thought and speech takes place in "Big Two-Hearted River," in which Nick speaks aloud only three times: "'Go on, hopper,' Nick said, speaking out loud for the first time. 'Fly away somewhere'" (SS 212); "'I've got a right to eat this kind of stuff, if I'm willing to carry it,' Nick said. His voice sounded strange in the darkening woods. He did not speak again" (215). But he does, one more time: "'Chrise,' Nick said, 'Geezus Chrise,' he said happily" (216). Hemingway, a celebrated master of dialogue, shows in these narratives his power of selection in allowing his solitary characters to monologize.

The prize catch at the end of *The Old Man and the Sea* would have been mental stability. Santiago knows that the acuity of his thoughts is in jeopardy, and, through the narration, the reader is cautioned about the stakes. Santiago reminds himself aloud of clarity's importance and then silently: "'You must devise a way so that you sleep a little if he [the marlin] is quiet and steady. If you do not sleep you might become unclear in the head.' I'm clear enough in the head, he thought. Too clear. I am as clear as the stars that are my brothers" (77). At the same time that his physical exertion reaches its most taxing level, he notices when his thoughts become less lucid. After imagining that he would not care if his cramped hand were amputated, the narrator intrudes in order to state, "When he thought that he knew that he was not being clear-headed" (85). After Santiago—in his thoughts—taunts the fish to come and kill him, because "I do not care who kills who," it might be read as mythological identification with the fish. However, he quickly amends the sentiment, reprimanding himself, "Now you are getting confused in the head, he thought. You must keep your head clear. Keep your head clear and know how to suffer like a man. . . . 'Clear up, head,' he said in a voice he could hardly hear. 'Clear up'" (92). Four times, Santiago exhorts himself to maintain mental clarity despite his physical struggle, and his success or failure in this task will determine whether *The Old Man and the Sea* is read as an improbable triumph or the tragic fall of a classic hero. "Keep my head clear" (95), he tells himself again, and then, later, when he tries to appraise the value of the marlin, he realizes he cannot do so without a pencil. "My head is not that clear" (97). Then, in an unspoken monologue: "All I must do is keep the head clear. . . . Then his head started to become a little unclear" (99). The attention on this aspect of Santiago's mental state is the actual drama of the novella, far more important than anything external, including anything regarding the marlin.

This lapse in clarity perpetuates the blurring of identity between predator and prey. Santiago thinks, "is he bringing me in or am I bringing him in?" (99). As Santiago prepares to kill the shark, it seems as if the old man has defeated his internal weaknesses: "The old man's head was clear and good now" (101).

Santiago makes the distinction between sustaining physical energy to fulfill the mission and withstanding mentally as he tries to move the marlin: "Pull, hands, he thought. Hold up, legs. Last for me, head. Last for me. You never went" (91). Of course, Santiago may be speaking too soon: it would be more accurate to say, "you haven't gone yet."

The persistent issue is not simply alertness as opposed to mental fatigue. It is clear that from the outset, Santiago considers himself a "strange" man (14, 66), and the stakes that emerge are nothing short of either salvaging sanity or else lapsing into madness. It must be recalled that one of the elements that motivated Hemingway to write the story of the old man was that, at the end of the actual incident that inspired the idea, the old man had been driven "half-crazy" by the ordeal. In *The Old Man and the Sea*, too, Santiago attests to his mental soundness, although he engages in the unusual practice of speaking while alone at sea. "'If the others heard me talking out loud they would think that I am crazy,' he said aloud. 'But since I am not crazy, I do not care'" (39). With this in mind, his battle with the fish takes on symbolic importance. As he aims to harpoon the marlin—with whom he has associated as if they were one being—Santiago thinks, "I mustn't try for the head. I must get the heart" (91). With the different practical ways of killing marlin and sharks accepted as a given, the larger effect emerges of Santiago sparing the marlin's head as a way of sparing his own, unlike his method of striking the brains of the scavenging sharks. The old man kills one shark by hitting the "location of the brain . . . with resolution and complete malignancy" (102), a savage attack he never would have imposed on the marlin. As the second wave of sharks attacks, Santiago drives the knife into the line on a shark "where the brain joined the spinal cord" (108). Santiago is proud of his ability: "I wonder how the great DiMaggio would have liked the way I hit him in the brain?" (103–4). The old man never identifies with the sharks, so his own consciousness is not affected.

Another manifestation of Santiago's focus on his own interiority is demonstrated in the text's dialectic between intelligence and stupidity. Santiago's pride in his own intelligence runs counter to the traditional reading of him as a simple, unthinking fisherman. His endurance is famous, but he is never mentioned as an unconventional example of Hemingway's surreptitiously cerebral heroes. However, the old man is not always so self-congratulatory. The old man thinks, "You must do nothing stupid" (48), and, soon after, "I must be getting very stupid" (56). After realizing that he has mismanaged his food intake and preparation, he laments, "If I had brains I would have splashed water on the bow all day and drying, it would have made salt" (80). He then criticizes himself in harsh terms: "You're stupid, he told himself" (85). In both cases, he equates stupidity with a lack of concentration, with thinking about baseball, and by considering the small bird rather than focusing on the fish. Etymologically, "stupid" connotes the state of being stunned or benumbed, as in "to be stupefied"; intelligence is not the issue. Conversely, one of Santiago's points of pride is that, despite the respect he has for his prey and the fish, he knows he is able to outsmart them: "But, thank God, they are not as intelligent as we who kill them; although they are more noble and more able" (63); "I wish I was the fish, he thought, with everything he has against only my will and my intelligence" (64); and later, "The *dentuso* is cruel and able and strong and intelligent. But I was more intelligent than he was. Perhaps not, he thought. Perhaps I was only better armed" (103). The sharks are described as behaving "in the stupidity of their great hunger" (107). Finally, to return to the final image of Santiago's struggle: "He was past everything now and he sailed the skiff to make his home port as well and as intelligently as he could" (119). Despite this sentence that describes his mental void, the adverb that describes the intelligence may mean that he is not sailing "stupidly," that is, he is not distracted, and will not perform his final task carelessly.

It is always a temptation for Hemingway heroes to imagine performing their tasks like a machine, to be reduced to an unfeeling zombie, a creature that does not allow introspection or fear or memory to intrude on the cold execution of an action. Philip Young describes Nick's "mechanical movements" in "Big Two-Hearted River" that allow him to allay thought and to succeed in his physical task (46), similar to the mechanical prayers and movements Santiago performs. "The Undefeated," from *Men Without Women*, also speaks to the automating of the mind during a tense activity, in this case bullfighting. The matador Manuel's thought processes are carefully described:

> He thought in bull-fight terms. Sometimes he had a thought and the particular piece of slang would not come into his mind and he could not realize the thought. His instincts and his knowledge worked automatically, and his brain worked slowly and in words. He knew all about bulls. He did not have to think about them. He just did the right thing. His eyes noted things and his body performed the necessary measures without thought. If he thought about it, he would be gone. (SS 260)

Manuel has a level of expertise and a depth of experience to the extent that he has consigned conscious deliberation of bullfighting to habitual processing. For Manuel, to "think" would be to "doubt" or to "overthink."

The tension that drives *The Old Man and the Sea* is that Santiago is naturally ruminative, introspective, and even nostalgic, although placed in a dire situation, one that renders such thoughts unhelpful. Young describes the situation by pointing out, "But much of the time [Santiago] is too busy to think . . . his hands are cut badly, he is nearly blind from exhaustion, and he is too tired to think of anything" (122). Santiago's attention must be focused exclusively on the landing of the fish, but, as his health is weakening and the futility and then failure of his task grow evident, his instinct to ruminate and analyze the situation emerges. Although Santiago famously claims that "man is not made for defeat. . . . A man can be destroyed but not defeated" (103), the true defeat portrayed at the end of *The Old Man and the Sea* is not the loss of pride or manhood or dignity or the marlin. The defeat is not even the loss of Santiago's life. The defeat is signaled when the old man loses consciousness and sanity and when he fails in heroic efforts of mental control. This loss is precisely the victory of "Big Two-Hearted River," the fragile triumph with which that story ends. The tragic moment of *The Old Man and the Sea* is announced at the end to indicate the old man's void, his doomed existence without a psyche: "He sailed lightly now and he had no thoughts nor any feelings of any kind. He was past everything now" (119).

Santiago's psychological vacuum echoes "Big Two-Hearted River," for precisely the opposite reason. Nick's relief at the beginning of his hike in the Michigan woods comes from realizing his own objective: "He felt he had left everything behind, the need for thinking, the need to write, other needs" (SS 210). The optimism at the end of Nick's story stems from his confidence that, although he has left behind his compulsion to ruminate, he will be able to recover it when he can better withstand such painful self-scrutiny. The hopeful last sentence of "Big Two-Hearted River" promises, "There were plenty of days coming when he could fish the swamp" (232). While Nick has the cautious confidence to suspend thinking so he might relax his tortured psyche, Santiago does not have that luxury and therefore must plunge into the swamp of the psyche that Nick so fastidiously avoids. What ultimately dooms Santiago is not a fish of prey but his decision to enter the domain of the unknown and unpredictable, the equivalent of Nick's swamp. Santiago understands that his hubris was the undoing of himself, the fish, and the sacred ritual of fishing. Later, when Santiago—who had proudly recalled being nicknamed "The Champion" (70)—must admit defeat, the cause to which he attributes his demise is clearly articulated: "Bed will be a great thing. It is easy when you are beaten, he thought. I never knew how easy it was. And what beat you, he thought. 'Nothing,' he said aloud. 'I went out too far.' (120). Hemingway's Nobel Prize acceptance speech—for an award given to him largely because of the achievement of *The Old Man and the Sea*—reiterates Santiago's mentality, which is that a writer must seek something "beyond attainment" and must use the inspiration of previous great writers to be "driven far out past where he can go, out to where no one can help him" (qtd. in Bruccoli, *Mechanism* 135), suggesting an artistic mission that is inherently reckless, dangerous, and certain to fail.

Nick is cautious enough not to risk going out too far, careful not to stake his psyche on an unknown, since it has all the potential of tragedy, the "tragic adventure" with which he associates that part of the river (SS 231). The unknown regions of the gulf waters are actual for Santiago but also carry important psychological implications. The further a character goes out, the further he must go within, and Hemingway chronicled both the outward and the inward journeys in these narratives of protagonists in solitude.

3

Memory in A Farewell to Arms

Architecture, Dimensions, and Persistence

> Remembrance has a rear and front,—
> 'T is something like a house;
> It has a garret also
> For refuse and the mouse.
> Emily Dickinson

> the war that matters is the war against the imagination
> all other wars are subsumed in it.
> Diane di Prima, "Rant"

_T_wo weeks after the publication of _A Farewell to Arms_ in 1929, William Faulkner's Quentin Compson futilely attempts to destroy time by mutilating its instrument of measurement, recalling his father's lesson that "clocks slay time . . . time is dead as long as it is being clicked off by little wheels; only when the clock stops does time come to life" (_Sound and Fury_ 85). Quentin's father cautions that the watch should not encourage "constant speculation regarding the position of mechanical hands on an arbitrary dial which is a symptom of mind-function" (77). _A Farewell to Arms_—unlike Faulkner's more strikingly experimental work—is not widely recognized as a profound statement about the nature of memory, nor is it praised as an incisive investigation into the psychological or philosophical implications of time. For many critics, the novel is emblematic of Hemingway's nonthinking characters, an ode to Behaviorism or anti-intellectualism.

A failure to recognize the temporal element in *A Farewell to Arms* results in viewing the novel as flat, plodding, a one- or at most two-dimensional work. However, one of Hemingway's earliest aesthetic statements about his own fiction appears in a 1925 letter to his father, in which he proclaims his determination to create multidimensional characters and texts. Hemingway, then writing his early work in Paris, outlines his approach: "You see I'm trying in all my stories to get the feeling of the actual life across—not to just depict life—or criticize it—but to actually make it alive. So that when you have read something by me you actually experience the thing. . . . It is only by showing both sides—3 dimensions and if possible 4 that you can write the way I want to" (SL 153). Hemingway often alluded to this bold literary project, while always insisting on the word "dimensions." Taken together, his remarks read as sly challenges to subsequent critics, since he never explicitly defines his terms.

The aptly named "Banal Story" from *Men Without Women* refers absurdly to the same idea: "Think of these things in 1925—Was there a risqué page in Puritan history? Were there two sides to Pocahontas? Did she have a fourth dimension?" (SS 361). In *Green Hills of Africa*, Hemingway tells his interlocutor Kandisky: "How far prose can be carried if any one is serious enough and has luck. There is a fourth and fifth dimension that can be gotten. . . . It is much more difficult than poetry. It is a prose that has never been written" (26–27).[1] As Hemingway recalls in *A Moveable Feast* of his efforts of the mid-1920s, "I was learning something from the painting of Cézanne that made writing simple true sentences far from enough to make the stories have the dimensions that I was trying to put in them" (13). To Charles Scribner in 1951, Hemingway writes of his forthcoming *The Old Man and the Sea*: "This is the prose that I have been working for all my life that should read easily and simply and seem short and yet have all the dimensions of the visible world and the world of a man's spirit. It is as good prose as I can write as of now" (SL 738). These excerpts illustrate that this focus on dimensions spanned Hemingway's entire writing life, even while he understood that most readers might overlook the hidden complexity at the core of his texts.

Supplementing the three dimensions of the visible world with psychological, spiritual, ethical, and emotional dimensions remained central to Hemingway's vision until the end. As he explained late in his life, "If you describe someone, it is flat, as a photograph is, and from my standpoint a failure. If you make him up from what you know, there should be all the dimensions" (Plimpton 33).

Hemingway supported his claim in his own Nobel Prize speech, in which he states that the staying power of a writer's work depends in part on the "degree of alchemy that he possesses" (qtd. in Bruccoli, *Mechanism* 134). Hemingway answers his imaginary critics by speaking of "secrets that we have that are made by alchemy and much is written about them by people who do not know the secrets or the alchemy" (MF-RE 222). The word "alchemy" implies the existence of additional value, power or matter not present in the raw elements. In a fragment, Hemingway elaborates on this claim: "a writer is both the mine from which he must extract all the ore until the mine is ruined, the mill where the ore must be crushed and the valuable metal extracted and refined, and the artizan and artist who must work that metal into something of enduring worth. Sometimes there is no mine and the writer must make his gold by alchemy. No one believes this nor knows anything about how it is done. The writer himself does not know. All he knows is that he cannot do it often" ("Prologue" 3). In an interior monologue in *Islands in the Stream*, Thomas Hudson attempts to compose a line of extemporaneous poetry: "*The solvent alchemist that in a trice our leaden gold into shit transmutes.* That doesn't even scan. *Our leaden gold to shit transmutes* is better" (197, emphasis in original).[2] Hemingway once told a journalist, "I believe that critics know very little about the alchemy of the production of literature" (Breit, "The Sun Also Rises" 1). All of these remarks come from the 1950s. Whether hinting vaguely at artistic alchemy, mysterious dimensions, or things not immediately discernible, Hemingway was challenging his readers to look beyond the simple language and syntax, to the submerged part of the iceberg and even beneath and beyond that to things invisible and metaphysical.

In *The Garden of Eden*, for example, David Bourne's quiet victory at the end of the novel—much like Nick Adams "holding something in his head" at the end of "On Writing" (NAS 241)—is his ability to capture this mysterious prose that is more difficult to create than poetry. The novel's penultimate paragraph proclaims David's triumph: "He found he knew much more about his father than when he had first written this story and he knew he could measure his progress by the small things which made his father more tactile and to have more dimensions than he had in the story before. He was fortunate, just now, that his father was not a simple man" (247). David's aim, and not a surprising one, is identical to Hemingway's own: the transformation of the writer's knowledge into multidimensional, complex prose. For David, as for Hemingway, the measure of quality in writing was to achieve this multidimensional effect.

How literally are we to take these references to added dimensions? Is Hemingway referring to a metaphorical model in which elements that seem simple combine not by addition but exponentially to create a web of relations, a prose elaborate and elegant, infinitely complex if the reader is willing to explore the permutations of the text? Or, did Hemingway have a specific corollary to these ideas; did the fourth dimension refer to one specific concept, while the fifth denoted another?

Generally, the fourth dimension is associated with "time" and its relation to subjective human perception. Einstein believed as much. The Russian mystic P. D. Ouspensky posited that "Time, as we feel it, is the fourth dimension" and that "eternity is the fifth dimension" (210). This view is substantiated by Proust's reference to the aura of the church at Combray, which, his protagonist recalls, "made of the church for me something entirely different from the rest of the town: an edifice occupying, so to speak, a four-dimensional space—the name of the fourth being Time" (83). Here, Proust is putting forth a decidedly Bergsonian notion, in which the present perception of an object includes the individual's subjective perspective and memory. In *Time and Free Will*, Bergson writes of the cognitive processing of the motion of a pendulum as a continuum: the pendulum's movements "are first preserved and afterwards disposed in a series: in a word, we create for them a fourth dimension of space, which we call homogenous time" (109).

H. G. Wells—who is needled in one of the few parodic touches of *A Farewell to Arms*[3]—anticipates the Einsteinian concept of the fourth dimension. In Wells's *The Time Machine*, The Time Traveller says: "There are really four dimensions, three which we call the three planes of Space, and a fourth, Time. There is, however, a tendency to draw an unreal distinction between the former three dimensions and the latter, because it happens that our consciousness moves intermittently in one direction along the latter from the beginning to the end of our lives" (2). Although Wells's novel might be dismissed as the fantasy of science fiction, the excerpt demonstrates that such a notion of additional dimensions that transcend Euclidian geometry existed in the imagination of writers and thinkers as early as the late nineteenth century.

In *The Wild Palms*, William Faulkner introduces a different—but perhaps not contradictory—idea of a fourth dimension, in which "the convict, glaring up again saw the flat thick spit of mud which as he looked at it divided and became a thick mud-colored log which in turn seemed, still immobile, to leap suddenly against his retinae in three—no, four—dimensions: volume, solidity, shape, and another: not fear but pure and intense speculation" (216). In Proust, Faulkner, and Hemingway, the added dimensions of their texts contribute to the depth and intensity of consciousness, which is informed by a vivid, complex memory.

Hemingway's public pronouncements that draw attention to these difficult-to-attain dimensions have invited the curiosities and speculations, as well as the abject scorn, of critics. In Michael F. Moloney's opinion, Hemingway's prose "not only lacks a fourth and fifth dimension; it lacks, for the most part, a third" (191). Reviewing *Green Hills of Africa*, Bernard DeVoto dismisses Hemingway's overtures at new dimensions, advising, "He ought to leave the fourth dimension to Ouspensky and give us prose" (212).

Other critics have viewed Hemingway's quest more sympathetically. Michael Reynolds speculates on the substance behind the claim in *Green Hills of Africa*, suggesting that Hemingway was:

> creating a prose more complicated than any of his earlier writing, a prose that stops time, twists time, escapes outside of time. If Einstein could imagine more dimensions than three, just maybe a writer can work through the fourth dimension of time and into a timeless fifth dimension: a continuous present tense both *now* and *then*, *here*, and *elsewhere* simultaneously. (*The 1930s* 181)

Other critics have joined Reynolds's view of this ubiquity in time featured in Hemingway's prose.

Barbara Lounsberry discusses this mysterious dimension as it pertains to *Green Hills of Africa*, the book from which Hemingway's "fourth and fifth dimension" remark sprang. For Lounsberry, the fifth dimension refers to "the plane of imaginative recall" (24) or "imaginative or artistic recall" (31). Lounsberry continues: "Any given moment, by definition partakes of all four dimensions: length, breadth, depth, and time. Yet it is the fifth dimension of memory which permits that moment to live again, and, in the living, be transformed through the associations of art into something new and eternal" (31). By linking the added dimension with the writer's creative process, Lounsberry's point recalls an essay by Robert Graves, who himself would publish a classic World War I narrative in 1929 and who deemed the fifth dimension integral to poetic creation, the realm of artistic genius.[4]

When Hemingway was bringing *Across the River and into the Trees* to publication in 1950, he spoke bombastically about his achievement. He called it his best novel, Proustian in conception; his self-praise was as brazen as his protagonist's challenge of Dante and Shakespeare. During his exegesis of the new work, Hemingway explicated the difference between *Across the River and into the Trees* and *For Whom the Bell Tolls*. Unlike the new novel, which was filled with "three-cushion shots," Hemingway thought *For Whom the Bell Tolls* was simpler and more straightforward: "In the last one I had the straight narrative; Sordo on the hill for keeps; Jordan killing the cavalryman; the village; a full-scale attack presented as they go; and the unfortunate incident at the bridge" (Breit, "Talk" 14). Hemingway might have forgotten, in his enthusiasm, that his interest in "three-cushioned shots" had begun more than a decade early; he had made the same assertion in a July 1929 letter to Owen Wister, written during the serialization and just before the book publication of *A Farewell to Arms.*

One of Hemingway's most intriguing riddles, though, is his claim about *Across the River and into the Trees* that "In writing I have moved through arithmetic, through plane geometry and algebra, and now I am in calculus" (Breit, "Talk" 14).[5] Although sympathetic critics have strained for literal explanations for Hemingway's boast (how exactly does one write algebraically?), the most relevant point is certainly his invitation to read his prose on a nonlinear level, with dimensions transcending Euclidean geometry. In the novel, Colonel Cantwell comments on his memory of war experience, claiming that "terrain is what remains in the dreaming part of the mind" (ARIT 117); a similar articulation comes in *The Garden of Eden*: "The distances did not matter since all distances changed and how you remembered them was how they were" (182). The subjectivity of the protagonist transcends the apodictic facts of history.

These various explanations of Hemingway's lifelong treatment of time, memory, and the added dimensions of fiction resonate powerfully in *A Farewell to Arms*. During the epic retreat at Caporetto, Frederic and his ambulance corps plod through the wet Italian countryside, and the description that ends chapter 29 is telling: "We walked along together all going fast against time" (208). Here, although the soldiers are walking, their movement is presented in the context of time, not space. Human beings move through space in "real life" or plane geometry; we move through time only in memory. Even on the rigidly realistic surface of the novel, the soldiers' description, through memory's lens, becomes an unexpected, impressionistic image. In a converse rendering, during Frederic's convalescence earlier in the novel, Catherine takes off three nights from caring for Frederic at the hospital, and, when she returns, Frederic remembers, "It was as though we met again after each of us had been away on a long journey" (111). Just as the soldiers' progress through space is expressed through the measure of time, with this formulation—the last sentence of chapter 17—the lovers' time apart is expressed in terms of distance. This metaphorical distance is akin to Stephen Kern's invaluable point about the works of Proust and Joyce, in which "travel took place in the mind as much as in the world, and distances depended on the effect of memory, the force of emotions, and the passage of time" (218). Taken together, Hemingway in these two instances of fusion manipulates the time-space continuum, the characteristic of a fourth dimension.[6]

In an analysis of Hemingway's short stories, Meyly Chin Hagemann writes that Hemingway "expressed verbally Bergson's 'movement in time,' just as

Cézanne had done it pictorially" (112). Richard Eriksen's formulation of this phenomenon demonstrates this tactic:

> In memory we move freely through time independently of the events in objective space, and in so far as space is present in the pictures and presentations of memory it is there only as a servant of our psychic movement through time. So we may say that in the physical world we move (for instance, when we are walking or writing) through space by means of time, while in the psychic world we move (in memory) through time by means of space. . . . Time is in the 'psyche' the dominant dimension . . . (51)

The three activities Eriksen uses as examples—walking, writing, and memory— are also the ones Hemingway employs in the examples of the retreat: Frederic is writing a memory of soldiers walking through the rain. For this reason, Frederic's non sequitur literary reference to "Time's wingèd chariot hurrying near" (154) and Catherine's immediate recognition of the Marvell couplet draws further attention to time's function in the novel. One of the discarded titles for *A Farewell to Arms* was "World Enough and Time" (Oldsey 15), part of the first line of "To His Coy Mistress," the Marvell poem from which the reference is drawn.

Hemingway's fellow Oak Park citizen Frank Lloyd Wright suggested the possibility of a fourth dimension in architecture, endeavoring to create buildings with an added dimension in which the space outside a building "becomes a natural part of space *within* a building. All building design thus actually becomes four dimensional" (Kaufmann and Raeburn 313). By creating a space that is characterized by the intangible rather than the physical, Wright was creating at once "theatres of memory" and "theatres of prophecy," to fuse the past and future (Hayden 11). Wright's project echoes the modernist conceit of T. S. Eliot's "Burnt Norton": "Time past and time future / What might have been and what has been / Point to one end, which is always present" (118). This notion of a place out of time also mimics Frederic's narrative perspective, employing the past and hinting at the future to include the added dimensions of memory and time manipulation.

In the same vein, Hemingway quite conspicuously made the protagonist of *A Farewell to Arms* an aspiring architect. Hemingway conveyed the senselessness of World War I by characterizing Frederic Henry as a man who more or less wandered into military service and who is not performing a mandated or even personally inspired duty. Catherine asks him why he joined the army, and Frederic's response is feckless and feeble: "I don't know. . . . There isn't always

an explanation for everything" (18). The slim amount of background information reveals that Frederic was in Italy because he wanted to be an architect.[7]
Unlike other Hemingway protagonists whose vocations inform their actions,
Frederic's interest in architecture does not provide obvious insight into the text.
Readers have no way of inferring that the protagonist is singularly passionate
about architecture. However, the disclosure of Frederic's interest in architecture alerts the reader to Hemingway's project with the novel itself: in his creation
of *A Farewell to Arms*, Hemingway explores the architecture of memory, his
stripped version of Proust's "vast structure of recollection" (64) or Augustine's
"vast mansions of memory" (*Confessions*, X, 8, 12: 244). Frederic's passion for
architecture is revealed by the method of storytelling itself.

Frederic Henry's narration assumes a shape, with a rear guard and an
Italian front; the student of architecture claims no professional achievement,
except to erect the elaborate structure of the narrative we read. *A Farewell to
Arms* is a memory in a much different sense than is *The Sun Also Rises*. Although
the action of *A Farewell to Arms* takes place almost a decade before that of *The Sun
Also Rises*, it was written four years later: Hemingway's postwar novel preceded
his war novel. Thus, the journalistic detail that pervades *The Sun Also Rises* gives
way to a broader, more sweeping historical chronicle in *A Farewell to Arms*.

Fiction writing as a form of design or construction is consistent with
Hemingway's approach to writing. Hemingway recalls his growth as a young
writer by pointing out that he was endeavoring "to make instead of describe"
(MF 156). During one of the didactic moments in *Death in the Afternoon*—the
publication that followed *A Farewell to Arms*—Hemingway explains, "Prose is
architecture, not interior decoration, and the Baroque is over" (191).[8] Were
Frederic an interior decorator, therefore, it might be more inviting to scrutinize
the details and ornamentation of the narrative. However, Hemingway's alle-
giance was clearly to narrative structure, to erecting the textual edifice that
would best support his artistic vision.

The importance placed on the dimensions and architecture of memory in *A
Farewell to Arms* emphasizes the relationship that Frederic has to his own past
and the effect this relationship has on his retrospective narration. In 1931,
Salvador Dalí's surreal masterwork "The Persistence of Memory" showed
melting clocks on a desolate landscape, suggesting—as did Mr. Compson—
the inapplicability of linear chronology to modern life and its irrelevance to
the way human consciousness truly operates. By concerning himself with the
"persistence" of memory, Dalí clearly was not alluding to pleasant memories.
"Persistence" connotes a dogged, unyielding force that, even when temporarily
repelled, returns unbidden. In Daniel L. Schacter's study *The Seven Sins of*

Memory, he lists "persistence" as a major problem affecting the way we remember and are able to incorporate the past into consciousness. Schacter includes "disappointment, regret, failure, sadness, and trauma" as the "primary territory of persistence" (162). Hemingway's fiction always exists in the arena where such persistent memories are in play: Nick Adams, Jake Barnes, Richard Cantwell, Robert Jordan, Thomas Hudson, and Frederic Henry all either cope with traumatic memory of the war after the war or cope with sadness and regret and failure during the war. "Persisting memories," Schacter writes, "are a major consequence of just about any type of traumatic experience" (174), including war.

The famous first sentence of *A Farewell to Arms* reads, "In the late summer of *that year* we lived in a house in a village that looked across the river and the plain to the mountains" (3, emphasis added). When Frederic begins his retrospective narrative by specifying "that year," he immediately signals that he intends to embark on a distant and particular memory. It may be "the . . . summer," "a house," "a village," "the river," "the plain," and "the mountains," but "*that* year" chooses one particular moment in time. By introducing his narrative in this fashion, the narrator denotes the process of selection when conjuring up a past experience that is the responsibility of any storyteller and the role of any individual consciousness in calling forth an intentional memory.

By pinpointing the year 1915 as significant in his past, the narrator introduces a novel in which the artistic canvas will be his own autobiographical memory. Although the Italian Army's clash with the Austro-Hungarian forces, the ramifications of Frederic's desertion of the army, and Catherine Barkley's health form the three external tensions, the understated or unstated psychological tension rests in the inherent unpleasantness of the memories that the narrator chooses to recount, causing Frederic to negotiate with and at times reject the nature of his own memory.

Frederic is unlike Jake Barnes, who might be recounting incidents from the weekend before; Frederic's memory manipulates time, and time manipulates Frederic's memory, so that events are seen through telescopic, microscopic, and binocular lenses, depending on the aspect of his life that Frederic decides to impart. The narration utilizes what Flaubert called "the lengthening of perspective which memory gives to things" (85). As in Flaubert, when Harry, the protagonist of "The Snows of Kilimanjaro," laments his inability to write all he wants before he dies, he realizes how time can be "telescoped" in moments of urgency or inspiration so that experience can be compressed and clarified through lucid narration.

Autobiographical memory describes "the capacity of people to recollect their own lives" (Baddeley 26), a term that can also be simply defined as "memory for information related to the self" (Brewer 26). If Proust is the acknowledged master at mining autobiographical memory for literary purposes, *A Farewell to Arms* might also be productively examined as its own search for lost time, although the styles that convey these memories are famously disparate. Frederic relates to memory in a manner far different—at times opposing— from that of Proust's Marcel. Rather than luxuriating in the free introspective exploration of his memory, Frederic is uneasy about surrendering his consciousness to a chaotic, unfettered investigation of the past. His reluctance complicates the story he is trying to tell, even if it does not expand it in the way that does Proust's liberated memory.

If *A Farewell to Arms* is constructed as an extended autobiographical memory from the first sentence, the novel in its manuscript stage puts forth Hemingway's most explicit analysis of the phenomenon of human memory. In so doing, he provides a valuable key to the narrator's attitude and unfolds a central theme in the collective consciousness of the Hemingway hero in all its incarnations. In chapter 17 of the novel's manuscript—which takes place following the operation on his leg—Frederic offers the following meditation:

> Nothing that you learn by sensation remains if you lose the sensation. There is no memory of pain if there is no pain. Sometimes pain goes and you can not remember it from the moment before but only have a dread of it again. When love is gone you can not remember it but only remember things that happen and places. There is no memory of love if there is no love. All these things, however, return in the dark. In the dark love returns when it is gone, pain comes again and danger that has passed returns. Death comes in the dark.[9] (qtd. in Grebstein 213)

In this fascinating rumination, Frederic reveals the kind of antagonism toward thought and introspection that is a hallmark of the Hemingway hero. However, Frederic's surface criticism and scorn for thought and memory must be examined closely; it is by Hemingway's consistent denial of its importance that he betrays his understanding of its centrality in the intellectual life of human beings, even that of his characters who are famously men of action.

Frederic's thesis on memory appears at first glance to be nonsense. The gap in logic that mars Frederic's argument is no less than a rejection of memory itself. To suggest that, without an equivalent present sensory experience, there is no attendant memory or that the present lack of pain or love eliminates the memory of pain or love is essentially to deny the way memory works. In Augustine's *Confessions*, one of the defining statements on memory, a description of a functional memory offers virtually a point-by-point refutation of Frederic's stance:

> memory also records emotions previously experienced in the mind, not in the same way as the mind experienced them at the time, but in the mode proper to the power of memory. I remember having been happy, without feeling happy now; I recall my past sadness but feel no sadness in so doing; I remember having been afraid once, but am not frightened as I remember; I summon the memory of how I once wanted something, but without wanting it today. (X, 13, 20: 250)

Augustine draws the distinction between recalling something and reliving it. If one needed to relive something in order to conjure up an experience in the past, then memory would have no utility. Memory depends not on a reimmersion in an identical sensory experience but simply on the individual imagining and recognizing (re-cognizing) the emotions connected to the experience. Augustine supplies another useful illustration: "I can distinguish the scent of lilies from violets even though I am not actually smelling anything, and honey from grape-juice, smooth from rough, without tasting or feeling anything: I am simply passing them in review before my mind by remembering them" (X, 8, 13: 246). Augustine is describing memory the way most of us process it; we don't need to touch an object to imagine the way it feels, since we have already experienced it and can access the stored sensation. Frederic's rumination from the manuscript overstates Bergson's point that the present circumstance informs the context of the memory. "The memory-image itself," Bergson writes, "if it remained pure memory, would be ineffectual. Virtual, this memory can only become actual by means of the perception which attracts it. Powerless, it borrows life and strength from the present sensation in which it is materialized" (*Matter and Memory* 127). With this formulation, Bergson is characteristically urging the practical utility of memory, the dynamic relationship between the past and the present, the way humans apply the past to shape or ease the present situation.

However, it is by protesting too much against the incessant tide of stored sensations and experiences that Frederic unwittingly provides the greatest insight into his character and the utter sadness with which his relationship with the past is framed. Even the imagery each writer uses is indicative of his opposite stance with respect to the past: Augustine speaks of making the willing effort to "call for" and to have "brought out" and "summon" and "fetch" senses and experiences from the past. Frederic, on the other hand, uses not verbs that convey the individual's control of consciousness but those that describe consciousness preying on the individual. In the manuscript excerpt, we read of death "coming" and love "returning," emotions acting of their own volition, not through the will and mental control of the individual.

Hemingway analyzed the same phenomenon of the memory of a sensory experience within a wartime context in his short story "A Natural History of the Dead," claiming:

> The smell of a battlefield in hot weather one cannot recall. You can remember that there was such a smell, but nothing ever happens to you to bring it back. It is unlike the smell of a regiment, which may come to you suddenly while riding in the street car and you will look across and see the man who has brought it to you. But the other thing is gone as completely as when you have been in love; you remember things that happened, but the sensation cannot be recalled.[10] (SS 443–44)

As snidely as the distinction is articulated in this excerpt, in each example the narrator suggests that in order to retrieve a sensation from the past, you must experience a similar sensation in the present. This speaks either to the unmatchable profundity of the original experience or to the inadequacy of human memory. These faulty sensory recollections of war suggest the presence of a dissociative element. In Hemingway's less urgent settings, an odor can freely be recalled; the narrator in *Green Hills of Africa* reports, even while smelling the other scents around the camp (roasting meat, the smoke of the fire, Hemingway's boots, another person), "I could remember the odor of the kudu as he lay in the woods" (239). During a relaxing moment in *For Whom the Bell Tolls*, also, Robert Jordan identifies the "odor of nostalgia" (260), the scent of fresh pine bringing him back to his Montana boyhood.

However, through the enormity of the power of the wartime experience, memory distorts. When William James defines memory as an *"object in the past . . . to which the emotion of belief adheres"* (*Principles*, I: 652, emphasis in original), he does not mention fact or truth or reality. Memory—even of an object—becomes a subjective phenomenon, particular to an individual consciousness. As Hemingway himself acknowledged, "Memory, of course, is never true" (DIA 100). Such subjectivity in the realm of memory adds an inherent complication to any first-person narrative.

By suggesting that no emotion remains and that no memory exists of what has come before, Frederic reveals the unconscious posttraumatic coping mechanism of dissociation, in which an individual's errant memory allows him not simply to be removed from his past, but ultimately to be divorced from his own identity, his very self. William James prizes memory as providing "the principle *unity* of consciousness" (297, emphasis in original) and fostering "the consciousness of personal sameness" (331). "Where the resemblance and the continuity are no longer felt," James writes, "the sense of personal identity goes too" (335). Augustine claims that, through memory, "I come to meet myself" (*Confessions*, X, 8, 14: 246): Memory is the principal component by which an individual forms a distinct sense of self. In Garry Wills's lucid commentary on Augustine's *Confessions*, he remarks, "Without memory we would have no sense of our own identity. . . . To wake with no memory of who one is, what one has done, what one's relations to others are, is to be denuded of one's very nature, since that depends on maintaining a continuity with one's former actions" (*Memory* 11–12). Wills's description of Augustine's autobiographical testimony also aptly describes Frederic's motivation, which is to detach himself from his painful past, to deny the overwhelming force of memory by believing that his unpleasant experiences did not exist. Frederic, by rejecting the memory, disowns the experience, and, by rejecting the past experience and denying continuity, he breaches his own identity, jettisoning the painful aspects of his former self.[11] The separate peace he declares is also a separation from his old identity and former attitudes.

The psychologist Elizabeth Waites discusses dissociation as a "subversion of memory" and identifies it as a common reaction to a traumatic situation such as Frederic's (146). Waites writes, "Most psychologists who specialize in the study of trauma view dissociation rather than repression as the typical dynamic in posttraumatic memory loss and recovery" (144). In a novel in which the turning point—Frederic being blown up—depicts the hero floating out of himself, literally having an out-of-body experience, it seems as if his imperfect memory has perpetuated this phenomenon, where he has come back, but not all the way. One of the central elements of dissociation is "depersonalization," described as "a sense of being disconnected from one's body" (McNally 172). Waites sheds further light on Frederic's monologue on memory from the manuscript. She remarks that the emotions forgotten in a dissociative reaction may be "altogether lost to recall until reactivated" (145), which explains why Frederic's claim that, to him, memories of his emotions are lost serve as more than just obstinate declarations. The memories of this period of Frederic's life may indeed be depersonalized and dissociated to the extent that he is not able to recall them with the "warmth and intimacy" that characterize an autobiographical memory (James, *Principles*, I: 223, et passim).

Although most people would regard the idea of waking up with no tie to one's past as horrifying, for Frederic this separation is the one state that provides a semblance of stability; it offers an existence where sensations corresponding to the deaths of Catherine and their baby, the deaths of his friends, the man he killed, his own traumatic injury, and the sum of his other brutal war experiences might abate and allow him a vacuum in which to cope with current perceptions and sensations without memory acting as a sniper that unpredictably—in Bergson's phrase—"imports the past into the present" (*Matter and Memory* 73).

The denial or avoidance of memory in chapter 17 of the manuscript of *A Farewell to Arms* is merely a more explicit articulation of the denial or distrust of thought that appears in so many other Hemingway texts, such as "Big Two-Hearted River," in which Nick Adams "felt he had left everything behind, the need for thinking, the need to write, other needs" (SS 210). Nick finds a geographical location that affords him the solitude he needs to be less susceptible to the trauma of past experience, the swamp of his mind that represents his "tragic adventure" (231). Implicit in Frederic's stance against memory, however, is the inescapable truth that we are reading his memory. The basis of retrospective narration is an imaginative investigation of the past through memory. Frank Budgen once asked James Joyce about his theory of imagination. Joyce, Budgen reports, "brushed it aside with the assertion that imagination was memory" (187). As delicious as Joyce's pithy comeback is, it may be more accurate to say that the reverse is true. Joyce's aphorism implies that, in order to write, the artistic mind must summon up past experiences, emotions, and perceptions to create anew. This axiom is not altogether original, of course, since the ancient muses were linked to memory long before *Ulysses* was written (or even *The Odyssey*). However, when examining the function of memory, modern psychology, led by William James, is careful to distinguish between the idea of memory as a tangible object embedded in the person's brain and an idea conjured up by the powers of imagination that the person believes to be real, an experience that has occurred in actuality. James is positing an individual's role in creating his own autobiography through memory, which is to say the power of his own imagination. This notion might be most memorably rendered in fiction in the sixth chapter of Faulkner's *Light in August*, which opens with the salvo "Memory believes before knowing remembers" (119).[12] A corollary in Hemingway's own work appears in a conversation between Santiago and Manolin in *The Old Man and the Sea*:

"How old was I when you first took me in a boat?"

"Five and you nearly were killed when I brought the fish in too green and he nearly tore the boat to pieces. Can you remember?"

"I can remember the tail slapping and banging and the thwart breaking and the noise of the clubbing. I can remember you throwing me into the bow where the wet coiled lines were and feeling the whole boat shiver and the noise of you clubbing him like chopping a tree down and the sweet blood smell all over me."

"Can you really remember that or did I just tell it to you?"

"I remember everything from when we first went together." (12–13)

When Santiago asks the boy if he can *really* remember it, he is in effect asking him: Is this an experience that you can recall through your own autobiographical memory, or does the "emotion of belief" adhere to this image in your mind because I have retold the story so many times? Although Manolin insists that this is out of a page of his autobiographical memory, Santiago teases the boy that the story belongs to the boy's *biographical* memory, of which the old man himself has been perhaps the principal author. Paul Ricoeur comments on such occurrences, remarking that the "constant danger of confusing remembering and imagining, resulting from memories becoming images in this way, affects the goal of faithfulness corresponding to the truth claim of memory" (7). This phenomenology of memory is a strain in *A Farewell to Arms* that is always pervasive, even if always implicit.

"Warmth and intimacy," the phrase used by James several times to describe an individual's recognition that something recalled in memory belongs to his personal, private consciousness, are states that Frederic is desperately trying to avoid, whether or not he believes it is possible. Although he has committed himself to tell his narrative as best he can, Frederic wishes to rid himself, by his flights of denial, of the "emotion of belief" that the tragedies of his war experiences are actually his. The emotion is too unpleasant. James references this aspect of conscious suppression or unconscious repression by quoting Théodule Ribot: "Oblivion, except in certain cases, is thus no malady of memory, but a condition of its health and its life" (I.681).[13] In *The Psychopathology of Everyday Life*, Freud writes that "*forgetting in all cases is proved to be founded on a motive of displeasure*" (79, emphasis in original). The motivation is for the benefit of the organism, for its ease in existence, moving forward.

In an early passage, Frederic concludes a reverie that describes his leave from the Italian Army, chronicling how he spent his time whoring, rather than more placidly visiting the priest's family in Abruzzi. In a rare break of linearity in the novel's narration, Frederic uses beautifully intricate language to draw a contrast between his selves (present and former) and the priest: "He had always known what I did not know and what, when I learned it, I was always able to forget. But I did not know that then, although I learned it later" (14). Frederic uses his temporally remote perspective to plot his knowledge and memory in time and to compare them to the priest's. In this meticulously crafted pair of sentences, Hemingway's architecture provides perfect symmetry: the priest *always* had known, while Frederic was *always* able to forget the same thing. The priest knew what Frederic *did not know*, and then, even though he learned it and subsequently forgot it, he insists that he *did not know* at the time of the action. The phrase *I learned it* is likewise repeated in each sentence, so that the skeleton of the two sentences reveals: ". . . always . . . I did not know . . . I learned it . . . always . . . I did not know . . . I learned it. . . ." Frederic gestures at his easy control over memory, being "always able to forget" the knowledge that the priest had, which is almost certainly intended to be a sense of the divine or holy.[14] However, Frederic's is an inexact use of the word "forget." After Frederic learns what the priest "had always known," he clearly does not forget this knowledge but instead disregards or disobeys it in favor of his immediate gratification. As the battler in an ongoing war on memory, Frederic declares himself the victor, although it is implicit that the winner may indeed take nothing in this circumstance, as well as elsewhere in Hemingway.

A second example demonstrates the way memory can be unwelcome, an unhappy function of consciousness to be mastered or overcome. As Book Three concludes and Frederic completes his abandonment of the Italian Army, he lies on the floor of the flatcar of a freight train, cataloguing his consciousness in an acutely introspective way:

> Doctors did things to you and then it was not your body any more. The head was mine, and the inside of the belly. It was very hungry in there. I could feel it turn over on itself. The head was mine, but not to use, not to think with, only to remember and *not too much remember.*
>
> *I could remember* Catherine but I knew I would get crazy if I thought about her when I was not sure yet I would see her, so *I would not think about her, only about her a little.* . . . Hard as the floor of the car to lie not thinking only feeling. . . .
>
> I wished this bloody train would get to Mestre and I would eat and stop thinking. I would have to stop. (231–32, emphasis added)

This passage must not be read reflexively as Hemingway's renunciation of thought or memory. The gesture is ironic: a rant against consciousness told in a lush, stream-of-consciousness mode. Likewise, Frederic's position that his head should be reduced to the proverbial hat rack and should not be a tool of introspection or retrospection—in his ungrammatical rendering, "not too much remember"—is immediately followed by "I could remember," emphatically leaving useless his self-exhortation. The unstated point of reminding himself that it would be best to "not too much remember" is the sheer impossibility of this challenge, particularly for someone like Frederic. If a nonintrospective, noncerebral man were lying on the train, he would not need to remind himself. Furthermore, Frederic immediately modifies his policy not to think of Catherine, rescinding her absolute banishment from his consciousness to a softened, more realistic stance: "only about her a little."

A third example: in the novel's most quoted passage, one of its thematic centerpieces, Frederic describes his new attitude toward the war and, as he does, perpetuates the negative characterization of memory's role in his consciousness. On his train ride to Stresa, Frederic recounts his attitude: "I had the paper but I did not read it because I did not want to read about the war. I was going to forget the war. I had made a separate peace" (243). Directly preceding Frederic's "separate peace" declaration, he proclaims that not only will he abstain from fighting in the war but also that he will not even remember that it exists. However, these statements must not be taken at face value. Frederic may be able to control the veracity of the first statement, but he is not in complete command of his memory simply by claiming that he is. "I was going to forget the war" is phrased as if Frederic is recalling the formulation and execution of a plan; however, the sentence is better paraphrased: "At that time, my naïve idea was that I would be able to forget the war." Frederic's retrospective stance conveys his new perspective, gained through experience, rather than the simplistic and inaccurate "I succeeded in forgetting the war." It is through Frederic's somewhat ambiguous, understated phrase that the retrospective narrator imbues his character's sentiments with ironic meaning. Clearly, the war was not and could not be forgotten, and Frederic (and his creator) knows all too painfully that memory does not work in such a convenient, take-it-or-leave-it fashion.

In a biographical parallel, Hemingway once expressed remorse for the anguish he caused his second wife, Pauline Pfeiffer, and his method for coping with his guilt is resonant: "The wave of remembering has finally risen so that it has broken over the jetty that I built to protect the open roadstead of my heart" (SL 737). The "jetty" to which Hemingway refers was not impregnable in everyday life, and, no matter the stoic pose of his protagonists, they too must inevitably succumb to their memory.

Voluntary memory consists of experiences in the past that the individual summons intentionally, as in Augustine's example. The controllable aspect of memory, however, is only one aspect of memory. Involuntary memory, on the other hand, involves associations that spring of their own volition from the past, such as the mysterious associative sensations that Proust's Marcel experiences after eating his madeleine. "Where did it come from?" asks Marcel. "What did it mean? How could I seize and apprehend it?" (60). Although Frederic and Marcel are both objects acted upon by involuntary memory, Marcel's tasty cake is an "exquisite pleasure" and an "all-powerful joy" (60), while, for Frederic, his personal history is the nightmare from which he is trying to awake. Like Nick in "Big Two-Hearted River," Frederic can remove himself from stimulation that would tempt involuntary memory to find logical associations — Frederic does go to Switzerland in an attempt to replicate a scene of Edenic domestic bliss with Catherine — but minimizing the likelihood of memory's intrusion is the best that can be done. It is senseless to declare, "I was going to forget the war." Ultimately, that is for the war to decide. Frederic can physically detach himself from the war and the army and declare peace more easily than he can ever separate himself from memory's persistence.

In these three representative excerpts from *A Farewell to Arms,* along with the extended passage from chapter 17 of its manuscript, memory is viewed as an impediment to stability, a burden that must be shed in order to gain enjoyment or to forge a separate peace of mind. Frederic knows that he is able not to "forget" the mystery that the priest knows but simply to ignore it; he knows intellectually that his mind cannot stop its own relentless cognition, nor can it fend off the force of memory, but he beseeches it to leave him alone. Frederic's separate peace, like that of Nick Adams before him, can be declared eloquently and sincerely, but no declaration equals a guarantee that war is to be forgotten.

At the end of Frederic's ruminations on memory in the manuscript excerpt, a qualification appears in a curious addendum: "All these things, however, return in the dark" (qtd. in Grebstein 213). The memories that have been assiduously avoided during the day cannot be repelled in the night. Georges Poulet's articulation of this moment of vulnerability in the Proust text is "the chiaroscuro wherein the consciousness is less prepared to withstand the phenomena that trouble it," often inspiring "a feeling of apprehension and even of horror" (*Proustian Space* 11). This theme recalls countless examples in Hemingway's work that underscore the difference in the operation of human consciousness in the daytime and in the night. Hemingway's soldiers and veterans are virtually without exception afraid of the dark and usually suffer from insomnia. "A

Clean, Well-Lighted Place" epitomizes this idea, as is evident from the title itself. In *The Sun Also Rises*, after Jake studies his naked body in the mirror of his armoire, he tries to go to sleep, but, in the quiet night, he cannot control his thoughts: "My head started to work. . . . I lay awake thinking and my mind jumping around. Then I couldn't keep away from it. . . . It is awfully easy to be hard-boiled about everything in the daytime, but at night it is another thing" (SAR 38, 39, 42). The short story "Now I Lay Me" contains an even more devastating examination of the problem, in the portrayal of Nick's dreams of death and his wounding: "I tried never to think about it, but it had started to go since, in the nights, just at the moment of going off to sleep, and I could only stop it by a very great effort" (SS 363). In "Big Two-Hearted River," as chapter 1 explores, Nick's main intention in hiking such a great distance is to tire himself out so that he can fall asleep quickly, bypassing the stage of lying awake, a vulnerable target for his thoughts and memories. Before Nick falls asleep for the night, he narrowly avoids this danger: "His mind was starting to work. He knew he could choke it because he was tired enough" (SS 218). Freud describes this liminal state as the most fruitful moment to analyze a patient:

> the point is to induce a state which is in some degree analogous, as regards the distribution of psychic energy (mobile attention), to the state of the mind before falling asleep—and also, of course, to the hypnotic state. On falling asleep, the "undesired urges" emerge, owing to the slackening of a certain arbitrary (and, of course, also critical) action, which is allowed to influence the trend of our ideas; we are accustomed to speak of fatigue as the reason of this slackening; the merging undesired ideas are changed into visual and auditory images. (*Interpretation of Dreams* 14)

Frederic's recognition of the powers of nighttime echoes Jake and Nick's experiences. His posturing about how memory does not apply since he has dissociated himself from his past leads to a significant exception: when his defenses are lowered at night. Each of the last three sentences of the manuscript excerpt from chapter 17 contains the phrase "in the dark," just as "in the rain" serves as an ominous refrain in the published novel. Before Frederic is blown up, he views the nights as representing celebration and hedonism, the likes of which cannot be enjoyed in the daytime. Of his explanation to the priest: "I tried to tell about the night and the difference between the night and the day and how the night was better unless the day was very clean and cold and I could not tell it; as I cannot tell it now. But if you have had it you know" (13).

After his traumatic wound, however, his opinion changes dramatically. Frederic candidly tells the priest that, although he does not love God, he fears God "in the night sometimes" (72). Later, he tells Count Greffi that he is a believer, or "*Croyant*" (261), only at night and that his religious feeling "comes only at night" (263), brought on by his fear of death.

One of the main gifts that Frederic's relationship with Catherine has given him, ultimately, is a temporary relief from the mindset of war. In another meditation, Frederic ruminates about the comfort he finds in the nighttime when he is with Catherine:

> I know that the night is not the same as the day: that all things are different, that the things of the night cannot be explained in the day, because they do not then exist, and the night can be a dreadful time for lonely people once their loneliness has started. But with Catherine there was almost no difference in the night except that it was an even better time. (249)

The deleted manuscript passage, then, remains a crucial piece of information for understanding Frederic Henry, as well as his relationship with his past self through memory. When he is happy, in love, and together with Catherine, frightening images or bad memories do not lurk in the dark to prevent him from a peaceful sleep. However, the fear of God, pain, danger, lost love, and death return in the dark when he does not have the comfort and protective company of the woman he loves.

The antagonistic feature of memory belies the reductive critical view of memory in Hemingway's work and life as being equivalent to nostalgia. Describing one of his most maliciously created female characters, Hemingway's preface to his play *The Fifth Column* explains, "There is a girl in it named Dorothy but her name might also have been Nostalgia" (vi). The moniker is not meant as a compliment. In *Islands in the Stream*, Thomas Hudson observes: "*Nostalgia hecha hombre*, he thought in Spanish. People did not know that you died of it" (233). This notion that nostalgia "makes a man" is further evidence of the danger of allowing the past to interfere with the urgent necessities of the present situation. Hudson enjoys the pleasant balm of nostalgia while indulging in a gin and tonic with lime and Angostura, a drink that provides a "pleasantly bitter" taste, much like the memory it induces: "it reminded him of Tanga, Mombasa, and Lamu and all that coast and he had a sudden nostalgia for Africa. Here he was, settled on the island, when he could as well be in Africa. Hell, he thought, I can always go there. You have to make it inside of yourself wherever you are. You are doing all right at that here" (21).[15]

Tony Tanner calls *A Moveable Feast* "an exercise in nostalgia" (rev. of MF 477), just as Faith Norris links Hemingway's memoirs to the "nostalgic passages" in Proust's magnum opus (101). However, accompanying the indisputably nostalgic tone of *A Moveable Feast* is a more complex, instructive attitude toward the functioning of memory.[16] Although much of *A Moveable Feast* casts a surface innocence on Hemingway's Paris years, the workings of memory also transcend simple nostalgia. In the vignette "A False Spring," for example, Hemingway's first wife tells him, "Memory is hunger" (57). If, as an aphorism, that statement does not mean a great deal, the rest of the volume pursues "hunger" as a significant theme in Hemingway's life during the 1920s. Hunger implies a lack, and memory also indicates the pursuit of something lost, be it time past, abandoned love, stolen manuscripts, broken relationships, the death of innocence, or the extinction of a former way of life. Later, Hemingway coaches himself on avoiding "hunger-thinking," in other words, harebrained thoughts emanating from a hysterical, food-deprived mind. The equating of "memory" and "hunger" also reveals the inherent inadequacy of recollection. Hemingway's memory of Paris may be a moveable feast, but William James explains that all a man's memory can provide is "a few of the crumbs that fall from the feast" (*Principles*, I: 276). Just as *Death in the Afternoon* acknowledges the unavoidable falsity of memory, James says that memory takes an object or an emotion from the past and "either makes too little or too much of it" (276). Distortion of some kind is unintentional and inevitable.

Although the content of memories make up much of *A Moveable Feast*, there are also exquisite examples of the iceberg theory, in which secret or painful memories are withheld from the reader, activating the reader's imagination and deepening the mystery of the narration. In this way, Hemingway's text rises to his own challenge of multidimensionality in writing. In what seems to be an inane construction, Hemingway interrupts a conversation with his friend Ernest Walsh to tell us: "I thought of Joyce and remembered many things" (126). Why not share them? Since they are obviously relevant, it would seem to behoove Hemingway to divulge these memories in detail. Hemingway's memories of Joyce are apparently so rich, so personally rewarding and pristine, that he would not waste them on a bull session with Walsh, to say nothing of any generosity toward the reader. Joyce is given more explicit memories elsewhere in the memoir, but in this case the submerged memory speaks to its value, not to be wasted during casual chatter.

Similarly, in the most powerful example of the iceberg technique that Hemingway would ever crystallize into a single sentence, he recalls the anguish of realizing that his precious early manuscripts were stolen from his wife: "It was true all right and I remember what I did in the night after I let myself into the flat and found it was true" (74). Here, the memory is so unspeakably painful that he does not voice it. The writing style represses the detail because the narrator must repress the memory in order to preserve his well-being.

In 1952, the year *The Old Man and the Sea* was published, Dalí painted a sequel that reexamined his most famous work, which he called "The Disintegration of the Persistence of Memory." Like Hemingway's novella, Dalí's landscape was now immersed in water, with a great fish at the center of it. Daniel L. Schacter joins Dalí in picking up the phenomenon of disintegration in the wake of trauma; however, he points not to memory's persistence being disintegrated but rather the disruption of a sense of a continuous self. Survivors of hellacious firestorms, for example, "reported disturbances in their sense of orientation in time: they felt that time had stopped or that the present was no longer continuous with the past or the future" (175). Schacter's point elucidates the same mental trap we see with Hemingway's heroes: "Temporal disintegration in response to a trauma thus foreshadowed later troubles in people who remained stuck in the past, prisoners of persistent memories" (175). Although Frederic in theory would welcome a relief from the persistence of his own memory, he is in effect also pulling the plug on his own self, his own consciousness. Elsewhere, Hemingway relates, "although we usually tried not to think about a war when it was over it is always impossible not to think or remember sometimes" (UK 387). Memory inevitably does persist: *A Farewell to Arms* is a war memory, recollected a decade or more after the events related occurred. In a discarded ending to *A Farewell to Arms*, Hemingway writes: "It is a good thing too [*sic*] not to try too much to remember very fine things because if you do you wear them out and you lose them" (qtd. in Reynolds, *Hemingway's First War* 293). Like the awful memories that he wishes he could avoid, Frederic likewise has anxiety about even enjoying the nostalgia or happy reminiscences of the past. It is only by the gift of memory that Frederic can assemble the fractured emotions of the past to form the narrative of his life, to wage his war on memory in order to write his memory of war.

4

"The Stream with No Visible Flow"

Islands in the Stream and the Thought-Action Dichotomy

For man's everyday needs, it would have been quite enough to have the ordinary human consciousness. . . . It would have been quite enough, for instance, to have the consciousness by which all so-called direct persons and men of action live.

Fyodor Dostoevsky, *Notes from the Underground*

One must act like a man of thought and think like a man of action.

Henri Bergson

*A*s Hemingway was composing *To Have and Have Not* in 1936, he received an admiring letter from fellow Scribner's author Marjorie Kinnan Rawlings, who wondered how Hemingway balanced his internal conflict "between the sportsman and the artist" (Reynolds, *The 1930s* 238).[1] Hemingway replied that he received "great inner pleasure and almost complete satisfaction" from hunting and fishing and that writing brought him "the same pleasure" (SL 449).

One year earlier, in a letter to a critic, Hemingway acknowledged, "A life of action is much easier to me than writing. I have greater facility for action than for writing. In action I do not worry any more. Once it is bad enough you get a sort of elation because there is nothing you can do except what you are doing and you have no responsibility" (SL 419).

This apparent conflict—between a man of action and a man of thought—not only defines Hemingway's public persona but also represents the essential tension in his work. Nick Adams and David Bourne are fiction writers who go to war as young men; Frederic Henry is a student of architecture who goes to war; Robert Jordan is a Spanish teacher and writer who goes to war; Thomas Hudson is a painter of seascapes who goes to war; Harry in "The Snows of Kilimanjaro" is a writer who pursues dangerous game in Africa. Jake Barnes, a wounded aviator, is also presumably a closeted fiction writer. However, the phrase "thought-action" in the title of this chapter is intentionally reductive, and what seems a clear dichotomy is a false choice. The power in Hemingway's fiction emerges when these two impulses, rather than being two separate and distinguishable entities, operate dysfunctionally, with one compromising or even crippling the other.

Leon Edel referred to Hemingway's fiction as taking place in a world "of superficial action and almost wholly without reflection—such reflection as there is tends to be on a rather crude and simplified level" ("Art of Evasion" 170). Michael F. Moloney concludes of Hemingway's corpus, "His heroes are men of action rather than thinkers" (188). This view stems in large part from accepting two disparate archetypes, one focused only on killing, drinking, fishing, carousing, brawling, and mindless activity, the other a caricature of the feeble intellectual confined to his cork-lined bedroom. Henri Bergson draws the distinction between these two polar existences, elucidating the practical differences between them:

> To live only in the present, to respond to a stimulus by the immediate reaction which prolongs it, is the mark of the lower animals: the man who proceeds in this way is a man of *impulse*. But he who lives in the past for the mere pleasure of living there, and in whom recollections emerge into the light of consciousness without any advantage for the present situation, is hardly better fitted for action: here we have no man of impulse, but a *dreamer*. (*Matter and Memory* 153, emphasis in original)

Bergson's quote echoes William James's chapter on "Habit": "There is no more contemptible type of human character than that of the nerveless sentimentalist and dreamer, who spends his life in a weltering sea of sensibility and emotion, but who never does a manly concrete deed" (*Principles*, I: 125). Although Bergson and James introduce these states as polar and hypothetical, these points resonate with their attention to the psychological dimension to action and the physical practicalities of psychology. As we have seen in chapter 3's discussion of the complexity of the memory of war, the physical activity in Hemingway's fiction is remarkable only for the corresponding internal reaction of the character. Bergson emphasizes the memories that a person brings to the current situation, informing it and allowing him to act in a way that is specifically his own. Bernard DeVoto's venomous charge in his review of *To Have and Have Not* encapsulates the anti-Hemingway stance:

> So far none of Ernest Hemingway's characters has had any more consciousness than a jaguar. They are physiological systems organized around abdomens, suprarenal glands, and genitals. They are sacs of basic instinct. Their cerebrums have highly developed motor areas but are elsewhere atrophied or vestigial. Their speech is rudimentary, they have no capacity for analytical or reflective thought, they have no beliefs, no moral concepts, no ideas. Living on an instinctual level, they have no complexities of personality, emotion, or experience. (223)

As Faulkner observed in his withering putdown during his Nobel Prize acceptance speech, Hemingway tends to be associated with prose "not of the heart but of the glands" (*Essays* 120). Wyndham Lewis raised this stereotyping of Hemingway into high art and even higher comedy, particularly in his "Dumb Ox" essay.

The distinction that must be made between these characterizations of Hemingway and the more complex world that exists in the text corresponds to what the neuroscientist Antonio Damasio calls "core consciousness," as opposed to "extended consciousness," the animal, sensory awareness as well as the more self-reflective, abstract ruminations of the mind. It would be foolish to suggest that the works of Hemingway present the typical protagonist purely as an intellectual. However, Hemingway's work constitutes a revolution in the fictional investigation of modern consciousness, not an avoidance of it. Hemingway's focus on action incorporates consciousness into an urgent external situation and does not ignore it or fail to understand the functioning of the mind.

From childhood, the figures Hemingway idolized all struck a swaggering balance between action and thought. Michael Reynolds points out, "From his youthful admiration for Teddy Roosevelt, Hemingway developed his need for both the active and the contemplative life, neither satisfying without the other" (*Final Years* 33). Elsewhere, Reynolds expands on this idea: "From d'Annunzio, T. E. Lawrence of Arabia and Lord Byron, Hemingway gradually developed a public role for the writer in his time: a physical, passionate, active life balanced against the contemplative life while actually writing" (*Young Hemingway* 211). Reynolds also observes, "On the one hand, he desperately wanted to be a writer of fiction, living on his earned income. However, the contemplative role of writer did not satisfy a deeply embedded need in Hemingway to be a man of action" (*Paris Years* 25). Reynolds finds that, throughout Hemingway's life, his "contemplative life and his active life are jammed together so tightly that only minutes separate them" (*The 1930s* 48). Denis Brian sees this tension as ultimately a destructive one for Hemingway: "He was not the first man of action to take to the pen," Brian writes. "Walter Raleigh, Teddy Roosevelt, Gabriele D'Annunzio, Rudyard Kipling, and T. E. Lawrence among others led the way. But they never denied or belittled their interest in literature. The secret core of fear and rejection stirred by the traumas of his early life was the wellspring of much of his writing" (320). Brian's conclusion is psychoanalytic speculation; far from denials, Hemingway made innumerable comments about literature. Those who fail to see the literary, cerebral side to Hemingway are swept up by the seductive distractions of stereotype. Reynolds traces an internal tension to Hemingway's life that is identical to the tension between thought and action that takes place within every Hemingway text, both the successful efforts like *For Whom the Bell Tolls* and the inferior examples such as *To Have and Have Not* and *Islands in the Stream*.

Dostoevsky's Underground Man anticipates the anguish of the Hemingway hero: consciousness gets in the way; it becomes a burden from which the protagonist suffers as the thoughtful man must perform an action. Hemingway's most vehement detractors perpetuate a stereotype and contrive a problem where none exists. The notion that a scene must have either thought or action is almost childish in its conception, a sophomoric criticism that taxonomizes films or novels as being either "character-driven" or "plot-driven." In his New York Edition Preface to *The Portrait of a Lady*, Henry James lauds his own scripting of Isabel Archer's drawing-room vigil in chapter 42 as "obviously the best thing in the book" (15). James intended to fuse thought and action in the scene, claiming that the vigil "throws the action further forward than twenty 'incidents' might have done. It was designed to have all the vivacity of incident and all the economy of picture" (14). James adopts the Bergsonian notion of thought in action and action in thought.

Henry's brother William begins *The Principles of Psychology* by defining psychology as being concerned with "(1) *thoughts and feelings*, and (2) *a physical world* in time and space with which they coexist and which (3) *they know*" (I: vi, emphasis in original). Stuart Hampshire's 1959 study *Thought and Action* picks up on James's definition, striving to reconcile the incessant stream of human thought with the immediate, external contingencies facing an individual. The significance of this framework rests in the fusion of human beings' consciousness and real-life situations. A satisfactory psychological novel must include all three elements that James enumerates: the thoughts and feelings of an individual; the external situation; and the relationship of one to the other. In his Preface to *The Princess Casamassima*, Henry James explains that "the figures in any picture, the agents in any drama, are interesting only in proportion as they feel their respective situations; since the consciousness, on their part, of the complication exhibited forms for us their link of connexion with it" (*Art of the Novel* 62). The Preface continues with an analysis of this aim of literature, stating, "What a man thinks and what he feels are the history and the character of what he does; on all of which things the logic of intensity rests" (66), an aphorism used by Leon Edel in his important study *The Psychological Novel: 1900–1950*.

Wyndham Lewis wrote that Hemingway's "muse is married to Action" and that he bought into the twentieth century "veneration for action, and for men of action" (*Rude Assignment* 35). This common view of Hemingway's prose simplifies and diminishes an inherent complexity that defines the tension of even his minor works. In actuality, Hemingway crafts a kind of triangulation among Hemingway's artistic muse, action, and thought, an interplay of the active hero in thought, and the thinking hero in action. This nuanced formula works most powerfully in *For Whom the Bell Tolls*, in which a consciousness under pressure must restrict its full scope in order to fulfill an external, physical duty. A dialogue between Robert Jordan and Pilar underscores the importance Hemingway places on the thought-action dichotomy. Pilar opens the exchange by asking Jordan if he has any fears:

> "Not to die," he said truly.
> "But other fears?"
> "Only of not doing my duty as I should."
> "Not of capture, as the other [Kashkin, the deceased dynamiter] had?"
> "No," he said truly. "Fearing that, one would be so preoccupied as to be useless."
> "You are a very cold boy."
> "No," he said. "I do not think so."

"No. In the head you are very cold."

"It is that I am very preoccupied with my work."

"But you do not like the things of life?"

"Yes. Very much. But not to interfere with my work."

"You like to drink, I know. I have seen."

"Yes. Very much. But not to interfere with my work."

"And women?"

"I like them very much, but I have not given them much importance."

"You do not care for them?"

"Yes. But I have not found one that moved me as they say they should move you."

"I think you lie."

"Maybe a little." (91)

This excerpt presents Jordan as a creature of either subhuman emotion or superhuman discipline, apparently unfazed by worldly things such as wine, women, and mortal trepidation. However, Pilar's knowing interrogation soon gets to the truth, that a person does indeed lurk beneath the dutiful soldier, a lover or thinker or sentient being within the focused man of action. As Erik Nakjavani points out: "as a man of action, or as a *guerillero*, it is required of Robert Jordan to suspend from time to time the flow of thinking, or what may be called surplus thinking, so that he can redirect it and refocus it" ("Nonthinking" 178). Jordan, after all, tells the journalist Karkov (more wishfully than accurately), "My mind is in suspension until we win the war" (245). Yet, minds cannot be suspended. The dialogue between Pilar and Jordan exemplifies the critical debate in interpreting the Hemingway hero through the decades: Is the typical Hemingway protagonist an unemotional, stoical brute, or has the crisis of the present fictional situation forced him to compromise aspects of his normal behavior and cripple the power of of his consciousness?[2]

Rose Marie Burwell posits that, with *For Whom the Bell Tolls*, Hemingway became more explicit in his presentation of the interiority of his characters. She cites Hemingway's letter to Maxwell Perkins about a crucial lesson from his experiences in World War II: "You see it is all done with people, not just weapons, nor logistics, but always people—and I'm finally getting so I know about people a little" (54). This observation is evidenced in *For Whom the Bell Tolls* when Jordan retains his individuality, despite his devotion as a soldier: "He was serving in a war and he gave absolute loyalty and as complete a performance as he could give while he was serving. But nobody owned his mind, nor his faculties for seeing and hearing, and if he were going to form judgments he would form them afterwards" (136). As Burwell puts it, "the iceberg theory had begun to dissolve with the interiority of Robert Jordan" (54).

A novel of heightened action does not disqualify itself from being categorized as a novel of consciousness. In fact, action—even urgent and dangerous action—is required to determine the extremes of the character's psychological response to the external world in which he finds himself. Although this strain runs through the entirety of Hemingway's work, it is illustrative to examine the thought-action dichotomy in one of Hemingway's minor, less artful novels, the posthumous *Islands in the Stream*. This novel's serious structural and dramatic flaws aside, the raw presentation of consciousness during the action of the narrative is suggestive of Hemingway's similar efforts in his more masterful texts. Comparing Hemingway's presentation of thought within action, and action within thought in *Islands in the Stream* to its rendering in *For Whom the Bell Tolls* can illuminate the failure of the second by examining how he succeeded in the first.

Hemingway's best novels are also his most linear. Although *The Sun Also Rises* and *A Farewell to Arms* contain subtle temporal manipulations, they are retrospective narratives told from a single point of view, first-person narrators that remind most readers of Hemingway himself. A major decision that Hemingway made when editing *The Sun Also Rises* was to present the action chronologically, rather than by using the in medias res technique with which the manuscript opens. *For Whom the Bell Tolls* and *The Old Man and the Sea* are each compressed into three days of action and told from a third-person perspective. The scope of *For Whom the Bell Tolls* allows it to take more adventurous turns, with the omniscient eye of the narrator occasionally abandoning Robert Jordan for extended periods of time, notably for the novel's two most spectacular moments, Pilar's embedded narrative recounting the massacre of the fascists and El Sordo's final battle on the hillside. Readers are also permitted to see—without the focalization of the protagonist—Andres's fruitless errand to military headquarters, which demonstrates the Republic's chaotically disorganized bureaucracy. Another embedded narrative recounts, from her own perspective, the brutal rape of Maria, heightening Jordan's emotional investment in the mission.

When Hemingway is praised as an experimental storyteller in the modernist tradition, critics almost unanimously point to *In Our Time* as the best example, the stories and interchapters forming, to D. H. Lawrence and others, a "fragmentary novel" itself (93). Along with *To Have and Have Not*—essentially its companion novel—*Islands in the Stream* most closely replicates the fragmented modernist structure that makes *In Our Time* so innovative. Although Hemingway never achieved in a published novel the level of technical experimentation that distinguished his volume of early stories, his two minor Gulf Stream novels examine several characters from various perspectives, using temporal shifts and disruptions of setting to an extent unseen in his other novels. Ultimately, the result of these techniques is in the eye of the beholder. His detractors describe these works as haphazard, unfinished, and scattered, rather than fragmented and suggestive. Although *Islands in the Stream* falls short of Hemingway's most convincing work, it remains a crucial text in his effort to represent consciousness through more ambitious narrative techniques.

In the 1977 film version of *Islands in the Stream*, an early scene shows the artist-protagonist Thomas Hudson (portrayed by Hemingway-in-winter lookalike George C. Scott) welding a metal sculpture. Although Hemingway would surely have balked at the transformation of his naturalist painter of maritime scenes into a contemporary sculptor with a blowtorch, the image mimics the writing of the narrative. Hemingway referred to his task of unifying the disparate parts of his "sea novel" as "a welding job" (qtd. in Ricks 17). Linda Wagner-Martin concludes that the ambiguity of Hemingway's authorial intentions required the editors of *Islands in the Stream* "to weld the three sections comprising the novel into a coherent structure" (218). Just as Joyce named his alter ego after Daedalus, the craftsman of the gods, a character who claims he will "forge in the smithy of my soul the uncreated conscience of my race" (*Portrait* 253), Hemingway often compared the artistic process to construction, handiwork, and craftsmanship.

If the italicized interchapters of *In Our Time* are jarring enough to cast a shadow of ominous violence over the narratives themselves, creating a kind of textual subconscious, for most critics, the seams of *Islands in the Stream* still show, yielding a confused, often frustrating text. "Nothing," Christopher Ricks judged of the components of *Islands in the Stream*, "could ever have welded these together—they desperately don't fit, which is both why Hemingway had to write the book and why he didn't publish it. The fissures can't even be leaped, let alone welded. Part III is At Sea [the title of the section] and so is the book" (18). *Islands in the Stream* is an extreme case that resembles a matryoshka doll: a three-part novel that itself was intended to be a part of a four-part opus, Hemingway's never-completed Land, Sea, and Air trilogy, which was to focus on World War II and for which *The Old Man and the Sea* would have served as an anthemic epilogue. Hemingway explained in July 1951 that "This book about the sea could be broken up into four books and each one of them published separately. . . . That is the way the book works. . . . But I plan the complete book, in one volume, to consist of parts one, two, three and four" (SL 730–31).

If Joyce was Hemingway's modernist exemplar in employing the cinematic technique of shifting perspective, *Ulysses* serves as an explicit touchstone for both

To Have and Have Not and *Islands in the Stream.* However, Hemingway's analysis of Joyce's masterpiece is ultimately more revealing of his own aesthetics than of Joyce's dizzying accomplishment. Hemingway told John Dos Passos in 1932 that "Bloom and Mrs. Bloom saved Joyce" (SL 354), preferring the characters he judged more distant from Joyce than his alter ego Stephen Dedalus. This argument echoes Nick Adams's review of *Ulysses*, revealed in the fragment later titled "On Writing": "That was the weakness of Joyce. Daedalus [*sic*] in *Ulysses* was Joyce himself, so he was terrible. Joyce was so damn romantic and intellectual about him. He'd made Bloom up. Bloom was wonderful. He'd made Mrs. Bloom up. She was the greatest in the world" (NAS 238). In this passage, Nick anticipates arguments that would be leveled more accurately and with greater vehemence against Hemingway for, among other works, *Islands in the Stream.* Although Michael Reynolds claims that Hemingway read all of Joyce, all we can be sure of is that he owned all of Joyce. According to Noel Riley Fitch, Hemingway's personal copy of *Ulysses* was uncut except "the pages of the first half and the last portion" (121), which includes Molly's soliloquy.

Molly's soliloquy is the primary referent of Joyce's influence and pervasive presence in the texts. Just as chapter 7 of *For Whom the Bell Tolls* ends with Maria in the throes of passion à la Molly—"'Yes,' she said almost fiercely. 'Yes. Yes. Yes.'" (73)—*To Have and Have Not* explores the feminine consciousness in two extended interior monologues in ways not featured in any of Hemingway's other published work. Marie Morgan and Dorothy Hollins are given, like Molly, direct treatment of their consciousness, not merely the feminine consciousness refracted through their male counterparts, as with Margot Macomber and Lady Brett Ashley. During one of *Islands in the Stream*'s departures into reverie about Thomas Hudson's Paris days, Joyce is named as one of his best friends, as well as an intimate friend of his eldest son, young Tom. During this extended dialogue, in which Joyce is referred to as "Mr. Joyce" some thirty-four times, the last chapter of *Ulysses* gains further prominence in the Hemingway text. "A nude by papa would be nothing like that chapter by Mr. Joyce" (75), his son says. Hudson later refers to the Molly soliloquy, alluding to "the secret Mr. Joyce knew all about in that last chapter" (76). The characters in *Islands in the Stream* show the same reverence for Joyce that Hemingway shows in *A Moveable Feast.*

If Joyce revolutionized the presentation of the stream of consciousness in fiction, Hemingway was fond of implying the link between the Gulf Stream and the stream of consciousness. As David Bourne characterizes writer's block in the manuscript of *The Garden of Eden,* "Today was just as though they'd shut the water off. No, that's wrong. There isn't any 'they,' and it isn't piped. That's the water closet, boys. It was like going to the stream you'd lived by all your life and finding it dry" (JFK 422, folder 35). Thomas Hudson explains the character of a stream: "A river can be treacherous and cruel and kind and friendly. A stream can be completely friendly and you can trust it all your life if you do not abuse it. But the ocean always has to lie to you before she does it" (IIS 358). *Green Hills of Africa* contains perhaps the most evocative sequence Hemingway ever wrote, a passage about nature that ends with the phrase "the stream" in prose so fluid that the writing functions like a glorious stream itself (148–50).

The importance of consciousness in *Islands in the Stream* can be intuited from the title itself: although Thomas Hudson's eventual goal is ostensibly to hunt Nazis in his Q-boat, his entire life is structured to provide himself shelter from the stream of his own thoughts, memories, and emotions. Haunted by his failed marriages (particularly his first one) and by his three absent sons (initially in the custody of their mothers, then dead), Hudson arranges his life in various ways to protect himself from the force of his own consciousness, leading to a limited, lonely life spent in constant internal struggle. Only by contriving external battles can he relieve his internal anguish. Once the tragedies and loneliness of Hudson's life are established, beginning with "Cuba," the second of three parts, he begins to adopt mental strategies in an attempt to manage sorrow.

Hemingway's career-long project of representing protagonists who for various reasons were forced to "not think" about things forms the thematic centerpiece for *Islands in the Stream*. An exasperated Christopher Ricks asked in his review of the novel, "was there ever a book so obsessively about not thinking about things?" (18). Erik Nakjavani refers to Hudson's efforts to avoid thinking about his problems as "ceaseless" ("Nonthinking" 180). Unlike "Big Two-Hearted River," in which Nick Adams chooses *not* to act recklessly, to maintain better his scheme of controlling his thoughts and memories, Hudson chooses a path of high-stakes adventure in order to replace the need for introspection. Such a charge is quite damning to Hemingway, because it reduces "At Sea" to a self-indulgent curiosity and minimizes the hunting of Nazis to Hudson's vain exercise of occupying himself with anything so that he does not have to withstand unpleasant thoughts. This realization exposes the ultimate weakness of *Islands in the Stream* and renders the third part of the novel a juvenile exercise in wish fulfillment, much like the nonsensical action scenes in Hemingway's Spanish Civil War play, *The Fifth Column*. Upon its publication, one review derided the action in the "Cuba" section as being "not very far removed from the Hardy Boys and Tom Swift in intellectual content" (qtd. in Anderson 326). Irving Howe claimed that the action "could thrill five-year olds" (122). Even Arnold Gingrich, Hemingway's own publisher at *Esquire*, refers disparagingly to the

"Rover Boys chase at the end of the book" (12). Rather than quarrel with these judgments, it nevertheless is instructive to observe Hemingway's portrayal of cognition in a character so willfully immersing himself in action. Even if the action is not authentic, the thought-action challenge for the character remains valid.

In trying to steer clear of thoughts of his happier past as well as his failed marriages and memories of his dead children, Hudson employs four strategies to erase unwanted thoughts: work/duty, habit, the consumption of alcohol, and not-thinking. In the first part, "Bimini," Hudson the artist immerses himself in work to avoid introspection or rumination, disciplining himself to paint every morning, even forgoing time spent with his visiting children. Hudson, with the elaboration of the more knowing narrator, describes ways to combat the unwelcome emotions that sad memories bring:

> He thought that on the ship he could come to some terms with his sorrow, not knowing, yet, that there are no terms to be made with sorrow. It can be cured by death and it can be blunted or anesthetized by various things. Time is supposed to cure it, too. But if it is cured by anything less than death, the chances are that it was not true sorrow.
> One of the things that blunts it temporarily through blunting everything else is drinking and another thing that can keep the mind away from it is work. Thomas Hudson knew about both these remedies. (195)

This investigation comes at the end of the first section, during which it is observed that "Thomas Hudson kept on painting." Hudson cannot even look at his children, although he "was having a difficult time staying in the carapace of work that he had built for his protection . . . he knew he must keep on working now or he would lose the security he had built for himself with work. . . . Work, he told himself" (188). Just as it demeans the later mission in World War II if Hudson is captaining a Q-boat merely to block out bad memories, it trivializes Hudson as an artist if the motivation for his productivity and prolific discipline is less inspiration and his creative muse than the need for busywork, a time-consuming shield from thoughts about his ex-wives, his sons, and the misfortunes of his life. Hudson's painting takes the place of Nick Adams's coffee in "Big Two-Hearted River," Santiago's arm-wrestling exploits, or the imaginary streams of "Now I Lay Me"; it is something to concentrate on that might distract from the pressing problems of his life. As the novel opens, readers are told that Hudson "had exorcized guilt with work insofar as he could . . . He had been able to replace almost everything except the children with work and the steady normal working life he had built on the island" (13). Even this description warns the reader that the solution is far from ideal—"insofar as he could" and "almost everything except" indicate that there are weaknesses to the practice of thought avoidance through disciplined labor.

In Hemingway's other writings, such as *A Moveable Feast* or *The Garden of Eden*, art is described as a true calling, with other people impeding the protagonist from its successful production. While attempting to write in the cafés of Paris, intruders constantly distract Hemingway. Zelda Fitzgerald is portrayed as an even more insidious figure, smiling when she knows her husband will be too drunk or too distracted to write. Hemingway recalls that Scott Fitzgerald attempted to interrupt him and that "drunk, he took almost as much pleasure interfering with my work as Zelda did interfering with his" (184). From Harry's bitter perspective in "The Snows of Kilimanjaro": "The people he knew now were all much more comfortable when he did not work" (SS 59). Hemingway always bemoaned intrusions, saying once, "You can write any time people will leave you alone and not interrupt you. Or rather you can if you will be ruthless enough about it" (Plimpton 23–24). One way in which Robert Cohn is shown to be a socially graceless outsider in *The Sun Also Rises* is by his cluelessly intruding on Jake Barnes's workday as a journalist, eventually falling asleep to the clacking of the typewriter while Jake hammers out dispatches. Likewise, in the manuscript of *The Sun Also Rises*, Jake is able to fulfill his ambition of writing a novel only after he removes himself from the distractions of the fiesta and his cadre of friends. Hudson, to the contrary, uses his art to distract from his life.

The "work" that Hudson the artist does in "Bimini" is more plausible than the "duty" that Hudson the renegade soldier performs "At Sea." One of Hemingway's clumsy missteps with respect to this book rests in his blurring the two words "work" and "duty," leaving a muddy impression of the protagonist's motivation and passions. Therefore, when Hudson tells Willie, "I don't think about anything except work" (353), he is talking about hunting Nazis, rather than creating seascapes in the tradition of Winslow Homer, as in the former connotation. Instead of an invigorating fragmentation that suggests complexity of character, the execution is careless, so that a painter's military adventure in the high seas falls anywhere from irrelevant to comical. One critic throws up her hands in defeat, unable to wrest meaning from Hudson's action: "What he is doing is done through some sense of Duty, but his heart is not really in it" (Hughes 47). Therefore, when Michael Reynolds pithily dubs the dramatic trajectory of *Islands in the Stream* Hudson's "redemption by duty performed" (*Final Years* 257), it is unclear what redeeming elements he discerns in a duty without qualities, except gratuitous danger.

One moment of interior monologue provides an essential explication of the merits of duty, the allure of work, and the distinction between the two concepts.

> He had been thinking so long in their [the enemies'] heads that he was tired of it. I am really tired finally, he thought. Well, I know what I have to do, so it is simple. Duty is a wonderful thing. I do not know what I would have done without duty since young Tom died. You could have painted, he told himself. Or you could have done something useful. Maybe, he thought. Duty is simpler. (401)

Hudson, here, is disclosing what should be a profound revelation: his acceptance of the mission is principally as a distraction from the memories that haunt him. The simplicity of duty allows him to thrust himself into action in order to shield himself from thought. Hudson would not even characterize his actions as "useful." According to Edmund Wilson's derisive (and somewhat obtuse) summary: "You are never allowed to know exactly what has happened in Thomas Hudson's past. He is always admonishing himself that he must not allow himself to think about it, so in order to avoid this he orders a drink. The reader clearly sees the drink but not the memory that is being stifled . . . the experiences that have been pushed out of sight are continually rising into consciousness; but not even here . . . are we told exactly what they are. In order to keep them out of his consciousness, Thomas Hudson takes another drink or plunges into his program of action" ("An Effort" 60–61). A point-by-point refutation of Wilson is unnecessary:[3] it is clear enough that Hudson is mourning the loss of his children and the failure of his marriages. It is clearer still that Hemingway's iceberg theory prohibits an explicitly detailed disclosure of painful memories if the protagonist in question would be actively suppressing them. Would Wilson lodge a similar complaint against "Big Two-Hearted River" or *The Sun Also Rises*?

Wilson's larger point, however, remains salient; if Hudson's "program of action" is a tool to salvage a brutalized consciousness, what does that reveal about his stance regarding World War II, and, furthermore, what can we deduce from Hemingway's own adventures, which are similar to those in which Hudson participated? After Pearl Harbor, Hemingway informed Maxwell Perkins that, if he became involved in World War II, "it would only be in order to get material for a novel" (qtd. in Burwell 53). The second of Hemingway's three sons confirms this claim, recalling, "Papa was all things—sportsman, father, hunter, soldier—in order to give him experiences for his writing" (P.

Hemingway, "My Papa, Papa" 264). As John Aldridge wrote of Hemingway, during the writing of *Islands in the Stream*, "he appeared to be almost frantically seeking distraction and taking advantage of any excuse, however trivial, to avoid full commitment to the big novel" (550–51). It is difficult to characterize Hemingway as avoiding "full commitment" to a novel on which he wrote a prodigious amount of material, regardless of subsequent evaluations of its quality.[4] However tempting it is to accept Aldridge's theory, the reality is more complex and infinitely sadder. Hudson first paints to avoid thinking and then hunts Nazis to avoid thinking; Hemingway's life mirrored that of his fictional alter ego. Hemingway claimed in a 1950 letter that the reason he was writing was to avoid thinking, mimicking Hudson's motivation for painting (Baker, *Writer as Artist* 380). The quality of the art is reflected in the defensiveness of its motivation.

Attempting to divine motivation for Hudson is a critical exercise that damns Hemingway by its necessity. If there is no moral imperative to hunt German sailors, then Hudson's credibility as a man of action falls short of the heroics of Robert Jordan, who believes that the future of mankind rests on the successful execution of his mission. To Jordan, the bridge he must blow up "can be the point on which the future of the human race can turn" (FWBT 43). When Jordan tells Pablo, "I come only for my duty . . . and I can promise you of its importance" (15), the mission that forms the action of the novel carries a level of gravity and authenticity entirely absent from *Islands in the Stream*.

Hudson cannot even be aligned with the disillusioned attitude of Nick Adams, Jake Barnes, or Frederic Henry, who are seen questioning, belittling, or abrogating their military duties, and the ignorant, inane orders of their superiors, the clueless masters of war. Hudson's mission is so gratuitous and ill defined that he floats meaninglessly through instances of life and death, where the outcome of "the cause" and the fate of our hero are fraught with vagueness but no tension. John Updike pinpoints this same deficiency: the aim of Hudson's mission, he writes, "was not demanded from above but invented and propelled from within" (489). Malcolm Cowley concurs, comparing where Hemingway went wrong with where he went right: "The sea chase of the final episode," Cowley writes, "should be the best sequence of all, and in fact it demands comparison with the dynamiting of the bridge in *For Whom the Bell Tolls*, but it loses by the demand. Hudson's grim sense of duty and implicit death wish seem pale when placed beside Robert Jordan's tangle of fierce emotions" ("A Double Life" 106). Likewise, Joseph DeFalco distinguishes between Hemingway's novel and *Moby-Dick*, writing, "The difference between the pair is that Ahab's quest is conscious and obsessive, while Hudson's rests limply upon the mechanism of duty and orders and does not originate from intense inner drives" (49).

These negative views suggest a plot contrivance, a life-or-death endeavor that seems to carry no authentic emotional weight for the protagonist. In one of the novel's more sodden moments, Hudson comes to a similar conclusion, that he ultimately has no deep moral investment in the mission: "Then why don't you care anything about anything? he asked himself" (344). Earlier in the same meditation, he outlines some of the mission's benefits: "Well, it keeps your mind off things. What things? There aren't any things any more. Oh yes, there are" (344).

As with all of Hemingway's postwar work, it is not dime-store psychoanalysis to equate his protagonist with the writer himself. In *The Dangerous Summer*, the African novel (*Under Kilimanjaro* [2005] and/or *True at First Light* [1999]), and *A Moveable Feast*, after all, Hemingway is his own protagonist. In each of the other novels, Colonel Cantwell, Santiago, and David Bourne—an epicurean soldier, a Cuban fisherman, and a writer in 1920s France, respectively—can safely be considered to be Hemingway's barely veiled alter egos. In response to *Islands in the Stream*, critics delighted in triangulating Hemingway with Thomas Hudson and Roger Davis, an old painter and a reputedly washed-up writer. The original draft of the novel did not divide the character of the painter and the artist as central characters.

Just as the twin commitments of "work" and "duty" occupy Hudson at various times, he clings to a compulsive routine of living that forms a rubric under which all of his other interests and vocations fall. His adherence to the habits he has devised is ultimately in place to combat intense loneliness. This structure to Hudson's life is clearly articulated, with reference to his children:

> He had been happy before they came and for a long time he had learned how to live and do his work without ever being more lonely than he could bear; but the boys' coming had broken up all the protective routine of life he had built and now he was used to its being broken. It had been a pleasant routine of working hard; of hours for doing things; places where things were kept and well-cared for; of meals and drinks to look forward to and new books to read and many old books to reread. It was a routine where the daily paper was an event when it arrived, but where it did not come so regularly that its nonarrival was a disappointment. It had many of the inventions that lonely people use to save themselves and even achieve unloneliness with and he had made the rules and kept the customs and used them consciously and unconsciously. (97–98)

Such a meticulous scheme was present in the novel's draft, in which the first-person narrator-painter, then named Roger Davis, divulges: "I had been lonely for a long part of my life but later I had learned how not to be lonely. But in avoiding loneliness my life had taken on certain forms and habits that were protections but were almost old-maidish even though they were, on the surface, the opposite" (qtd. in Burwell 63). Likewise, although stalking Nazis may appear to be the height of masculine courage, it actually is a cowardly retreat from the enemies within. In the published novel, as Hudson anticipates his children going away once they end their stay in Bimini, he senses a loss of balance and clings to the security of habit: "as he worked he felt a loneliness coming into him already. It was next week when they would leave. Work, he told himself. Get it right and keep your habits because you are going to need them" (188). In this case, the habit is used not to combat loneliness as much as it is employed in anticipation of future loneliness, truly a portrait of deep melancholy, if not abject depression.

Such protection can motivate unsympathetic readers to find in Hudson a caricature of the stereotypical Hemingway stoic or a farcical incarnation of the robotic discipline Jordan purports to have at the beginning of his mission. Referring to the second and third sections of *Islands in the Stream*, one critic writes that Hudson's "self-discipline is that of a zombie" (Justus 117). The critic's sentiment is a familiar reaction to Hemingway's heroes who endeavor to suspend the full workings of consciousness to execute a task or to withstand past traumas. A 2005 essay by Joyce Carol Oates echoes this point, noting that Krebs, the beleaguered protagonist of "Soldier's Home," "is so accustomed to keeping 'sensations' at bay that he's become a kind of zombie: a prototype of a generation 'lost' to wartime experience" (36).

The health afforded by habitual behavior is a staple of psychology; problems or dangers are addressed through the attention of consciousness, and what can be consigned to habit leads to a smoother, more efficiently functioning organism. William James called human beings "bundles of habits" (*Principles*, I: 104) and referred to habit as "the enormous fly-wheel of society, its most precious conservative agent" (121). Hemingway utilizes the same metaphor of the flywheel in a crucial passage in *For Whom the Bell Tolls*, which follows Robert Jordan's most extended interior monologue, about, among other things, his grandfather's Civil War legacy and his own father's suicide: "You better not think at all, he told himself. Soon you will be with Maria and you won't have to think. That's the best way now that everything is worked out. When you have been concentrating so hard on something you can't stop and your brain gets to racing like a flywheel with the weight gone. You better just not think" (340). A "flywheel with the weight gone" describes an unstable, erratic, unpredictable stream of thought, excitement that Jordan cannot afford to indulge. Jordan is inclined to shut off the power of thought, because he is afraid that once he begins, he will

not be able to control it. The habitual thinking during the unquestioning performance of duty provides the flywheel that controls consciousness. Although
Hudson's explanation of this technique is rawer and less poetic than Jordan's,
his attitude toward consciousness is strikingly similar.

Hudson's affinity for alcohol, as well as the description of the innumerable
series of drinks that would make Jake Barnes seem a teetotaler, is another
pronounced strategy to negotiate his relationship with his own thoughts and
the past. Of sorrow, Hudson knows that alcohol acts as an effective anesthetic,
but "he also knew the drinking would destroy the capacity for producing satisfying work and he had built his life on work for so long now that he kept that as
the one thing that he must not lose" (195). Hudson's drinks, as Joseph DeFalco
writes of the "Cuba" section, "represent another attempt to create an 'island'
that will give him a safe place away from the dangers of time and contingency. . . .
All the totally estranged Hudson can do is hope for momentary escape into
oblivion through the aesthetic [*sic*] of alcohol. Hudson's retreat from consciousness and headlong flight into oblivion emphasizes his lapse into total despair"
(48). Hudson's strategy, then, undoes the central illumination of *For Whom the
Bell Tolls*, which is articulated in John Donne's epigraph, stating that "No man
is an *Iland*, intire of it selfe." In *Islands in the Stream*, we reach the opposite, unhappy conclusion.

However, the novel's simplistic and quite monotonous stance on alcohol's
effect becomes complicated later, during a quiet moment in "At Sea." Drinking
gin and coconut water with lime, Hudson disobeys his vow not to drink "so
that he would not think of anything but work" (426). As with Robert Jordan's
mystical experience drinking absinthe, Nick Adams's meditative drinking of
canned apricot juice, and even Proust's tea, Hudson realizes, "A drink always
unlocked his memory that he kept locked so carefully now." Hudson sips his
drink, stares ahead into the keys and channel, and is reminded of his son as a
small boy and of their days trolling for tarpon. The reverie extends for several
pages, linked by phrases of retrospection: "He remembered . . . He remembered . . . Then he remembered," and so on, with the verb "to remember"
repeated six times (427–28). How does a drink "always" unlock the vaults of
memory when the novel uniformly treats alcohol as a deadening balm?

Although Hudson has been decidedly morose if not morbidly depressed for
the balance of the trip, triggered by his drink he asks himself, "What were the
happiest times?" (429). In a quintessentially Hemingwayesque reminiscence,
Hudson recalls moments in Paris and days following cycling races, in scenes
that seem culled from the writer's Paris memoirs or perhaps from *The Garden of
Eden*.

The man of action can function in Hemingway's fiction only by pretending he is not a man of thought. *Islands in the Stream* presents Hudson as embodying the tension found in all of Hemingway's work. When someone attributes internal stolidity to him, Hudson thinks:

> I wish I were as solid as Freddy Archer thinks I am. . . . I have certain unavoidable reactions. . . . I would like to be as solid as Freddy thinks instead of being human. I think you have more fun as a human being even though it is much more painful. It is goddamned painful right about now. . . . Don't think about that either. If you don't think about it, it doesn't exist. The hell it doesn't. But that's the system I'm going on, he thought. (252)

Hudson expresses envy over a robotic, automated, subhuman consciousness during action or times of trial. As Hemingway explains in his introduction to *Men at War*, the ability for a soldier to suspend his imagination during action is the most important of all the qualities a solider must have.[5] Hemingway goes on to say that this gift is the opposite of a writer's ability, which attests to the rarity, in his view, of good writing by good soldiers. Hudson's stance, however, denies the reality of the way the world works, which he understands all too well. "The hell it doesn't" openly admits the failure of such a strategy. In Jake's solitary rumination about his wound, he acknowledges that, despite the torturous frustration of his injury, it is a false option to erase it from the mind. Jake explains: "The Catholic Church had an awfully good way of handling all that. Good advice, anyway. Not to think about it. Oh, it was swell advice. Try and take it sometime. Try and take it" (SAR 39). The Church gives the Hemingway hero the same feeble advice that George offers in the last line of "The Killers," recommending to Nick Adams that the best way to get over the idea of the forthcoming murder of his friend is: "Well . . . you better not think about it" (SS 289).

In *Islands in the Stream*, Hudson's envy of those who can suspend thought resurfaces during what is intended to be the climax, the drawn-out confrontation that leads to his death. A chasm separates the resigned, resolved, stoical Jordan and the wooden, empty response of Hudson. In Jordan's final moments, to be sure, he is aware that death is imminent, and he shares Hudson's impulse to numb the pain. He searches for his absinthe—the "giant killer" (FWBT 467)—to keep his consciousness at bay but finds that the flask has fallen out during his acrobatic performance at the bridge. To his surprise and ours, Jordan accepts the lack of alcohol and tells himself: "You didn't need the giant killer at all" (468). Likewise, Jordan also considers adopting a Hudson-like scheme of thought avoidance, of willing a cessation of consciousness.[6] Jordan "looked at the hillside . . . looked at the pines, and he tried not to think at all. Then he looked at the stream and he remembered" (468). His effort to enact an unthinking gaze succumbs to the force of rich memory and contemplation, and, of course, it is the stream that triggers his cognition. Although Jordan in his role as a man of action has bravely led his band of guerrilla soldiers, he has never completely forsaken his simultaneous identity as a man of thought. Soon after Jordan's final contemplation begins, thoughts of suicide give way to the familiar self-exhortation: "Don't think about that. Don't think at all" (469).

In what must be read as a final conquest, in Jordan's final moments he is not an unthinking zombie but a man desperate to continue cognition, evidence that justifies Erik Nakjavani's descriptions of him as both "an intellectual militant" ("Nonthinking" 178) and an "intellectual hero" ("Knowledge as Power" 131). In a fierce internal dialogue,[7] Jordan repeatedly implores himself to think, thirteen times conjuring up twelve different images: his guerrilla friends being away; riding through the timber; crossing a creek; riding through the heather; going up the slope; them being O.K.; them traveling; them hiding tomorrow; "Think about them"; "God damn it, think about them" (470). Jordan struggles to think and protests that the extent of his thoughts has a limit: *"That's just as far as I can think about them, he said"* (470, emphasis in original). He responds with another series of plans to think: about Montana or Madrid; about "a cool drink of water" (470), which he soon equates with the feeling of being dead and the phenomenon of dying. This moment of elaborate internal debate emphasizes the two-hearted cognition of the soldier, the man of thought within the man of action.

In *Islands in the Stream*, on the other hand, Hudson's final reverie is a rare moment of rumination in a narrative dominated by action. *Islands in the Stream* as Hemingway envisioned it contained more explicit interiority, including extended passages that recall *For Whom the Bell Tolls*. An uneventful moment in chapter 11 of the published novel is only the tip of a far more salacious iceberg that alludes to scenes in *The Garden of Eden*, which Hemingway was also composing as he worked through *Islands in the Stream*, passages that Carl P. Eby refers to as a "familiar déjà vu of perverse fantasy" (264). The thoughts that readers do not see in the published version are memories of "the girl he always thought of when he was alone" (JFK 113). In the unpublished flashback, Hudson's first wife, Jan, incorporates sexual games of twinning, tanning, and the fetishization of hair that Hudson recalls in vivid detail. Hudson questions the wisdom of surrendering to this reminiscence: "Why should I think all this? he thought lying on the deck. . . . So think about her. . . . Think of her. . . . And do not think like that, you son of a bitch, because you still have work to do. . . . But think of her for fun. . . . Think some more about her. . . . Think about all the fun she could make about an un-important thing such as how you cut your hair. . . . I'll just think straight on with her" (JFK 113). Likewise, the discarded chapter 12 continues these moments of metacognition: "I might as well think about her some more. . . . It is fun to think about my wild girl. . . . I'm going to think about her some more" (JFK 113). Therefore, DeFalco's point that Hudson "practices a process of selected remembrance by suppressing the painful memories of the past and dwelling on pleasant memories only" does not explain even the half of it (46). In the manuscript version, the man of action is obsessively ruminative and for chapters at a time indulges in fond sexual reminiscences.

Hudson's reverie does more for the Hemingway reader than simply reference *The Garden of Eden* and provide grist for psychosexual readings of Hemingway; the moments removed from *Islands in the Stream* convey the value of thought for the Hemingway man of action. As he begins to ruminate on his rendezvous with Jan, the flashback abates, and Hudson evaluates the benefit or risk to this reminiscence. He asks himself, "Why do I think of all this?" and then discovers the reason, which is that he needs to avoid thinking about unnamed "other things" and to prepare his mind for the action to follow. Hudson assesses the value and practicality of this line of thought just as he would assess the value and practicality of a plan of action. Following Hudson's analysis of his own consciousness, he scolds himself: "Quit justifying" (JFK 112). If "Why do I think of all this?" is Hudson's metacognition, then "Quit justifying" is meta-metacognition, an evaluation of an evaluation of a thought. This suffocating self-scrutiny indicates the care with which a Hemingway hero engages in indulging a memory, allowing it to trickle out like precious absinthe from a flask. Hudson does not find it necessary to "choke it" as Nick did (SS 218); he has improbably found a moment where he can attain cautious enjoyment, a pleasant memory. Tellingly, Hemingway (or perhaps his fourth wife, Mary, who co-edited the novel) scrapped these fascinating sections where Hudson recalls the character that evokes associations with Hadley, Hemingway's first wife, thus robbing readers of a significant aspect of Hudson's psychological dimension.

These unpublished excerpts are replaced by a much more benign moment in the published *Islands in the Stream*:

> He knew there was no use thinking of the girl who had been Tom's mother nor all the things they had done and the places they had been nor how they had broken up.

There was no use thinking about Tom. He had stopped that as soon as he had heard. There was no use thinking about the others. He had lost them, too, and there was no use thinking about them. He had traded in remorse for another horse that he was riding now. So lie here now and feel clean from the soap and the rain and do a good job at nonthinking. You learned to do it quite well for a while. Maybe you will go to sleep and have funny or good dreams. Just lie quiet and watch the night and don't think. (369–70)

Therefore, the posthumous editing process largely removes rumination, depriving critics such as Edmund Wilson of the precise details of memories that are only hinted at in the published text. In the final version of the novel, as in the excerpt just given, Hudson wishes for "funny or good" dreams and does in fact doze off, dreaming of an innocent boyhood moment, riding a horse and watching a trout stream. He is awakened and then falls asleep later in chapter 11, dreaming of a burned cabin and the death of his buck and dog. "I guess dreams aren't the solution. . . . You will never have good dreams anymore," Hudson concludes (370). Ultimately, as the chapter ends, "he slept without dreaming" (371). In the same moment during the unpublished manuscript, Hudson's plan for dreaming contains a distinctly more sexual element.

Beginning with the third part, "At Sea," Hudson's means of confronting the Nazi boats involve not brute force as much as cunning and superior strategizing; he fancies himself a thinking man's action hero. He knows that he carries the responsibility as the brains behind the mission: "Now I must try to think it out. . . . You're supposed to be able to think" (326), he tells himself. As in other moments in Hemingway's work, this ideal is easier to strive for than to enact under the pressure of the situation. The narrator explains, "But he did not think" (327). Instead of "thinking" about the mission and the means for hunting down Germans, Hudson watches "the sculpture that the wind and sand had made of a piece of driftwood," a specimen beautiful enough to belong in the Salon d'Automne. Thoughts of duty/work (i.e., war) are replaced by thoughts of duty/work (i.e., art), frustrating Hudson's ability for coldly rational thought. Hudson understands that he must go back to thinking about the mission, but he is still drawn to his artistic yearnings: "he did not wish to . . . make all the practical thinking that he must make. I will enjoy the gray wood, he thought" (327). If abstract rumination is usually suspended in deference to the needs of the moment, here Hudson suspends pragmatic thought for a much-needed reverie, a sentimental reflection on art.

Hudson's plan of attack is reduced to a simplistic formula. The second chapter in "At Sea" opens with Hudson gazing at the skyline, and the information that Hudson "had it pretty well thought out. . . . He had tried not to think about it and to relax but it had been impossible" (327). This dubious description of the problems of the mission as needing to "be thought out" or of Hudson "thinking it out" recur throughout much of the book, reducing the seriousness and complexity of the mission to a pesky math problem in a middle-school workbook. Hudson tells one of his shipmates, "I'm trying to think in their heads," to which the man responds confidently, "You can think it out, Tom" (329). This formulation, which might sympathetically be construed as realistic ship-speak, in fact trivializes the demonstration of Hemingway's understanding of thought during moments of action. The silly phrase compromises what has been dramatized elsewhere, in Hemingway's more successful renderings of the thought-action dichotomy. Hudson tells himself to "think it out" twice (326, 370), in addition to the instance in which his shipmate encourages him to "think it out" (329).

Although critics have valid arguments when they decry *Islands in the Stream* as a sophomoric action adventure or a novel void of emotional depth, the more valuable reading of the novel is as a contribution to the larger project of under-standing Hemingway's work: the portrayal of moments of cognition in com-promised situations. While Ricks and others have criticized the book's "not-thinking," Hudson—like Robert Jordan and Harry Morgan—is actually a tactical thinker, with an eye toward action and pragmatic results.[8] The thought-action dichotomy is the tension that drives Hemingway's fiction. When Philip Young writes: "Thought is a kind of dis-ease with the hero, and it must be cured lest it become an impediment to carrying out the actions which were implicit in Harry Morgan's dying words" (111), he is paradoxically arguing for the value of thought, its preciousness to Hemingway's soldiers and men of action. The renunciation of thought is difficult for Hemingway's protagonists because it is so dearly prized, and the temporary quest to banish or control the stream of thought only attests to its importance.

The French philosopher Émile Boutroux contributed an ingenious mani-festo that attempts to reconcile the apparent thought-action dichotomy. To Boutroux, thought attempts to consider an object from all its perspectives, while action necessarily seeks to exclude all other options while fulfilling a single goal. "The end of Thought," Boutroux writes, "is truth. The aim of Action is success" (7). Georges Poulet advances this notion a step further, suggesting that men of action necessarily are not self-aware and do not consider their memories or emotions; while their memories do exist, they are submerged out of view. Boutroux's conclusion is so helpful with respect to Hemingway because he affirms that thought and action are not dissimilar; in fact, they are "far from being things heterogeneous" (23).[9] Ultimately, Boutroux sees that the link between thought and action is the presence of human emotion.

> While irremediably exterior and alien one to another as long as they are considered as the sole essential faculties of human nature, Thought and Action come nearer one to another, penetrate one another, and unite intimately, the moment Feeling is introduced as a thing of eminent value in itself and as the fountain of the superior manifestations of Thought and Action. Feeling is the living medium between Action and Thought. In Feeling lie the common principles of the highest Thought and of the most generous Action. (27)

In Hemingway, when thought and action are linked and manipulated with tension and a causal relationship, as in *For Whom the Bell Tolls*, the emotions of the protagonist resonate powerfully. As Boutroux indicates, the interrelated functions of thought and action, when portrayed shrewdly by the writer, allow the humanity of the protagonist to emerge without negating the plot of the narrative. In *Islands in the Stream*, however, action is overplayed to the exclusion of thought or to the minimization of thought's complexity. In fact, the action of *Islands in the Stream* suffocates thought to the extent that Hemingway was ultimately making a thematic point by the imbalance.

5

Beating Mr. Turgenev

"The Execution of Tropmann" and Hemingway's Aesthetic of Witness

> Dying is a very simple thing. I've looked at death and really I know.
> Hemingway, letter to his family, 18 October 1918

> He had been in it and he had watched it and it was his duty to write of it . . .
> "The Snows of Kilimanjaro"

*I*van Turgenev's influence on Ernest Hemingway has been widely appreciated, a literary relationship whose discussion was repeatedly invited by Hemingway himself.[1] Although critics have in the past discussed Hemingway with respect to Turgenev, important aspects of this link remain unmined. In this chapter, I propose to tie in Hemingway's attitude toward the aesthetics, ethics, and metaphysics of dying by addressing a new dimension to this line of comparative inquiry. One of Turgenev's most poignant works, his 1870 essay "The Execution of Tropmann," introduces a theme that Hemingway would spend an entire career negotiating: the artist's responsibility to witness violence in all its horror, to observe the most minute details that might challenge one's own humanity, and, finally, to render that scene with authenticity to inspire emotion (and with accuracy to convey authenticity). "The Execution of Tropmann"—entirely unremarked upon in conjunction with Hemingway—is a valuable illustration of the sensitivity of the challenge Hemingway presented to himself. This chapter will examine the thematics of Turgenev's essay and then explore Hemingway's own entrance into similar literary terrain.

In "The Execution of Tropmann," Turgenev dramatizes himself at the scene of an execution, squeamishly turning away from the beheading of a mass murderer at the moment of the coup de grâce. The essay is a twelve-part narrative that implicates those in attendance—primarily the writer himself—as being morally complicit in the government's action. Although Turgenev does indeed turn away at the moment of impact, he nevertheless spares no detail; the reader is constantly reminded of the horror of execution, the humanity of the executed man, and the moral ambivalence of the mob in attendance. Upon its publication, Fyodor Dostoevsky ruthlessly mocked the essay, citing Turgenev's disproportionate focus on his own reaction as overly sentimental and self-involved, revealing a hesitance to comprehend and then detail faithfully the full range of the behavior of man.

A disgusted Dostoevsky wrote of "The Execution of Tropmann" in a June 1870 letter:

> this pompous and finicky article exasperated me. Why does he get all flustered and maintain that he had no right to be there? Yes, of course, if he only came for the spectacle; but man on the surface of the earth does not have the right to turn away and ignore what is taking place on earth, and there are lofty *moral* reasons for this: *homo sum et nihil humanum* ["I am a man; nothing human is alien to me"], etc.[2] The most comic thing of all is that in the end he turns away and doesn't see how [Tropmann] is finally executed . . . all this over a decapitated head! (qtd. in Jackson 39)

To Dostoevsky, it would be immoral to turn away, not immoral to watch, contrary to Turgenev's conclusion. Clearly, Dostoevsky—who had an even more immediate experience with an execution (his own last-second commutation in 1849)—claimed different priorities than did Turgenev.

Dostoevsky continued his assault on Turgenev in his 1872 novel, *Demons*, with a passage that further satirizes Turgenev's "highly moral" stance.[3] Dostoevsky's writer Karmazinov is a stand-in for Turgenev and, in what Dostoevsky biographer Joseph Frank terms "a malicious but masterly caricature" and a "devastating depiction" (461), is lampooned for authoring a text reminiscent of "The Execution of Tropmann":

I had read an article of his in a magazine, written with a terrible pretension to the most naïve poetry and . . . to psychology. He described the wreck of a steamer . . . of which he himself had been a witness and had seen how the perishing were being saved and the drowned dragged out. The whole article, quite a long and verbose one, was written with the sole purpose of self-display. One could simply read between the lines: "Pay attention to me, look at how I was in those moments. . . . Better look at me, at how I could not bear the sight and turned away. Here I am turning my back; here I am horrified and unable to look again; I've shut my eyes—interesting, is it not?" (85)

Robert Louis Jackson refers to this dilemma as an "ethics of vision" (34), in which moral implications are attached to those in attendance. Jackson's focus on "The Execution of Tropmann" reveals what he calls "the accountability of sight" and the "moral-psychological experience of looking at violence" (4), notions crucial to Turgenev's piece, Dostoevsky's reaction, and Hemingway's career-long examination of bullfighting and war. Likewise, In *The Hanging Tree*, an analysis of executions in Britain in the eighteenth and nineteenth centuries, V. A. C. Gatrell observes that voyeurism can be "turned into a form of honest witness, avoiding cant and testing courage and manhood. One could not flinch at these realities; one needed to watch another's death in order to experience it vicariously, as one would one's own" (250). Jackson and Gatrell concur with Hemingway's judgment that the mettle to watch an execution provides the individual a moral and artistic quality that cannot be replaced if a writer does not bear witness.

William C. Brumfield, who judges Dostoevsky's reaction "unfair and overstated" (79), points out the compelling paradox of Turgenev's writing performance: "the skill with which Turgenev describes the execution . . . renders apologies and justifications irrelevant" (80). As Brumfield suggests, although the conceit of the article is that Turgenev turns away, somehow nothing escapes the writer's vision. With his unerring use of detail that evidences artistic courage, Turgenev probes the inhumanity he found inherent in executing a human being.

"The Execution of Tropmann" chronicles Turgenev's firsthand experience attending the 19 January 1870 beheading of Jean-Baptiste Tropmann, who was notorious for killing all six members of the Kink family in 1869. The sensational murder became a cultural touchstone—Tropmann is mentioned in works by Rimbaud, Céline, Henry James, and Georges Bataille—and also gained international attention as a sordid news event. Accounts of the trial in the *New York Times* refer to Tropmann as the "most inhuman savage of the present generation," "a monster" whose deeds were "so horrible and revolting that we can only imagine the universal voice of mankind crying for his blood." The editorial proceeds to suggest that the trial "is one of those cases in which almost every one is heard to declare that death is too slight a punishment for the offence" ("Traupmann").[4] Almost everyone, indeed: Turgenev disagreed.

Turgenev agreed to attend Tropmann's execution after receiving an invitation from his friend, the writer Maxime Du Camp. Almost immediately, Turgenev wished to rescind his acceptance, although his "[f]alse pride" and his fear of being called a coward kept him silent ("Execution" 245). With the essay, then, Turgenev punishes himself for his own moral failings and simultaneously instructs his readers about the realities of the execution, imploring them to reevaluate capital punishment as a moral issue.

Turgenev's chilling details and his proximity to a man about to die summon a moral deliberation from the reader, one that the vigilantly objective Hemingway would have avoided. In interchapters V and XV of *In Our Time*, for example, executions (those of six cabinet ministers and Sam Cardinella, respectively) are described in strictly objective terms. Turgenev describes the executioner's "pair of beautiful hands of remarkable whiteness" (250) and offers an extended description of the guillotine itself, its "sort of sinister shapeliness, the shapeliness of a long, carefully stretched out swan's neck" (253). The essay's most haunting image occurs in Turgenev's description of Tropmann's haircut before his execution: "Thick strands of wiry, dark-brown hair slid over the shoulders and fell on the floor; one of them rolled up to my boot" (264). The description is an intensely humanizing gesture, focusing on the most fragile aspects of Tropmann's anatomy, along with the "slender, youthful" neck, which Turgenev cannot imagine being severed by the guillotine. As with the seeming purity of the executioner's hands, Tropmann's neck is "so smooth, so white, so healthy" (265). Tropmann's neck has the same virginal whiteness as the hands of the lovely Anna Sergyevna Odintsov in his great novel, *Fathers and Sons*. Turgenev finds signs of human vulnerability in three quite different people and positions.

In a poignant moment early in "The Execution of Tropmann" that suggests the witnesses' culpability, Turgenev is himself mistaken for the executioner as he walks to the prison. With a dry, sardonic reaction, Turgenev exclaims: "A lovely beginning!" (246). This initial confusion of identities prefigures a stretch of time during which Turgenev is sickened by his own decision to associate himself with the execution and is repulsed at state-sponsored executions, even while obviously never condoning Tropmann's murders. Just as he was mistakenly taken for the executioner, he writes that, as the crowds wait during the night, "we wandered about like condemned souls" (252), conflating himself and the other witnesses with the man to be executed. When he later observes horses chewing oats, he considers them "at the moment to be the only innocent creatures among us all" (255). For Turgenev, "there was one thing I was sure of, namely that I had no right to be where I was, that no psychological or philosophic considerations excused me" (249). Dostoevsky later scoffed at such a solipsistic account of someone else's execution, but Turgenev's disgust with himself leads logically to the essay's ultimate commentary on capital punishment.

Through the intense introspection in "The Execution of Tropmann" that made him such an easy target for Dostoevsky's contempt, Turgenev realizes that he does not want to be an unflinching, unreflective eyewitness to violent death. As the execution nears and the dropping of the guillotine blade is rehearsed, Turgenev already cannot bring himself to watch, expressing the sensation of "some unknown transgression . . . some secret shame" (255), until he eventually feels—like *Hamlet*'s beleaguered night watchman Francisco—"terribly sick at heart" (256). In the moments preceding the execution, Turgenev recalls that he "suddenly felt cold, so cold that I almost felt sick . . . my legs gave way under me" (266). In the same way that Hemingway uses the early pages of *Death in the Afternoon* to accuse his literary predecessors of meekness and averting their gaze both actually and psychologically, Turgenev does just that. As Tropmann is wrestled into position to be killed, Turgenev writes, "But here I turned away" (267). His moral disgust leads to physical nausea, and then, capturing the mood of the gathered throng, he reports, "everyone tried to turn away in spirit" (268). Turgenev concludes with the hope that capital punishment will be outlawed, arriving at a political statement via a sobering psychological crisis.

Elizabeth Cheresh Allen argues that this repulsion that necessarily leads to a compromised eyewitness account allows Turgenev to "maintain his sanity, his identity, his very humanity" (52). However, to Dostoevsky and, later, to Hemingway, such a sacrifice distorts the reality of the scope of human behavior that includes the ugly, the evil, and even the inhumane, all of which are necessary elements to inform authentic art. What they would term Turgenev's excess of sensitivity also prevents him from maintaining his purity of craft and his fidelity to reporting violent experience.

Although Turgenev is preoccupied with the ethics of the execution, Hemingway's aim, along with Dostoevsky's criticism of "The Execution of Tropmann," is concerned with the writer-citizen's responsibility to the true portrayal of violent experience. For Dostoevsky, it was moral timidity to turn away from an execution. For Hemingway, who revered both Turgenev and Dostoevsky, it was an artistic and aesthetic shortcoming, softness, and a diluted approach to writing. "The Execution of Tropmann," to Hemingway, exposed

Turgenev's glass jaw; Hemingway would publicly promise a more faithful representation of violence in his own work.

In the opening pages of *Death in the Afternoon*, Hemingway presents the book's raison d'être:

> The only place where you could see life and death, *i.e.* violent death now that the wars were over, was in the bull ring, and I wanted very much to go to Spain where I could study it. I was trying to learn to write, commencing with the simplest things, and one of the simplest things of all and the most fundamental is violent death. (2)

This proclamation at once justifies *Death in the Afternoon* and sheds light on Hemingway's larger aesthetic aim. Hemingway not only positions himself as a writer striving toward a specific objective but also distinguishes himself from previous writers who he believes failed to portray authentically someone (or some thing) being killed. In the same passage, he elaborates:

> I had read many books in which, when the author tried to convey it, he only produced a blur, and I decided that this was because either the author had never seen it clearly or at the moment of it, he had physically or mentally shut his eyes, as one might do if he saw a child that he could not possibly reach or aid, about to be struck by a train. (2–3)

Such an unseemly flinching, argues Hemingway, would leave the writer to present the anticipation of death as the source of tension and emotion of the violence, thus sparing the readers and the writer himself from the shock and immediacy of the death blow. However, Hemingway also suggests an important exception to this instinct to shield oneself: "But in the case of an execution by firing squad, or a hanging," he writes, "this is not true, and if these very simple things were to be made permanent, as, say, Goya tried to make them in *Los Desastros* [*sic*] *de la Guerra*, it could not be done with any shutting of the eyes" (3). Hemingway stresses that a writer's inclination toward self-protection leads to robbing the reader of a true presentation of the death.

Hemingway made sure to name Goya when citing a particularly authentic, courageous nineteenth-century artist. Hemingway frequently went outside the literary medium—to painters like Goya, Brueghel, Bosch, and Cézanne[5] and to a composer such as Bach—to name paradigms of irreproachable artists. Although he did not specify any of the "many books" or identify any of the timid writers who failed to make the simple matter of life and death "permanent," his implication does indict Turgenev, just as it supports Dostoevsky's outrage.

Although his criticism is couched in generality, Hemingway, here, surreptitiously castigates those literary forebears he typically held in high esteem.

Hemingway responds to his literary mentors when he makes such brazen claims in *Death in the Afternoon*'s opening pages. Portrayals of executions were at the center of the debate framed by Turgenev and Dostoevsky that forced most major nineteenth-century writers to choose sides. Byron, Hugo, Dickens, Thackeray, Turgenev, Twain, and Tolstoy all witnessed executions. These writers found themselves in the roles of citizens who may have been uneasy about state-sponsored killing, while simultaneously working as writers who were impelled to witness and report vividly and honestly on beheadings and hangings. Although Hemingway enters in the wake of this formidable debate, his thoughts and fiction on the topic transcend political commentary on capital punishment; they provide a key to his aesthetic of violence and ethic of writing.

From the beginning of his writing career, Hemingway seems to have absorbed this test of ethics and embraced the challenge. In Hemingway's early poetry, efforts such as "Ultimately" and "To Will Davies" reveal that element of Hemingway's imagination that Michael Reynolds describes as "fascinated with executions and the demeanor of the executed" (*Young Hemingway* 215). This fascination was part of the inspiration of Hemingway's earliest work. Verna Kale argues that the early poems demonstrate Hemingway's intention to write accurately and honestly about even the most violent activity. Kale points out that, just as "Ultimately" begins with a condemned man who "tried to spit out the truth" (Poems 39), Hemingway is engaging in the same task as a writer. These early works, Kale writes, represent "a testament to the frustrations of a young author who knows that he wants to write truly" (62). Hemingway's memory of his early challenge to himself as articulated in *Death in the Afternoon*, then, is evidenced even in the work that predates his first publication.

Hemingway's same fixation on executions and on holding his gaze to violence emerges in a bizarre dream in *Under Kilimanjaro*, during which Hemingway and the safari crew member Keiti hang the Informer. Even in this random, somewhat gratuitous aside in the narrative, Hemingway's attitude on execution is clearly revealed:

> Recounting this I gave him the exact procedure: where, how, why, how he had taken it, and how we had taken him out, afterwards, in the hunting car, to be eaten by the hyenas. . . . I gave him some more details of the execution. . . . I could remember all the details of the execution of the Informer in about the third of the nightmares and I was ashamed of having even such a nocturnal imagination. (120, 120–21, 123)

This articulation in *Under Kilimanjaro* is consistent with even the earliest evocation of this theme in Hemingway's writing. He is focused on the "demeanor of the executed" or "how he had taken it," dying well or badly, as he would put it elsewhere. Hemingway's imagination, his dreamscape, both his unconscious and his consciousness, is attuned to the possibility and intrigue of sudden death and to presenting it in good prose.

This ethic also translated to the way Hemingway lived his life, as if a writer must behave in the same disciplined, professional way as when he is at his desk. Robert McAlmon relates an anecdote from 1924, in which he and Hemingway, on a trip to Madrid, saw a dog in a dreadful state of decay. McAlmon freely admits that he turned away from the awful sight, at which point:

> Hemingway gave a dissertation on facing reality. It seemed that he had seen in the war the stacked corpses of men, maggot-eaten in a similar way. He advised a detached and scientific attitude toward the corpse of the dog. He tenderly explained that we of our generation must inure ourselves to the sight of grim reality. I recalled that Ezra Pound had talked once of Hemingway's "self-hardening process." (160)

The characterization of Hemingway endeavoring to undergo a process of "self-hardening" invites a sexualizing of violence, as it describes the callousness or shell of objectivity that Hemingway believed a writer—particularly a modern writer—needed to convey violent death authentically. This ethic runs throughout the course of Hemingway's career, with a similar episode recounted in *Under Kilimanjaro*, when Hemingway realizes that "Nguili had never seen a dead wild dog so we stopped and examined one" (366). The way the characters study the carcass in the safari is reflected in the subsequent paragraph, in which the details are recorded, much in the "detached and scientific" manner that McAlmon recalls.

Hemingway directly confronts the issue of beholding violence and transmuting that experience into fiction in the discarded four-page coda to "A Natural History of the Dead," in which the narrator describes the tragedies that he has witnessed in his time.

> I have never been much impressed by horrors so called, due perhaps to a great curiosity which forces me to look at them closely whereupon the horror is difficult of persistence [*sic*] and the greatest horrors I can recall are, first a child being lifted with his legs dangling oddly after being run over by a bus on the stone road between Grau and Valencia and an old man in Madrid struck by a

motor car and fallen from his bicycle. . . . I suppose I must have turned away from both of these since I remember them with no element of the grotesqueness that replaces horror when the object or occurrence is closely observed. (qtd. in Beegel, *Craft of Omission* 46)

This passage introduces a paradox similar to Turgenev's in "The Execution of Tropmann." As Susan F. Beegel wonders in her explication of this passage, "Would a man who had averted his gaze from such scenes have such flawless recollection of their details?" (46). The dichotomy arises between the natural history of the dead and a dramatic narrative of violent death. The human being must ask if his morality and psyche will allow him to witness a violent death, but the writer knows that, without such an experience, his text will lack this crucial element.

In an unpublished fragment, "The Way Fish Die," Hemingway offers a related examination of the dead, posing as a naturalist interested in the science of the dead and not in the emotion. In this disturbing piece, Hemingway offers his inflection of Vardaman Bundren, the grieving young boy in Faulkner's *As I Lay Dying*, who conflates his dead mother with a dead fish. Hemingway declares that studying dead fish is easier and more practical than waiting for your friends or family to die so that you can study them. Hemingway, presumably writing in the 1930s, following his father's December 1928 suicide, laments that if a naturalist would be unfortunate enough to have a parent commit suicide, he might be "deprived of this moment of observation" by being elsewhere and not having the opportunity to be an eyewitness. This naturalist, Hemingway continues, would then have to rely on the description of anyone who might have happened to be there at the time, which as Hemingway's thoughts on the topic consistently make clear, would inevitably be unreliable and distorted. As Hemingway remarks ruefully, if the person who happened to be on hand at the moment of the suicide of one of his parents were "untrained," then he would be likely to be "impressed by the picturesque rather than the essential" (JFK 812).

As in the stated objective of *Death in the Afternoon*, Hemingway stresses the training—the discipline and experience—required to render the essence of the violent moment, rather than the ornamental, the expected, and the unnecessary. By using the tasteless example of a parent's suicide that one must treat as if one were a disinterested party, Hemingway emphasizes the cold objectivity that the writer must have, a standard that Turgenev admitted that he failed to achieve. Turgenev was unable to be objective even in the execution of a mass murderer, much less the death of his father. For Hemingway, capturing a parent's suicide and a dead dog on the road required the same ethic of vision. Hemingway, like his doctor in "Indian Camp," does not hear the screams, because they are not important.

In *For Whom the Bell Tolls*, the absence of observing the moment of an execution is a source of implied frustration for Robert Jordan. While Pilar is able to describe in excruciating detail the mass execution of Fascists in her town, Jordan cannot claim a similar experience. For this shortcoming, he is the target of Pilar's condescending taunt: "thou hast seen nothing" (99), a particularly galling charge to Jordan. In response, he describes to Pilar and Maria his attending a wedding in Ohio as a seven-year-old, a visit that coincides with a racial lynching. However, when questioned by Pilar, Jordan must admit that he is unable to represent the experience with perfect accuracy. "I saw it only looking out from under the blinds of a window in the house which stood on the corner where the arc light was. The street was full of people and when they lifted the Negro up for the second time . . . my mother pulled me away from the window, so I saw no more" (116–17).[6] The image neatly reverses a moment from Pilar's extended narrative, in which she scrambles onto a chair to see through a window, the better to view the violence. Jordan, a writer, has obviously witnessed more than his share of violence since that childhood incident (including killing his friend Kashkin), but it is crucial to note that Jordan's mother made the decision to spare him the sight of the execution, and not Jordan himself. Jordan is careful to point out this detail when recounting the anecdote.[7]

The viewing of an execution is also given prominent attention during the climactic moment of the Caporetto retreat in *A Farewell to Arms*. Frederic Henry notices a disturbance of flashing lights on the other side of the bridge that sits on the bank of the Tagliamento River. In his careful narration, Frederic provides a meticulous litany of what he captures in his field of vision: he declares that he "sees" eight separate things in a single sequence: the carabinieri and officers in silhouette; one of the officers picking out another officer; the man selected for questioning; the stars on the sleeve that make the accused man a lieutenant-colonel; one or two officers looking at Frederic himself; the carabiniere approaching Frederic; the carabiniere's face after Frederic hits him; and the flashes of the rifle as the lieutenant-colonel is executed. This faithful reporting of his field of vision speaks to the unavoidable receptivity of sight, what James Joyce in *Ulysses* calls "the ineluctable modality of the visual" and "what you damn well have to see" (3.1, 9.86). However, Frederic soon directs his vision and powers of attention; as in the difference between "hearing" and "listening," he remarks that he "looked at the man the officers were questioning" (223). This conscious decision to pay attention to the incident has repercussions when the man is executed, and Frederic's vision omits the moment of impact and the instant of death; as he recalls, "I did not watch them shoot him but I heard the shots" (224). Frederic uses the verb "watch" rather than "see," which suggests that he could have physically witnessed the killing had he not turned away. No tangible impediment blocks his view. Although seeing something is not a choice—it is ineluctable—watching something does connote intentionality. Watching requires sustained attention. As the narrator, Frederic creates a harrowing near-death experience, but he cannot provide the vivid detail of death for his readers.

After Frederic avoids the sight of the execution, the burden of vision remains important in the scene but assumes a much different tone. In a famously mordant articulation, Frederic states, "I saw how their minds worked; if they had minds and if they worked" (224). With this figurative vision, sight equals understanding and corresponds to an analysis of behavior. For the rest of the chapter, the tone changes markedly: "I looked at the carabinieri. They were looking at the newcomers. The others were looking at the colonel" (225). After noticing what people are "looking" at—that is, what they are paying attention to—Frederic discerns that he may escape. He breaks free, reaches the Tagliamento, and then dives into the river.

Even during his swim to freedom, vision is a crucial theme. "I saw a piece of timber ahead of me," Frederic recalls. "I kept my head behind it and did not even look over it. I did not want to see the bank" (225). However, soon after, once the shots have died down, he "looked at the bank." In this critical passage, what Frederic has seen and what he has chosen to see and to avoid reveal his mental state. The chapter ends with Frederic gliding down the river, swept up by the current and noticing, "The shore was out of sight now" (225).

The notion of sight during the crisis of the war story in *A Farewell to Arms* returns during the crisis of the love story, in the depiction of Catherine Barkley's fatal childbirth. In a scene that echoes Hemingway's earlier "Indian Camp," Frederic's narration of the event not only discloses what happens but is also careful to specify what he saw and what he did not see. When the nurse invites Frederic to sit on one of the benches, it recalls a sporting event; indeed, the operating room is described as a "bright small amphitheatre" (324). The language of the delivery emerges as a spectacle, a performance, rather than as a life-or-death operation.

As Frederic's fear sets in, he chooses to stay outside the operating room and, instead of witnessing Catherine on the main stage of activity, his visual attention, tellingly, is directed elsewhere:

I looked out the window. It was dark but in the light from the window I could see it was raining. I went into a room at the far end of the hall and looked at the labels on bottles in a glass case. Then I came out and stood in the empty hall and watched the door of the operating room. (324)

In this sequence, Frederic *looks* out the window and is able to *see* the rain, which in this novel is an insistent harbinger of doom. He *looks* at the labels on the bottles and then *watches* the door. He turns down the opportunity to see, look at, and watch the operation.

After the delivery of his son, Frederic reports that the doctor "held him up for me to see" (324). Again, the violence and morbidity attached to the child are reflected through Frederic's choice of vision. Frederic narrates, "I saw the little dark face and dark hand, but I did not see him move or hear him cry" (325). As the doctor attends to the baby, Frederic states:

I did not wait to see it. I went out in the hall. I could go in now and see. I went in the door and a little way down the gallery. The nurses who were sitting at the rail motioned for me to come down where they were. I shook my head. I could see enough where I was. . . . I knew as I watched I could have watched it all, but I was glad I hadn't. I do not think I could have watched them cut, but I watched the wound closed into a high welted ridge with quick skilful-looking stitches like a cobbler's, and was glad. (325)

The focus of Frederic's narration is less forgivably solipsistic than Turgenev's, referring more to his role as a witness than to Catherine's danger and her role as a victim. When the doctor emerges from the operating room, his focus, too, is on Frederic as much as Catherine. Their exchange is bizarre: the doctor asks Frederic, "Did you watch?" to which Frederic responds, "I saw you sew up" (325). The disproportionate focus on what Frederic sees, as opposed to what happens to Catherine, is not egotistical rambling but rather a testament to the fidelity of first-person narration. *A Farewell to Arms* is not the work of omniscient narration but the limited retrospective vision of a man who occasionally averted his eyes.

Anticipating Frederic Henry, in the early story "Indian Camp" the young Nick Adams is plunged into the role of witness to an unexpectedly violent operation. Through Dr. Adams's lack of foresight, Nick's own vision becomes the defining element of the narrative. After his father explains what labor is and identifies the source of the Indian woman's screams, Nick responds, "I see" (SS 92), with vision again suggesting comprehension. Dr. Adams continues his explanation, beginning his next point by saying, "You see, Nick, babies are supposed to be born head first" (93). However, Nick's sight and his role in witnessing the traumatic situation are not so simple. After the baby is delivered, Dr. Adams addresses his son in the same particular way: "See, it's a boy, Nick."

Nick, however, does not see. His vision is intentionally obscured. Although he affirms his father's good news, the narrator reports: "He was looking away so as not to see what his father was doing." Dr. Adams continues the postoperating procedure, but the one-sentence paragraph that follows it reads, "Nick didn't look at it." Dr. Adams perhaps finally intuits that the operation is too much for his son; he assures him, during the suturing of the woman's wound, that "you can watch this or not, Nick, just as you like." The decision is obvious: "Nick did not watch." Nick chooses to avoid the unfamiliar ordeal of a difficult childbirth, but, even more unexpectedly, he "had a good view" of the suicide in the upper bunk (94).

"Indian Camp" delineates the distinction between observing the harsh realities of life and avoiding them and between having the authority over the power of vision and having that authority controlled by someone else. Nick is probably the same age as Robert Jordan was when Jordan's mother blocked his view of the Ohio lynching. Nick only damn well had to see the suicide because of his father's insensitivity and dedication to professional responsibility.

Hemingway's vow to himself in this challenge and his kinship with Dostoevsky rather than Turgenev highlight an essential aspect of the personality of Brett Ashley in *The Sun Also Rises*. When Jake introduces Brett to bullfighting, his main concern is that she may not have the stomach to watch the bulls gore the steers.[8] During the unloading of the first bulls, they have a brief exchange, at which point Brett surprises him:

> "Don't look," I said to Brett. She was watching, fascinated.
> "Fine," I said. "If it doesn't buck you."
> "I saw it," she said. (144)

When Jake somewhat irrelevantly approves her continuing to watch if it doesn't disturb her, Brett merely says that she saw it, not that she saw it and it did not "buck" her. While Jake was holding Brett to a standard of watching only those incidents that did not disturb her, Brett wanted to see the full spectacle of the bullfight and made sure that she did. Brett's willingness to look at the most violent situations is prefigured in Book I, when Jake observes of Brett: "She was looking into my eyes with that way she had of looking that made you wonder whether she really saw out of her own eyes. They would look on and on after every one else's eyes in the world would have stopped looking. She looked as though there was nothing on earth she would not look at like that, and really she was afraid of so many things" (34). Even at this early stage of the novel, Jake incisively distinguishes between Brett's gaze and the things that frighten her. Jake's singular flight into mysticism—it reads as his improbable restatement of Emerson's "transparent eyeball" passage—turns out to be true; during her infatuation with Pedro Romero, Brett admits, "I can't look at him" (188). As Pedro fights a bull whose own vision is impaired, Brett says, "It's the sort of thing I don't like to see." Jake acknowledges this reality: "It was not nice to watch if you cared anything about the person who was doing it" (221). Ultimately, Brett is "bucked" more by love (or lust or infatuation, perhaps any emotional attachment) than violence.

Jake's attitude toward Brett fictionalizes a similar characterization in *Death in the Afternoon*, in which Hemingway writes: "Women that I felt sure would enjoy the bullfights with the exception of the goring of the horses were quite unaffected by it; I mean really unaffected, that is, something that they disapproved of and that they expected would horrify and disgust them did not disgust them or horrify them at all" (4). In the appendix, entitled "Some Reactions," Hemingway profiles a woman—Mrs. E.R.—whose response recalls Brett's:[9]

> Did not want her to see horses in bullfight, but believed she would enjoy rest of corrida. Had her look away when bull charged horse. Told her when not to look. Did not want to shock or horrify her. Found she was not shocked nor horrified by horses and enjoyed it as a part of bullfight which she enjoyed greatly first time and became great admirer and partizan of. (467)

As a contrast to Brett, Bill advises Robert Cohn how to avoid being disgusted when the bulls gore the horses. Similarly, Jake tells Brett: "Don't look at the horses, after the bull hits them. . . . Watch the charge and see the picador try and keep the bull off, but then don't look again until the horse is dead if it's been hit. . . . Just don't watch when it's bad" (165–66). Several times during the bullfight that follows, Jake seems obsessed with respective reactions of Brett and Cohn. As in Hemingway's own gauging of artists' response to violence such as executions, Jake discerns a moral barometer from his friends' responses, just as Hemingway himself did in the "Some Reactions" section of *Death in the Afternoon*. Jake finds that "Brett did not look upset" (168). After the bullfight, Brett is asked how she handled the spectacle of the horses being killed, and she reports, "I couldn't help looking at them." Mike confirms: "She couldn't take her eyes off them. . . . She's an extraordinary wench." Brett then says, "They do have some rather awful things happen to them. . . . I couldn't look away, though" (169). The others distinguish between sadism and a healthy interest in watching every detail of the bullfights. The line is not always clear. Susan Beegel attributes Hemingway's inclusion of violence in "A Natural History of the Dead" to his "half-sadistic creative impulse" (49). In response to Cohn's similar charge, Mike defends Brett: "Brett's not a sadist. She's just a lovely, healthy wench." When Jake asks Brett if she is, in fact, a sadist, she replies, "Hope not" (170). In our time, is it sadism to stare without blinking at the most violent moment in a violent scene; or, instead, is it every mature person's responsibility, particularly that of our artists?

Of all the moral judgments that can be made about Robert Cohn, one of his most damning sins is that he flinches at the realities of violence and the violence of reality. Cohn—a working novelist, after all—was not a participant in World War I, unlike Jake and Brett herself. Jake's scorn for Cohn's lack of personal bravery matches Hemingway's frustration with writers who show the same timidity in their work. The passage that opens *Death in the Afternoon* indicates that with Cohn and Brett—as Dostoevsky did by juxtaposing Turgenev with himself—Hemingway emphasizes the difference between two moral and aesthetic sensibilities that illuminate his quest for representing authentic violence. When Hemingway boasted of beating Mr. Turgenev, he might have felt that in "Big Two-Hearted River" and *The Sun Also Rises* he had rendered nature and landscape even more evocatively than his hero. His real test of moving beyond his artistic idols, however, was to realize the challenge he proclaims in the beginning of *Death in the Afternoon*: the vivid, accurate representation of violence, putting into a sharp focus that which had previously been a blur.

6

That Supreme Moment of Complete Knowledge

Hemingway's Theory of the Vision of the Dying

and yet the whole is somehow felt as one pulse of our life
William James, *A Pluralistic Universe*

He arrives at the unknown: and even if, half crazed, in the end, he loses the
understanding of his visions, he has seen them!
Arthur Rimbaud, *Illuminations*

Although Hemingway's interest in death and dying has become so accepted and well covered that any further comment risks retreading the stereotype of his frequently lampooned death "obsession," I wish in this chapter to examine a strain of this subject more traditionally applied to Hemingway's contemporaries and more conventionally metaphysical literary forebears. Hemingway's career coincided with modernism's emergent attitude toward the phenomenology of dying, one that includes a proposition that a person facing an urgent situation—such as drowning, or falling from a cliff, or execution—experiences a rapid life review, that one's whole life "flashes before one's eyes."

In Conrad's *Heart of Darkness*, published in 1899, the year of Hemingway's birth, Marlow speculates about Kurtz's final instant: "Did he live his life again in every detail of desire, temptation, and surrender during that supreme moment of complete knowledge?" (139). Marlow is not wondering about the most prominent image that entered Kurtz's consciousness but is instead proposing that his entire life, down to the most minute experience and emotion, might be replayed instantaneously.

For a writer so notoriously fascinated by death, Hemingway's speculation about an individual's dying moments becomes an intriguing area of inquiry. Hamlet's meditation "For in that sleep of death what dreams may come" is by definition unsolvable—the prince is, after all, talking about a country as yet undiscovered. A related question is somewhat more testable: What occurs in the distorted, traumatized, or even reconciled consciousness of a person who is dying or who faces a similarly urgent situation? What goes on in such a frantic or fatigued mind? Or, as Hemingway's literary icon Ivan Turgenev asks, "What will I think when the time comes for me to die, if I'm in any condition to think at that time? . . . Will I review the past, and dwell on the few delightful moments I've experienced, on precious images and faces? Will my bad deeds come to mind, and will my soul be filled with the burning anguish of belated remorse?" ("Poems in Prose" 882). As Turgenev might have restated Hamlet's notion: At that moment of dying what thoughts may come?

The content of such a vision is the ultimate flight of imagination, the impossibility of apprehending the human consciousness during the crisis of its own extinction. It is a mystery hidden from the living, which heightens the allure and adds an inherently mystical or transcendent element to the topic. However, one small sector of society granted access to these visions consists of those who experience intense danger or near-death experiences, those who in their peril are granted a look beyond the range of vision normally granted to human experience. Hemingway—who had at least two near-death experiences, one as a young man in World War I and one following his plane crashes in 1954—used his insight of these moments to demonstrate the way his characters mark the moral judgments of their lives and assess their present circumstances.

A look at one of Hemingway's earliest presentations of this idea is instructive of the way he handled such moments. The single paragraph of *In Our Time*'s chapter XIV portrays the final moments of the dying matador Maera. During the frenetic scene in the bullring, Maera "felt everything getting larger and larger and then smaller and smaller. Then it got larger and larger and larger and then smaller and smaller" (SS 207). Following this cyclical expansion and concentration of consciousness that allegedly precedes death, "everything commenced to run faster and faster as when they speed up a cinematograph film" (207), a trope already familiar by the mid-1920s. Since Maera was still alive at the time of the scene's composition, Hemingway evidently used this bullfight setting to contemplate the subjective experience of death. In this way, the moment of death fascinated Hemingway not only as a barometer of manhood or as a test of decorum but also as a rich, rare phenomenological experience. According to Michael Reynolds, Ezra Pound exhorted Hemingway to challenge his imagination to create a death, to murder the matador, even though Hemingway could not report it objectively or accurately at the time (*Paris Years* 139–40), since Maera was still living.[1] Therefore, chapter XIV becomes an important text because Hemingway used the vignette to imagine the consciousness of a dying man, the last instant before the narrator can state: "Then he was dead" (SS 207), a return to objective reportage.

Just as Maera's subjective perception of time is distorted given his waning consciousness, Harry, the dying writer in "The Snows of Kilimanjaro," uses a suggestive phrase to lament the many memories of his life that he will never record in fiction: "There wasn't time, of course, although it seemed as though it telescoped so that you might put it all into one paragraph if you could get it right" (SS 68). With this articulation, Harry has introduced two important points. First, he reveals what we can assume to be a central tenet of his writing approach, which matches Hemingway's own famously concise, concentrated aesthetic. The italicized reveries to which Harry surrenders in "The Snows of Kilimanjaro" bring to mind the sketches that divide the longer narratives in Hemingway's first volume of short stories, *In Our Time*.

However, Harry's ambiguous sentence describing the telescoping of experience does not limit its concern to an artistic problem. Just as Harry is commenting on a focusing of narrative perspective, so too does he suggest that a man in his last moments of existence encounters the same phenomenon metaphysically. The sequence "*it* seemed as though *it* telescoped so that you might put *it* all into one paragraph if you could get *it* right" utilizes the word "it" in an intentionally allusive way. The reader might substitute the word "life" for "it" in the first three instances and then "the story" for the fourth use of "it." Or, more provocatively, "it" might replace "life" on all four occasions, which is to say that—keenly examined—an individual can encapsulate an entire existence into one visual articulation, a single instant that summarizes a lifetime, as in William James's epigraph to this chapter.

The Geneva School critic Georges Poulet makes great use of the scene in *The Scarlet Letter* in which Hester stands on the scaffold, vulnerable and on display before the townspeople.[2] Poulet refers to this moment of Hester's life—in a Conradian flourish—as "a supreme moment in which one sees the panorama of one's entire life unroll itself" (*Studies in Human Time* 327). Poulet's insistence on the word "panorama" is instructive. Elsewhere, in an article discussing this phenomenon with respect to Romantic poetry, Poulet writes: "All these recollections . . . are perceived by the mind in such a number and in such a short time that they appear quasi-simultaneous, in a sort of altogetherness, not one after the other with the ordinary successiveness of time, but as if forming a widely spread panorama" ("Timelessness and Romanticism" 5). A 1980 psychiatric study of individuals who had reported near-death experiences concluded that "Review of past events, or 'panoramic memory,' was reported by 27% of our respondents; memories were most commonly described as appearing all at once (38%) rather than in some particular sequence" (Greyson and Stevenson 1195). Despite the variance in the way the dying vision is articulated—as a short film, a photo album, or a single snapshot—the crucial element is this "panorama" that allows a dying person to see everything and then provide an emotional reaction to what he sees.

Therefore, the second revelation to be gleaned from Harry's description—the point with which this chapter concerns itself—is that the portrayal of the dying writer in "The Snows of Kilimanjaro" is one of Hemingway's most prominent depictions of the urgent, hypermnesic perspective of those dying or in mortal danger, a foray into a branch of speculative, metaphysical prose into which he would rarely stray. Although it is one of his greatest stories, one reason that "The Snows of Kilimanjaro" is among his least characteristic, in fact, is that Hemingway is so often characterized—even by himself—as an antiphenomenological writer, one whose commitment to concrete vision and reportorial fidelity avoids such abstractions or poetics.

Poulet's study of Henri Bergson unfolds a profound philosophical basis to the cliché of life "flashing before" one's eyes. For Bergson, these crisis moments are identified as a key to understanding the function of human memory. Like Freud and William James, Bergson believed that the memories of a person's life remain intact, hidden but available. Describing this "total memory," he writes: "We trail behind us, unawares, the whole of our past; but our memory pours into the present only the odd recollection or two that in some way complete our present situation" (*Creative Evolution* 167). Elsewhere, he writes: "the past is preserved even down to its slightest details, and . . . there is no real forgetting" ("Phantasms" 94). Bergson argues that these submerged memories often surge toward consciousness during moments of exceptional excitement. While not a strict anti-Bergsonian by any means, Hemingway does use his own experience to refute the French philosopher.

In the introductory passage to *Death in the Afternoon*, Hemingway expresses curiosity and a desire to learn about the authentic death experience through unflinching and diligent study. More than twenty years later, after his own near-death experience in the second of his two plane crashes in Africa in January 1954, Hemingway explicitly calls Bergson's conclusion into question. In "The Christmas Gift," his journalistic effort for *Look* magazine, Hemingway writes, "Your past life does not rush through your brain like a cinema film and your thoughts are purely technical. Perhaps there are people whose past lives rush through their brains, but so far in my life I have never experienced this sensation" (BL 446). As he recollects his consciousness during the crash: "My brain refused to have anything to do with my past life, contrary to the usual reports" (452). In portraying his own experience, Hemingway still casts his consciousness in the mode of action. He characterizes himself as understanding his specific objective, whose urgency precludes the indulgence of yielding to an uncontrolled and unhelpful series of memories. As Hemingway remarks, "Various people and several periodicals have asked me what one thinks at the hour of one's death, a rather exaggerated phrase. . . . I can answer truthfully that at the moment of an aircraft crashing and/or burning, your only thoughts are of technical problems" (446). Hemingway is describing a survival instinct, one in which the consciousness is focused on the concrete, practical challenge of the present situation.

This rigid discipline that Hemingway claims to have maintained is illustrated in *Islands in the Stream*, during an anecdote that the protagonist Thomas Hudson tells to Honest Lil, his favorite prostitute. Hudson recalls slipping into a river between logs that cover the surface of the water. He is trapped underwater and unable to break through the logs to come up for air. Although he faces the immediate prospect of drowning, Hudson does not experience a rapid series of flashbacks or an encapsulated version of his life. As with Hemingway's assertion of his own consciousness following the plane crash, Hudson becomes preoccupied with purely pragmatic concerns:

> I thought very hard and I knew I had to get through very quickly. I felt very carefully around the bottom of a log until I came to where it was pushed against another log. Then I put my two hands together and pushed up and the logs spread apart just a little. Then I got my hands through and then my forearms and elbows through and then I spread the two logs apart with my elbows until I got my head up and I had an arm over each log. (272)

Hudson relates a problem and then the enactment of a successful strategy, hardly the description of a mystical, visionary experience. The traditional notion of the life review during the process of drowning is utterly ignored. The four-sentence excerpt from *Islands in the Stream* deals entirely with Hudson's actions and his behavior. The characterization that Hudson "thought very hard" corresponds to devising a strategy pertaining to the physical action that immediately follows; "thought very hard" applies not to sentiments, reminiscences, introspection, or anything meditative or remotely emotional but simply to planning.

For a curious counterpoint, the memoirs of Hemingway's granddaughter, Mariel—she was born less than four months after his suicide—describes her own near-drowning experience. Mariel moves from a practical train of thought to a profoundly spiritual one:

> My mind started into overdrive, and all the thoughts were negative. . . . My instinct was to turn toward shore and fight the current with everything I had. . . . My mind started to think about my situation. *Where am I? How come I can't swim in this? What can I do?* And right in the flow of thoughts came a real stopper—*I'm going to drown.* . . . With all my spiritual training and seeming acceptance of death, I was no more ready to die than to fly. I could make no connection with my guru or with God. . . . Beneath the water again, yet now above the experience somehow, I could clearly see that I was drowning. It seemed all right. My frantic self was finally exhausted, and I became intensely aware of God and my guru. Surrender was possible with that awareness, and I succumbed to whatever was meant to be. (192–94, emphasis in original)

Like Mariel, the object of Hemingway's infatuation in the 1940s and '50s, Adriana Ivancich, once had a related experience. At the age of eight, Adriana nearly drowned in a whirlpool in the Tagliamento River and felt "an ecstasy," a sense of atonement such that "she was ready to enter heaven itself" (Doyle and Houston). She was reconciled to death beyond any need to struggle to stay alive.

Hudson never achieves Mariel's or Adriana's level of acceptance. Hudson's mind too actively seeks survival to ponder any benefits of surrender. Hudson, unlike Harry in "The Snows of Kilimanjaro," never says of death, "it meant nothing in itself. It was strange how easy being tired enough made it." "With the pain," Harry realizes, "the horror had gone" (SS 54). For Hudson, the balm of fatigue never eases his single-minded quest for survival. The key to this distinction might be contextual; Hudson's anecdote is of a younger man, slipping into the Michigan waters familiar from the Nick Adams stories. The younger Hudson, unlike Harry, is not prepared to look back and relive past joys or judge a life gone wrong.

The thrust of "The Snows of Kilimanjaro" compels discussion on this subject among Hemingway's body of work because it so forcefully rejects the previous examples that have been mentioned, the moments encountered in chapter

XIV of *In Our Time*, *Islands in the Stream*, and even Hemingway's memories of his own thoughts during the 1954 plane crashes. In "The Snows of Kilimanjaro," Harry initially joins the view put forth in the other writings by aligning himself with practical thoughts: to his wife Helen's almost mystical question, "I don't see why that had to happen to your leg. What have we done to have that happen to us?" Harry's response is absurdly literal: "I suppose what I did was to forget to put iodine on it when I first scratched it. Then I didn't pay attention to it because I never infect. Then, later, when it got bad, it was probably using that weak carbolic solution when the other antiseptics ran out that paralyzed the minute blood vessels and started the gangrene" (SS 55). However, this exaggerated gesture at the practical details of the situation is also offset by a more personal, phenomenological approach. Harry emphasizes the notion that fatigue eases the act of dying by introducing the first of his five italicized flashbacks with: "I'm tired" (55), suggesting a slackening of his defenses, a loosening of the reins that sets free the powers of memory.

This fatigue introduces a dichotomy on which Poulet puts an enormous emphasis; he differentiates between the various portrayals of the vision of dying as an acceleration, a hardening or constriction of consciousness in order to focus on survival, and as a relaxing and expansion of consciousness to surrender to the full vista of thought. The emotional fatigue that Harry betrays signals an acceptance that Hudson (and Hemingway himself) refused to proclaim. Poulet's study includes a portion of a pertinent passage from Bergson, which is quoted here more fully:

> It happens in exceptional cases that the attention suddenly loses the interest it had in life: immediately, as though by magic, the past once more becomes present. In people who see the threat of sudden death unexpectedly before them, in the mountain climber falling down a precipice, in drowning men, in men being hanged, it seems that a sharp conversion of the attention can take place, — something like a change of orientation of the consciousness which, up until then turned toward the future and absorbed by the necessities of action, suddenly loses all interest in them. That is enough to call to mind a thousand different "forgotten" details and to unroll the whole history of the person before him in a moving panorama. ("Perception of Change" 127)

Bergson here stresses that the key to an individual's consciousness in moments when that individual faces death rests upon an individual's instinctive urge to sustain life. On the surface, in sharing his thoughts with his wife, Harry has absolutely no interest in continuing his life. He is resigned and unsentimental about dying, even defiantly drinking liquor, knowing the physical damage it will cause. However, as the narrative progresses, Harry's life flashes back in rich, sometimes painful associations, simultaneously functioning as material for a writer who will not complete the corpus he believes is his obligation and also as the laments and memories of a man who cannot help but look simultaneously backward and within.

The paradox of "The Snows of Kilimanjaro" is that the full potentiality of Harry's consciousness is revealed only when it loses its technical bent, when he surrenders the physical realm to embrace the life of the spirit. In *Matter and Memory*, Bergson remarks, "we renounce the interests of effective action to replace ourselves, so to speak, in the life of dreams" (154). This same attitude is summed up poignantly in Cormac McCarthy's Pulitzer Prize–winning *The Road*, in which the father intuits: "the right dreams for a man in peril were dreams of peril and all else was the call of languor and death" (18). Thus, once Harry performs the irreversible renunciation that Bergson describes, the narrative allows us to experience his new life of dreams, the consciousness that expands to include the subconscious. As Poulet phrases it:

> With the certainty of death, when man convinces himself that it is useless to continue to pay attention to his present life, he falls in a state equivalent to the most profound reverie: "A human being who should *dream* his life instead of living it . . ." This human being, this absolute dreamer, is the dying man. Uninterested in any action, removed from the inhibitions that the necessities of life imposed on him, he effortlessly takes possession of his past and of his self. . . . Remembering everything . . . is the most natural thing in the world. And yet it is also the most unexpected thing, since by losing all and by losing ourselves, we gain everything and we gain ourselves. The visionary who experiences his death unforeseeably gains possession of his life. ("Bergson: The Theme" 493)

The possession of the life that Harry regains is indeed—to use Bergson's term—his "total memory," with visions of his forgotten past. However, Poulet's point specifies that this acquisition of the past is not gained through "a tension, a tautening, or a hyperactivity of the soul" but through "a relaxation of the soul's habitual tension" ("Bergson: The Theme" 492). The fatigue that Harry experiences, therefore, invigorates the life of the mind and unlocks his store of memories, which enables him to judge the sum of the actions of his life as a single entity.

Harry's illness and Mariel's near-drowning produce a fatigue not traditionally associated with a man who is about to be executed. Of course, most people who are set to be killed do not survive to report their state of mind in the final moments. Hemingway dramatizes a hanging in chapter XV of *In Our Time*, which divides the sections of "Big Two-Hearted River." As in Hudson's brief anecdote, the vignette in chapter XV describes in rigidly objective terms the condemned man, Sam Cardinella, being carried to the gallows: "*He had been like that since about four o'clock in the morning*" (SS 219, emphasis in original). "Like that" refers to the loss of physical control that makes him unable to walk to the gallows. Any of Cardinella's emotions beyond basic dread, along with any specific recollections, are effaced by the narration. The closest thing to emotion that is alluded to in the entire three-paragraph sketch is the disgust registered by the priests when Cardinella loses control of his sphincter muscle. Also, the three Negroes sentenced to hang are described as "very frightened" (219). Cardinella's fear is objectively reported through physical indicators—his wobbly legs and uncontrolled sphincter. Although Bergson believes those about to drown or to be hanged tend to experience a panoramic retrospective vision of their own lives, Hemingway in chapter XV never indulges that claim; the narration of his doomed man either suppresses or denies such a vision.[3]

To cast Hemingway's skeletal presentation of Cardinella's final moments into even more stark relief, the portrayal of chapter XV can be placed alongside Dostoevsky's *The Idiot*, which features a powerful investigation of a condemned man's consciousness.[4] During an anecdote in that novel, Prince Myshkin observes—in a description that for Dostoevsky might well have been autobiographical, given the commutation of his own death sentence in 1849—"It's strange that people rarely faint in those last seconds! On the contrary, the head is terribly alive and must be working hard, hard, hard, like an engine running; I imagine various thoughts throbbing in it, all of them incomplete, maybe even ridiculous, quite irrelevant thoughts . . . and meanwhile you know everything and remember everything" (65). To know everything and to remember everything refers to the omniscience and hypermnesia that Bergson promises, the "supreme moment of complete knowledge" envisioned by Conrad's Marlow. However, Dostoevsky portrays a man's mind "working hard, hard, hard," engaged in an intense inner gaze at his own past; Hudson describes himself likewise, as thinking "very hard" in his determination to avoid a tragic fate. The situation leads both men to an intensified level of cognition, but each instance of hyperactivity is engaged in a completely different task. One is directed at external elements, the other flooded with internal activity. The difference lies in Mariel's surrender and the young Hudson's absolute refusal to surrender.

Why would Dostoevsky's condemned man be burdened with irrelevant thoughts during the most pressing moment of his life? The phenomenon could be a result of "psychic protection" (Kletti and Noyes 5), a shield that makes one think about anything other than the impending catastrophe. This theory is also Hawthorne's narrator's suggestion for Hester's incongruous life review upon the scaffold in *The Scarlet Letter*. Cognitive science offers another compelling hypothesis. An ingenious recent study speculates convincingly that, in moments of great urgency, an individual will scan with amazing rapidity the full scope of his episodic memory, in the hope that he will find a prior circumstance that may be applied usefully to the current predicament. Of course, because the present urgency is unprecedented, all the various thoughts are inapplicable and appear inappropriate and confused.

The study is careful to distinguish experienced "decision makers" like fire-fighters, who expect to be placed in urgent moments and can instinctively make a decision, with "a person facing a complex, unexpected emergency situation," whose "memory retrieval mechanisms" would, the writers argue, "obtain, at times lacking a proper set of precedents, a number of irrelevant courses of action" (Linhares et al. 3). Hemingway makes a related observation in "The Christmas Gift": following a crash landing, he writes that a survivor's shock might be mitigated if he is "conditioned . . . by the practice of more or less contact sports" (BL 446). These "quite irrelevant" moments in Dostoevsky might be final, futile stabs at a previous experience that might come to the aid of the condemned man.

Once an individual ascertains that survival is impossible, the slackening of the will to live invites a gaze within, one with profound moral overtones. Poulet develops this crucial point with respect to *The Scarlet Letter*:

> But what is brought to light here is not only the more or less vast field of lived existence; it is also the moral significance of that existence, which enables the mind to understand and judge itself as it really is. In peering into the mirror in which the revivified past completely unveils itself to the consciousness, the being who reexamines his life once more sees not only deeds, gestures, actions and emotions that are over. He discovers that in withdrawing themselves from the present where each in turn had a fleeting life, these actions and emotions wound themselves together in the darkness to compose a continuous thread, a homogenous picture. (*Studies in Human Time* 327–28)

Poulet's inclusion of the moral element to this metaphysical phenomenon informs a reading of Harry's final moments upon Mount Kilimanjaro and of Robert Jordan dying in the mountains of Spain. The entire narrative of Harry's gradual death amounts to an inventory of the ethics of his life, whose most noble deed would be to fulfill his creative potential. "The Snows of Kilimanjaro" is a narrative of re-examination, in which the visions of past memories cease only when Harry embraces the vision of the present, his mystical ascent to the peak of Kilimanjaro. To recall the case of Admiral Beaufort, a canonical case of a near-drowning experience and the life-review, each act of his life encompassed by his panoramic vision was likewise accompanied by "a consciousness of right or wrong" (Dawson 2). Harry joins Beaufort by imbuing his retrospective view with intense self-judgment.

By terming the ultimate vision a "homogenous picture," Poulet reminds us of the image Harry uses, that life (and/or the story) might "telescope" and in fact become an entity, a single visual representation that encapsulates the entirety of an individual experience. During the intense moments in *For Whom the Bell Tolls* when Robert Jordan is engaged in the battle subsequent to blowing the bridge, he senses that "It was as though a reflex lens camera had been suddenly brought into focus" (453). As with Poulet's description, the concentrated final moments of Jordan's life enable his consciousness to crystallize and the disparate, vague elements of existence to become a unified panoramic vision.

Jordan's unfeeling, unreflective existence as a soldier ultimately merges with his identities as a reverential grandson, an ashamed son, a passionate lover, an academic, and a writer. Jordan's façade of stoicism, behind which he was capable of compartmentalizing his various concerns, ultimately vanishes, and he must finally assess the moral sum of his existence. The subtle difference between the final moments of Harry and Jordan is that Jordan has not completely stopped resisting the cascade of memories; although he is not able to maintain perfect discipline, Jordan remains poised to act until the last words of the novel and never completely succumbs to the onrush of the past.

A different inflection to such a slackening is illustrated during the climactic moments of *For Whom the Bell Tolls*, which give rise to the novel's theme of interpersonal awareness. Through the acceptance of his tragic fate and a slight loosening of his rigidly disciplined consciousness, Robert Jordan becomes aware of the full panorama of his memories and his mind. The capacity to approach this spiritual ascent would not have existed before he met and fell in love with Maria. On the night before he is to blow up the bridge, Jordan sheds his soldier's attitude, an act that is described unambiguously:

> Then suddenly surrendering to something, to the luxury of going into unreality . . . Then he surrendered again and let himself slip into it, feeling a voluptuousness of surrender into unreality that was like a sexual acceptance of something that could come in the night when there was no understanding, only

the delight of acceptance. . . . Now the making believe was coming back in a great rush and he would take it all to him. It had him now, and again he surrendered and went on. (342, 346)

Not only is Jordan's mental state the issue, but, to locate him within Poulet's dialectic, the narrator describes him as surrendering (four times) and slipping and accepting. This movement within Jordan is the ironic one, in which, by surrendering, Jordan is able to vanquish all obstacles and, by conceding the realities of his circumstance, is able to master the vast scope of his own consciousness.

Jordan's metaphysical conciliation is echoed in military terms by Golz, the Soviet general, who realizes too late that his attack should have been canceled: "*Rien à faire. Rien. Faut pas penser. Faut accepter*" (429). [Nothing to do. Nothing. You must not think. You must accept.] That which Golz accepts politically and strategically, Jordan accepts spiritually. Poulet captures this process of acceptance and explains its ramifications:

> Thus, distraction, reverie, and dreams are like successive steps in a long sliding, where the spirit abandons itself, without the sensation of resistance by any obstacle. It is as if, from within the spirit itself, all the past, all *its* past, all the life that it had already lived, moved toward a meeting with it because in renouncing action it ceased to prevent its past from invading its present. ("Bergson: The Theme" 493, emphasis in original)

For Whom the Bell Tolls anticipates this point. Poulet's characterization of the onset of the panoramic vision of one's past as a "long sliding" is nearly identical to Jordan's own; he "let himself slip into" the state of surrender. As Jordan awaits his target's approach, he "tried to hold on to himself that he felt slipping away from himself as you feel snow starting to slip sometimes on a mountain slope" (470–71). However, the "himself" that he is trying to keep from slipping is not only his biological life and the maimed leg he can no longer control but also his identity as a member of the guerrilla band who must maintain discipline and focus to kill those in pursuit of his Maria and the rest of the guerrilla band. When Jordan is described in the novel's last paragraph as "holding onto himself very carefully" (471), one understands that he is actually bracing himself physically to maintain a steady shot so that he can kill Lieutenant Berrendo and the band of pursuers. However, the explanation clearly doubles as a metaphysical gesture in which Jordan struggles to remain alive and aware and functional.[5]

The "slipping" that appears in *For Whom the Bell Tolls* mirrors that in *A Farewell to Arms*, during which a similar moment appears as the "sliding" to which

Poulet refers. The moment of this "slipping" occurs at precisely the instant of highest tension, when the protagonist Frederic Henry's life and identity are in the most jeopardy, when he is blown up during World War I:

> I tried to breathe but my breath would not come and I felt myself rush bodily out of myself and out and out and out and all the time bodily in the wind. I went out swiftly, all of myself, and I knew I was dead and that it had all been a mistake to think you just died. Then I floated, and instead of going on I felt myself slide back. I breathed and I was back.[6] (54)

Hemingway presents this occurrence in a decidedly ambiguous way: the bombing transcends a moment of life and death and exists as a dramatic moment of transfiguration or conversion, in which a person's identity is at stake, his psychological self, not just his biological self. In this way, readers are invested in the transformation of the protagonist, and the bombing has a psychological and spiritual impact, not merely a physical one. The function of this theme in Hemingway's work is the topic of the next chapter.

The autobiographical memories that rush back to Jordan during his moments of tension and concentration—of his grandfather as a heroic exemplar in the Civil War and of what he perceives to be his father's cowardice in committing suicide—are luxuries that the almost robotically detached Jordan early in the novel would not have permitted himself. In the stream-of-consciousness passage that serves as the novel's crescendo, Jordan shuts off his impulse to ruminate: "Think about Montana. *I can't*" (470, emphasis in original). While these two sentences seem like a simple tit-for-tat, delineating two opposing tendencies, given the circumstance with Jordan knowing that only minutes remain in his life, the choice is to succumb to the panoramic vision of his past life and the onrush of "useless" childhood memories or to maintain the "self," the professional mindset required to fulfill his final duty. For Jordan, it is a metacognitive civil war. One impulse is to ruminate and luxuriate in the full rush of his retrospective consciousness; however, his final task necessitates his being in complete control of his thoughts so that they will aid him in his actions. If he will think "hard," it will be to concentrate on killing Berrendo, not to savor memories of his hometown. An early theorist of such cases, Oskar Pfister, phrases the tension: "the endangered person sees his situation and flies beyond it into fantasies" (Kletti and Noyes 6), an acceptable explication, incidentally, of the final image in "The Snows of Kilimanjaro." Pfister's key observation distinguishes between the excited consciousness of the man struggling to survive and then relaxed reconciliation of the one accepting his demise.

Both "The Snows of Kilimanjaro" and *For Whom the Bell Tolls* end with a heartbeat. In "The Snows of Kilimanjaro," Harry's wife, Helen, is unable to hear the death knell of a hyena "for the beating of her heart" (77). In the last sentence of *For Whom the Bell Tolls,* Jordan "could feel his heart beating against the pine needle floor of the forest" (471). The symbolic power of the two heartbeats joins with William James's image that illustrates an occasion in which a single pulse might reveal an entire lifetime of experience and emotion. For Jordan, the image suggests his oneness with the earth; he is described as being "fully integrated now. . . . He was completely integrated now and he took a good long look at everything" (471). The broad description of a "good long look" conveys not only Jordan surveying his surroundings for signs of the enemy and scoping the woods for one final absorbing, appreciative gaze but also an internal view, a retrospective look at his integrated self and its development over the course of his final three days. This final moment of spiritual atonement departs from Hemingway's description in "The Christmas Gift." After he emerges, dazed, from his plane crash, Hemingway goes on to describe his brain as "something like your brother rather than a complete integrated organ" (BL 452). He allows for a closeness or kinship that qualifies as intimacy without being total oneness. The disparate presentation attests to Hemingway's quest to survive and his active pursuit of a plan of action, in contrast to Harry's and Jordan's understanding of the impossibility of surviving.

Like the scaffold from which Hester Prynne or the condemned man from Prince Myshkin's anecdote views the populace, Hemingway's narratives offer both physical and metaphysical perspectives from which to gaze backward and forward, inward and outward, to view the world and the self panoramically and omnisciently, all in a snapshot, a concentrated instant. Harry ends up in his metaphysical perch at the top of Mount Kilimanjaro, a soaring altitude that allows for a full range of vision, as well as a metaphorical location that allows for a retrospective and introspective review. Jordan, too, has his final moment in the mountains of Spain, which bring him back to his home state of Montana, of which, he summarizes, "Many mountains and very high" (207). Likewise, the altitude and high mountains of Spain afford him a full view of his past, as well as an integrated view of the present. The seemingly innocuous detail that, to Jordan, the bridge, following its successful destruction, "showed now at a new angle . . . without foreshortening" gestures at Jordan's expanded perspective (460), a widened scope of consciousness, his ability to see life panoramically rather than myopically, fraternally rather than solipsistically, and morally rather than shackled by the cold limits of military professionalism. The new angle transcends Euclidean geometry and becomes instead a multidimensional psychological vista. Harry's mountain and Jordan's bridge, like Sam Cardinella's scaffold before them, represent the metaphorical point of view from which to embrace an overview, an instantaneous autobiographical summary. The manner in which Hemingway portrays their visions of death reveals much about the way they viewed their lives.

7

Reading
Through Hemingway's Void

The Death of Consciousness as
Conversion or Annihilation

To be converted, to be regenerated, to receive grace, to experience religion,
to gain an assurance, are so many phrases which denote the process, gradual
or sudden, by which a self hitherto divided, and consciously wrong inferior
and unhappy, becomes unified and consciously right superior and happy,
in consequence of its firmer hold upon religious realities.

William James, *The Varieties of Religious Experience*

Any real change implies the breakup of the world as one has always known
it, the loss of all that gave one an identity, the end of safety . . . it is only
when a man is able, without bitterness or self-pity, to surrender a dream he
has long cherished or a privilege he has long possessed that he is set free—he
has set himself free—for higher dreams, for greater privileges.

James Baldwin, "Faulkner and Segregation"

$\mathcal{I}$n 1925, Hemingway considered several titles for the novel that became *The
Sun Also Rises*. Some of his discarded ideas deepen our understanding about the

eventual theme of the narrative: "Two Lie Together," "Rivers to the Sea," and "The Old Leaven." Hemingway's impulse to use these biblical phrases draws attention to the novel's emphasis on the cyclical nature of life and on the contrast between the fickle, fleeting fortunes of mankind and the permanence of nature. Michael Reynolds suggests that, along with *The Sun Also Rises*, these rejected titles "encompass mutability, permanence, and union" ("False Dawn" 172); to Matthew J. Bruccoli, the titles intend to "convey a sense of renewal or completion" (Hemingway, Facsimile I: xiii).

Further focus on the theme of renewal suggested by the discarded titles reveals that Hemingway's subtle evocation of Jake Barnes's interiority does signal profound character development, and a narrative that sometimes seems nothing more than a linked collection of drinking stories necessitates scrutiny of Hemingway's portrayal of Jake's mind. The strategy in *The Sun Also Rises* provides a skeleton key that allows us to read Hemingway's approach to portraying consciousness as plot development in other narratives. If Jake's character development seems to be underplayed, it was a strategy Hemingway was well aware of. In a defiant sentence in Hemingway's drafting of *The Sun Also Rises*, his narrator self-reflexively vows that "none of the significant things are going to have any literary signs marking them. You have to figure them out by yourself" (Facsimile I: 51).

The Sun Also Rises begins with an apparently irrelevant aside about the history of Robert Cohn's boxing, literary, and romantic life—remains from ramblings that F. Scott Fitzgerald referred to as "inessentials in Cohens [*sic*] biography" and that he recommended be eliminated (*Life in Letters* 144). However, the details of Cohn's boxing ability that are introduced in the first sentence foreshadow the importance of the melee that ensues two hundred pages later. After being called a pimp, Jake swings at Cohn, and the reader then recalls that this annoying, cluelessly cloying character was "once middleweight boxing champion of Princeton" (11) and knows how to handle himself physically, even if not socially. From Jake's perspective, Cohn delivers an impressive pugilistic performance: "I swung at him and he ducked. I saw his face duck sideways in the light. He hit me and I sat down on the pavement. As I started to get on my feet he hit me twice. I went down backward under a table" (195).

What seems on the surface like little more than a sensational bar brawl soon emerges as the pivotal event in the novel; Cohn has improbably ignited an abrupt psychological change in Jake. With a strange construction—"I tried to get up and felt I did not have any legs" (195)—Jake begins a kind of withdrawal or dissociation from his own body, an out-of-body experience during which his old self has faded away from the force of Cohn's blows. When, Jake recounts,

"Some one poured a carafe of water on my head" (195), this dissolution of identity is accompanied by a de facto baptism by an anonymous priest.

Mike informs Jake, "you were cold" (195), and, although Jake insists three separate times that he is "all right" (194–95), he also confesses, "My head's a little wobbly" (195). He prepares to leave the others and to go back to the hotel, recalling, "I had heard them talking from a long way away" (196). The description presents Jake as if he has been removed from his physical being into another plane of consciousness, a separation from his old self that for Hemingway characters often accompanies a traumatic physical disturbance, such as being bombed in war. Indeed, the narration that follows Jake's moment of blackout gives credence to the promise of a new incarnation:[1]

> Walking across the square to the hotel *everything looked new and changed.* I had never seen the trees before. I had never seen the flagpoles before, nor the front of the theatre. *It was all different.* I felt as I felt once coming home from an out-of-town football game. I was carrying a suitcase with my football things in it, and I walked up the street from the station in the town I had lived in all my life *and it was all new.* . . . *It was all strange.* Then I went on, and my feet seemed to be a long way off, and everything seemed to come from a long way off, and I could hear my feet walking a great distance away. (196–97, emphasis added)

Although Jake's knockout at the hands of Cohn physically replicates a relatively common boyhood football injury, combined with the events at Pamplona it represents a dramatic psychological change, in which the vocabulary of conversion—different, new, change, strange—is employed to dramatize Jake's growth, his insight.[2] Jake's conversion is secular, relating to religious experience but not bound to a specific denomination or creed.

The next morning, the physical effects of being knocked out are gone, but Jake's spiritual and psychological renewal remains and informs the conclusion of the novel. As Jake describes it: "I was not groggy now. . . . Everything looked sharp and clear" (200). Book II ends with another indication of a new self: "The world was not wheeling any more. It was just very clear and bright . . . I looked strange to myself in the glass" (228).[3] The world has a new clarity and brilliance because of the keenness of Jake's insight, the protagonist's illumination; as the novelist Robert Stone phrases it, the "touch of redemption through insight that finally justifies fiction" (84). Following this temporary death and reincarnation, Book II ends with a weathered but more mature and more realized version of Jake Barnes who is able to confront Brett and send her off on his terms, just as he sheds the raucous, ultimately debilitating hedonism of his Pamplona getaway and withdraws from the company of his unruly friends.

In his important essay about *The Sun Also Rises*, Mark Spilka concludes that the novel contains "no celebrations of fertility and change" ("Death of Love" 92). Fertility, certainly not; however, Spilka's oft-anthologized point underestimates the wry victory implicit in Jake's final line: "Isn't it pretty to think so?" (251). If Jake's change carries with it no overt celebration, the moment is more triumphant than jubilant; it is not joyous as much as a necessary casting off of frivolity and a solemn embracing of a new maturity, the pain and difficulty associated with the purging of the old leaven.

What does Jake do after he leaves Madrid and returns to Paris? Does he return to his old lifestyle, or has he had an enduring growth experience? To be optimistic about Jake's future beyond the narrative, one need not read *The Sun Also Rises* as a feel-good fairy tale and expect the festivities to which Spilka refers. Discussing the conversion experience, William James dismissed those who would disparage life-changing moments by cynically predicting a relapse into the old ways:

> Psychologically, as well as religiously, however, this is shallow. It misses the point of serious interest, which is not so much the duration as the nature and quality of these shiftings of character to higher levels. Men lapse from every level—we need no statistics to tell us that. Love is, for instance, well known not to be irrevocable, yet, constant or inconstant, it reveals new flights and reaches of ideality while it lasts. These revelations form its significance to men and women, whatever be its duration. So with the conversion experience: that it should for even a short time show a human being what the high-water mark of his spiritual capacity is, this is what constitutes its importance,—an importance which backsliding cannot diminish, although persistence might increase it. (*Varieties* 228)

To apply James's remarks to the conversion of *The Sun Also Rises*, then, what is important is to recognize Jake's capability to grow, his epiphany and metamorphosis and life-changing experience, whether or not he will stay completely and unalterably true to it at all times. James describes conversion as a dramatic shift in:

> the hot place in a man's consciousness, the group of ideas to which he devotes himself, and from which he works . . . *the habitual center of his personal energy*. It makes a great difference to a man whether one set of his ideas, or another, be the centre of his energy; and it makes a great difference, as regards any set of

ideas which he may possess, whether they become central or remain peripheral in him. (*Varieties* 177, emphasis in original)

Jake's shift marks his maturation from the fiesta lifestyle to the more sober life of reflection that he leads temporarily in San Sebastian and that he may pursue following his return to Paris. As James indicates, the relevant question is not whether Jake will ever attend another fiesta. Jake says himself that he will not accompany Bill to continue the party because he is "through with fiestas for a while" (236). While he is not necessarily banishing friends and fiestas and absinthe from his life, the conversion shifts such diversions away from his "hot place" to a more subdued, peripheral presence. This maturation would be more evident had not Hemingway removed the most important aspect of the manuscript draft: Jake's pronounced desire to write a novel. This revelation is a victim of Hemingway's iceberg theory, omitting literary landmarks and leaving some readers with the erroneous impression that Jake has experienced no legitimate change of direction. The timidity with which Jake's conversion into a writer is represented echoes the way the revelation of Nick's own writing was excised from "Big Two-Hearted River."[4] An examination of Hemingway's editorial process demonstrates the way Jake's rather dramatic conversion falls prey to the iceberg theory, remaining submerged, implied yet somehow present only in the vague impression that we are reading Jake's roman à clef.

The paragraph in question in *The Sun Also Rises* reads:

> At a newspaper kiosque I bought a copy of the New York *Herald* and sat in a café to read it. It felt strange to be in France again. There was a safe, suburban feeling. I wished I had gone up to Paris with Bill, except that Paris would have meant more fiesta-ing. I was through with fiestas for a while. It would be quiet in San Sebastian. The season does not open there until August. I could get a good hotel room and read and swim. There was a fine beach there. There were wonderful trees along the promenade above the beach, and there were many children sent down with their nurses before the season opened. In the evening there would be band concerts under the trees across from the Café Marinas. I could sit in the Marinas and listen. (236)

The same moment—although not isolated as its own paragraph—in the manuscript reads:

> At the café I read the papers and a copy of the New York Herald. It felt strange to be in France again. There was a safe, suburban feeling. I wished I had gone up to Paris with Bill except that would have meant more fiesta-ing in Paris and

I was through with Fiestas. It would be quiet in San Sebastian. The season did
not open until August and I could get a good hotel room and read and swim. It
was a splendid place to swim. You could lie on the beach and soak in the sun
and get straightened around inside again. *Maybe I would feel like writing.* San
Sebastian was a good place. There were wonderful trees along the promenade
above the beach and there were good looking children sent down with their
nurses before the season opened. In the evening there would be band concerts
under the trees across from the Cafe Marinas. There was a nice old port. It
would be quiet and solid and restful. (Facsimile II: 569–70, emphasis added)

Although the same basic idea is imparted in both passages—the wish to
unwind on the beach—the manuscript is significantly more revealing in three
major respects. First, Jake declares himself "through with Fiestas," which is
softened in the published version to "through with fiestas for a while." Although
at first glance it may seem that the manuscript demonstrates a more emphatic,
unequivocal conversion, it seems instead that Jake makes the same development but is just giving it a sneer of disgust in the published novel. Second,
declaring San Sebastian a "good place" is not a bland, meaningless aside but
rather an understated reference to the same divine place of refuge that Nick
reaches in "Big Two-Hearted River": "He had made his camp. He was settled.
Nothing could touch him. It was a good place to camp. He was there, in the
good place" (SS 215). As with Nick, Jake's concern is less a sandy beach for its
own sake than a place where he could "get straightened out inside again,"
another significant confession omitted from the published novel. Third, Jake's
speculation that he might feel like writing finally exposes his true desire,
which—again, as with Nick—is to become a writer of fiction. Clearly, the
impulse to write does not refer to journalistic dispatches. Jake is tentatively
embracing the same challenge that Hemingway faced after his actual experiences at the Fiesta de San Fermin in 1925, the awareness that it was time to
transmute his experiences into a novel. This moment is captured in *A Moveable
Feast*: "I knew too that I must write a novel. I would put it off though until I
could not help doing it. . . . When I had to write it, then it would be the only
thing to do and there would be no choice. Let the pressure build" (76).

The typescript clearly evidences Jake's literary aspirations. In chapter 2 of
the deleted typescript, Jake confesses: "Like all newspaper men I have always
wanted to write a novel, and I suppose, now that I am doing it, the novel will
have that awful taking-the-pen-in-hand quality that afflicts newspaper men
when they start to write on their own hook" ("Unpublished Opening" 11).[5]
Perhaps the fear of this cliché and his concern for abject self-reflexivity motivated Hemingway to eliminate overt mention of Jake's literary designs.[6]

Hemingway's method of demonstrating psychological development is intentionally subdued. As Hemingway explained to Maxwell Perkins soon after the publication of *The Sun Also Rises,* "Also have discovered that most people don't think in words—as they do in everybody's writing now—and so in Sun A.R. the critics miss their interior monologues and aren't happy—or disappointed I cut out 40,000 words of the stuff that would have made them happy out of the first Mss—it would have made them happy but it would have rung as false 10 years from now as [Louis] Bromfield" (SL 229). Frederic J. Svoboda, the author of the indispensable study of the *Sun Also Rises* manuscripts, confirms Hemingway's own opinion, arguing that one major improvement of the published novel over the draft is the reduction of explicit reportage of Jake's ruminations, "moving its emphasis from [Jake's] disordered thoughts to the presentation of the ordered world around him. . . . Thus Jake's anguished reflections have become part of the submerged seven-eighths. . . . The early-draft explanations of Jake's mental state have been replaced by a much more direct presentation" (83, 86). Although Jake is not as obviously compulsive as Nick Adams in "Big Two-Hearted River," apparently minor episodes like his balancing his checking account or obsessively recording the type and quality of food and drinks (and payment of same) indicate such a quest for order. More broadly, Jake's interest in bullfighting might also satisfy this need for order and design, even in areas of violence. Hemingway saw his task as conveying thought through action or behavior and in the space between the lines. Hemingway never suggests that his characters do not think or do not think in a complex manner.

Jake's conversion does not call for a festive celebration, nor does there need to be a false guarantee of permanence. Although Hemingway resists easy narratives chronicling personal growth, he does create men who, through lessons learned by trial and injury, are capable of insights that will mark either death-bed conversions (like Harry Morgan or Robert Jordan or Richard Cantwell) or pivotal moments that represent significant changes in their existences (like Jake). This theme makes *The Old Man and the Sea* a fascinating text, because the boy, Manolin, has a more profound psychic change than Santiago, who does not learn anything that he did not know before his trial. The boy, on the other hand, makes a significant change, which is to break from his parents' authority and to devote himself to fishing because of Santiago's example. This novella might be a surreptitious coming-of-age narrative, even though the boy entering maturity and independence does not appear during the main action of the novella.

Having examined the moments of Jake's secular conversion, it becomes compelling to put further pressure on Hemingway's proposed title, "The Old Leaven." The text of 1 Corinthians 5: 7 reads, "Purge the old leaven that you may be fresh dough, still uncontaminated, for Christ, our Lamb has been sacrificed." This passage urges the embracing of a new, more perfect existence and the distancing of the self from less holy and pure ways. In Jake's case, his rejection of further fiesta-ing and his brush-off of Brett are the early steps toward this transition to refinement. As the next verse of Corinthians continues: "Therefore, let us keep the feast, not with old leaven, nor with leaven of vice and malice and wickedness, but with the unleavened bread of purity and sincerity and truth." The title "The Old Leaven" illustrates the infamous "lost generation" lifestyle, but Jake's conversion, along with the title and the novel's epigraph from Ecclesiastes, alludes to the purging of these unhealthy, vulgar ways and the ascent to a new life.

The interpretation of the fight in *The Sun Also Rises* as the traumatic incident that incites change breaks from the prevailing view, which imputes baptismal implications to Jake's series of dives into the Bay of Biscay at San Sebastian. Such an interpretation is speculative; we see elsewhere, such as in *A Farewell to Arms*, that Hemingway does not hesitate to use specific language to indicate a washing of the past or sin. The claim that merely because Jake is diving and immersing himself in the sea he is automatically undergoing some kind of rite of conversion pales in comparison to a more convincing example in *A Farewell to Arms*, where the language of conversion is unmistakable.

Soon after Frederic Henry emerges from the Tagliamento River, he declares his separate peace with the war, which is to say his separation from his incarnation as a soldier, and a break from his past. Frederic makes this declaration when he is on the train to Stresa. He arrives, checks into his hotel, and heads toward the bar. Frederic drinks his first martini, which "felt cool and clean" (244). He drinks a couple more martinis, realizing again, "I had never tasted anything so cool and clean" (245). Looking at the reflection of himself in civilian clothes in the mirror behind the bar, Frederic recalls that he "did not think at all" (245), suggesting further that consciousness has receded under the cleansing elixir of the alcohol following his escape into the river. In response to a question from the barman, Frederic again articulates his quest for separation, which, to use one of Frederic's least favorite phrases, may well be "in vain":

> The war was a long way away. Maybe there wasn't any war. There was no war here. Then I realized it was over for me. But I did not have the feeling that it was really over. I had the feeling of a boy who thinks of what is happening at a certain hour at the schoolhouse from which he has played truant. (245)

The separate peace, it is clear, is more easily declared than maintained. The realization that the war is "over" is irrelevant, Frederic admits, if it does not have the accompanying feeling of peace. Planning to forget about the war and actually forgetting about the war are two vastly different enterprises. As daring as his maritime escape was and as boldly individualistic as his separation from the Italian Army may have been, Frederic has been reduced to the furtive, guilty feelings of childhood mischief, certainly not the psychological state he sought. Likewise, the recollection that he "did not think at all" rings hollow when followed by the feeling of being a boy whose thoughts are occupied by fears and anxiety. Frederic can claim to have forgotten the war, but the word "war" appears three times in the first three sentences of the excerpt; it does not appear in "Big Two-Hearted River" even once. Later, even while safely ensconced in Switzerland with Catherine, Frederic notes, "The war seemed as far away as the football games of some one else's college." The next sentence, beginning with the telling first word, introduces the reality behind the delusion: "*But* I knew from the papers that they were still fighting in the mountains because the snow would not come" (291, emphasis added). The dialectic between the two sentences evidences the chasm between "seems" and "is."

The cleansing that Frederic reports from his series of martinis continues the crucial transformation that he has undergone. The physical separation from the army, an escape into the waters following a frenzied dash through a hail of bullets, has triggered a psychological rebirth. The last sentence in chapter 30, the epic account of the retreat at Caporetto, is "The shore was out of sight now" (225). While this certainly describes the terrain and the physical safety of Frederic's removal from the Italian battle police, the "shore" also represents that which is known. As in *The Old Man and the Sea*, Santiago's removal from the shore is a symbolic venturing into uncharted waters to discover aspects of the self that could not have been ascertained by staying on the shore or in safer, familiar waters from which the safety of shore was visible and obtainable.

Frederic's escape inverts the movement of "Big Two-Hearted River"; Frederic moves from the river to the train, from the chaotic free-flowing current to the plodding segmented train on a linear set of tracks. After gaining convenient relief in a flatcar filled with guns and exhorting himself not to use his head to think or remember too much, he uses the language of a freshly converted individual. Addressing himself in the second person as if completely dissociated, Frederic says, "you seeing now very clearly and coldly—not so coldly as clearly and emptily. You saw emptily" (232). These adverbs—the same ones that will soon apply to martini after martini—suggest a new clarity and the refreshing of the soul and mind, now unburdened with responsibilities of warfare. "You were out of it now," as Frederic characterizes his new incarnation. "You had no more obligation" (232). The emphasis continues throughout the rest of chapter

32, which chronicles his escape to Milan: "Anger was washed away in the river along with any obligation. . . . I was through. . . . it was not my show any more . . . I would eat and stop thinking. I would have to stop. . . . That life was over" (232–33). As Proust's Marcel describes it, "a man cannot change if he behaves according to the dictates of his former self" (536). As in Proust, Frederic recounts his experiences by using the language of conversion, welcoming a new identity. Such a dramatic proclamation of conversion in *A Farewell to Arms* diminishes a similar reading of the San Sebastian scene in *The Sun Also Rises*, where, although Jake's diving is invigorating and perhaps even cathartic, the moment of conversion has already taken place.

Images of being far from shore recur in *A Farewell to Arms* when Frederic makes a second escape—this time from Milan—accompanied by Catherine Barkley. As Frederic embarks on his international rowboat odyssey, he recalls, "But for a long time we did not see any lights, nor did we see the shore" (270), and "the point was out of sight and we were going on up the lake" (271). Through the moonlight, however, Frederic tracks their progress through the coastal towns of northern Italy: "it was much lighter than it had been before and we could see the shore. I could see it too clearly" (271). During their escape, Frederic and Catherine are faced with a vicious catch-22: they need to see the shore to know where they are, but, if it is light enough to see the shore, then the coast guard will spot them before their boat reaches Switzerland. As their journey ends, Frederic highlights this tension: "When I knew daylight was coming I settled down and rowed hard. I did not know where we were" (275). However, soon after: "When it was beginning to be daylight we were quite close to the shore. I could see the rocky shore and the trees" (276). Finally, the tension is alleviated as Frederic tells Catherine: "I think we're in Switzerland, Cat" (276).

Conversion in *A Farewell to Arms* is introduced early in the novel, in terms that Hemingway would revisit throughout his career. As seen in the same passage discussed in the previous chapter, when Frederic is wounded, he recalls in poetic stream-of-consciousness language both the physical and the psychological effect of being bombed:

> I tried to breathe but my breath would not come and I felt myself rush bodily out of myself and out and out and out and all the time bodily in the wind. I went out swiftly, all of myself, and I knew I was dead and that it had all been a mistake to think you just died. Then I floated, and instead of going on I felt myself slide back. I breathed and I was back. (54)[7]

Frederic's moment, like Jake's before his, is only a particular inflection for what is essentially a trope in Hemingway's fiction. According to Philip Young's "wound" theory, the traumatic bombing that Nick Adams sustains in chapter VI of *In Our Time* resonates throughout the entire Hemingway canon. Young believes this brief vignette becomes a "climax for all of Hemingway's heroes for at least the next twenty-five years" (40). Young's thesis, too, seemed to dominate critical discussion of Hemingway for at least that long.

Young's observation also pertains to a discussion of Hemingway's use of the secular conversion as a device for theme, plot, and character in his narratives. Jake's injury in the bar brawl only gestures at the gravity of the war wounding that Hemingway's soldiers receive; perhaps Jake had already endured such a profound wartime death and rebirth before *The Sun Also Rises* begins through the wound that rendered him impotent. It is quite evident that Nick's wounding echoed throughout Hemingway's fiction, as Hemingway strove in various ways to fictionalize his own life-altering experience of being bombed. The woundings that Hemingway would fictionalize represent both a death and rebirth[8] psychologically and a near-death and rehabilitation physically, as underscored by both the title of Hemingway's poem "Killed Piave—July 8—1918" (the place and date of Hemingway's actual wounding) and the content, which speaks of:

> Desire and
> All the sweet pulsing aches
> And gentle hurtings
> That were you,
> Are gone into the sullen dark.
>
> (Poems 35)

Recalling the actual event in his own life, Hemingway described his own wounding even more poetically than he did in the poem: "I died then. . . . I felt my soul or something coming right out of my body, like you'd pull a silk handkerchief out of a pocket by one corner. It flew around and then came back and went in again and I wasn't dead anymore" (Cowley, "Portrait" 47). The same temporary loss of identity caused by a different retelling of Hemingway's bombing appears in "Now I Lay Me," another Nick Adams story: "I myself did not want to sleep because I had been living for a long time with the knowledge that if I ever shut my eyes in the dark and let myself go, my soul would go out of my body. I had been that way for a long time, ever since I had been blown up at night and felt it go out of me and go off and then come back" (SS 363). "Now I Lay Me" begins with the image of silkworms, which invites comparison to Hemingway's metaphor of the silk handkerchief. In fact, the typescript of "Now I Lay Me" contains a description of the image of "a red silk handkerchief being pulled out of your pocket if your pocket was your body" (qtd. in Smith, *Reader's Guide* 173). Also, a silkworm is a breed of caterpillar, an obvious creature of conversion; Saint Teresa of Avila, Jonathan Edwards, Thoreau, and Nikos Kazantzakis all use the silkworm as a metaphor for a creature refining itself into a purer form. William James quotes Hippolyte Taine: "One can compare the state of the patient to nothing so well as to that of a caterpillar, which, keeping all its caterpillar's ideas and remembrances, should suddenly become a butterfly with a butterfly's sense and sensations. Between the old and the new state, between the first self, that of the caterpillar, and second self, that of the butterfly, there is a deep scission, a complete rupture. The new feelings find no anterior series to which they can knit themselves on; the patient can neither interpret nor use them; he does not recognize them; they are unknown. Hence two conclusions, the first which consists in his saying, I no longer am; the second, somewhat later, which consists in his saying, I am another person" (qtd. in *Principles*, I: 376). For a writer like Hemingway, so concerned with representing the conversion of a character, the silkworm was a pitch-perfect objective correlative.

In *Under Kilimanjaro*, Hemingway refers obliquely to the bombing: "Once I had thought my own soul had been blown out of me when I was a boy and then it had come back in again" (220). Directly preceding this memory in the African novel, Hemingway engages in a remarkable speculation about the exact biological moment of metamorphosis:

> Before I woke I had been dreaming and in the dream I had a horse's body but a man's head and shoulders and I had wondered why no one had known this before. It was a very logical dream and it dealt with the precise moment at which the change came about in the body so that they were human bodies. (220)

The specific moment of conversion is crucial because the writer is able to freeze the action as the character passes through zero on his ascent from a negative condition to a positive one. It would be naïve to believe that, following this cessation in consciousness or temporary entrance into oblivion, the individual who is able to re-enter his former state emerges unchanged, exactly as he was before. One of William James's tenets about the stream of thought is that "*no state once gone can recur and be identical to what it was before"* (*Principles*, I: 230, emphasis in original). If such uniqueness to human thought is true of everyday experience, the singularity of this experience is magnified during a breach or cessation of consciousness subsequent to a traumatic incident.

Although the published version of *The Garden of Eden* does not reflect this aspect, Hemingway's sprawling manuscript makes great use of the theme of conversion. In the unpublished draft, the characters are explicitly inspired by Rodin's sculpture *The Metamorphoses of Ovid* (cf. Eby 160, Burwell 102). Mark Spilka describes the novel as an "externalized account of a psychic journey into the wilds of androgyny, as inspired by a mysterious Rodin statue of two lesbians making love" (*Hemingway's Quarrel* 12). In the manuscript, the precise title of the Rodin sculpture is crossed out, and the Rodin museum is referred to more generally. However, Hemingway's design demonstrates that the focus of the novel was on the devastating effects of a character changing his or her former self.

The "before" and "after" states in a conversion are fundamental to interpretation, since the emotional or psychic growth of a character is in many ways the raison d'être of fiction. Joseph Campbell's studies of the monomyth summarize the universal hero's journey as "leaving one condition and finding the source of life to bring you forth into a richer or mature condition" (152). Hemingway frequently emphasizes the change of his hero by evoking and exploring a harrowing moment: the instant in between these two before-and-after states, the zero point of conversion. This moment of nonbeing in which consciousness and selfhood have been eliminated is the fork in the road that leads, in Hemingway's work, to a conversion or to inescapable annihilation.

Perhaps the most memorable dramatization of this phenomenon in literature comes in the last canto of Dante's *Inferno*; the pilgrim's vision of Satan causes him such a paralysis of fright that his consciousness freezes, and, along with it, he literally ceases to exist: "I did not die and I did not remain alive" (XXXIV, 25).[9] The pilgrim, still referring to the state of nonbeing, then turns to the reader and apostrophizes, "now think for yourself, if you have any wit, what I became, deprived alike of death and life!" (26–27). This moment, as John Freccero points out, is a crucial moment of conversion in the poem, one that allows for the appearance of a new incarnation of the self that is able to enter purgatory. Freccero's discussion of Dante's conversion shows two nearly simultaneous changes in character: both "the leaving behind of sin" and "the movement to grace." As the pilgrim swooning at the sight of Satan is a moment of vacuum where, to Freccero, "corruption meets generation" (174), Hemingway's characters are often frozen within a similar void, although his narratives were not always divine comedies or narratives of new lives; sometimes, the characters confronted voids they could not escape.

The key to interpreting the voids in consciousness in Hemingway's work is to gauge the character's response to the void, as well as the response elicited from the narrative itself: Does the character—per Dante's pilgrim and per Campbell's outline of the universal hero—emerge with an expansion of consciousness and a richer existence? Or, does the void crack the character, become a tragic *nada* that kills him or dooms him to a tragic, unsatisfying existence? We can recall the famous aphorism in *A Farewell to Arms*: "The world breaks every one and afterward many are strong at the broken places." Of course, as the passage continues, "those that will not break it kills" (249). This dichotomy epitomizes conversion in Hemingway: characters either pass through a void into transformation or succumb to destruction. *The Old Man and the Sea* and "Big Two-Hearted River" demonstrate how the characters can take such drastically divergent turns. Nick leaves behind thoughts and needs in his solo camping trip but is confident that he can escape the void in the future, the "plenty of days coming" when his ambitious renewal will take place (SS 232). For Santiago, his "no thoughts nor any feelings of any kind" signals something far more desperate and discouraging (119). When the void comes at the end of an old man's life and the end of a narrative, the implications are bleak indeed.

The apotheosis of this phenomenon occurs during the final ten pages of *For Whom the Bell Tolls*, following the breaking of Robert Jordan's leg, from which he never recovers. Just as Frederic's growth in *A Farewell to Arms* is his recognition that his love affair with Catherine Barkley gave him a new perspective on war and life, Jordan's last moments following the successful destruction of the bridge afford him an appreciation of his own change, the touch of redemption through insight that Robert Stone describes.

In the paragraph preceding the blow that eventually leads to his death, Jordan experiences the epiphany that his brief relationship with Maria has prepared him to appreciate. Jordan, according to the text, "looked down across the slope to where the bridge showed now at a new angle he had never seen" (FWBT 460). Even though Jordan is an expert dynamiter who planned exhaustively and meticulously considered all aspects of his job, the moment before his fatal injury occasions complete illumination and fresh insight.

After being struck down, Jordan and his archenemy, Pablo, have a final encounter, during which Pablo ominously traces Jordan's fading fate: "there is not much time . . . there is little time. . . . There is no time" (462). Faced with this concentrated urgency, Jordan urges Maria to seek safety, claiming a metaphysical union with her: "I am thee also now. . . . You are me now" (463). He urges her to flee, referring to "The me in thee" and suggesting that "Thou art me too now" (464). At the end of the novel, when Jordan is described as "completely integrated now" (471), the image refers to his oneness not only with the earth, his heart beating against the pine needles on the ground, but also with his true love and the absorption of his spirit into hers. This integration reinforces earlier moments, as when Maria tells Jordan during their lovemaking, "we will be as one animal of the forest and be so close that neither one can tell that one of us is one and not the other. Can you not feel my heart be your heart? . . . I am thee and thou art me and all of one is the other. . . . I would have us exactly the same. . . . But we will be one now and there will never be a separate one" (263). Such moments emphasize the theme of a kinship among humans, as captured in the novel's title and epigraph, derived from John Donne's Holy Meditations.

As the rest of the guerrillas escape, Jordan is "soaking wet with sweat and looking at nothing" (465), the image of a man no longer in control of his senses, facing a void or vacuum of stimulation. The void is palpable and unavoidable; although Jordan must sustain consciousness to fulfill his final duty of killing the cavalry that will pursue Maria and the other members of the band:

> He felt empty and drained and exhausted from all of it and from them going and his mouth tasted of bile. Now, finally and at last, there was no problem. However all of it had been and however all of it would ever be now, for him, no longer was there any problem. (466)

This description echoes the concession that culminates *The Old Man and the Sea*, following Santiago's failed journey. The description of Jordan's exhaustion negatively restates Nick's optimistic break from memory and thought and obligation. An intentional movement toward the void is either suicidal or an act of faith that one will be able to transcend it. First, there must be a level of discontentment with the current situation that justifies the risk of giving one's self over to the void. In a negative enactment of this surrender, it becomes nihilistic or even baldly self-destructive.

Hemingway uses the notion of oblivion in disparate ways, both as a helpful temporary balm and as a tragic permanent realm. Nick's camping trip courts a semblance of oblivion, an existence with the bare minimum of stimulation, as a means of rehabilitation. As mentioned in chapter 2, William James quoted Théodule Ribot to support his belief that, in this sense, oblivion "is thus no malady of memory, but a condition of its health and its life" (*Principles*, I: 681).

On the other hand, the notion of oblivion can represent more than a temporary respite, the *nada* state from which Hemingway characters do not escape. In *Islands in the Stream*, for instance, Hudson snarls, "Fuck oblivion" and then warns ominously: "Don't you ever fool with that oblivion stuff" (157–58). As with Hudson, oblivion is no condition of health for Robert Jordan. With a broken leg, the cavalry fast approaching, and five pages remaining in the narrative, the void plainly relegates him to an imminent death, one—as in *The Old Man and the Sea*—that the narrative implies but does not show.

The deathbed conversion that Jordan has experienced, with a final illumination before he is killed, is the ultimate triumph before tragedy. As Jordan awaits the attack, he "tried to hold on to himself that he felt slipping away from himself as you feel snow starting to slip sometimes on a mountain slope" (470–71). The "himself" to which Jordan refers is a far different entity from the one that existed three days earlier, at the beginning of the novel, before he met and fell in love with Maria. Of course, stemming the slipping snow is only a temporary victory, and, soon after, the death of consciousness and the death of self both suggest Jordan's death following his final duty to the Republic.

When analyzing Pablo after he returns to the gang following his theft of Robert Jordan's explosives, Jordan muses about the nature of his character and his shady, malevolent ways: "I didn't think you had experienced any complete conversion on the road to Tarsus, old Pablo, Robert Jordan thought. No. Your coming back was miracle enough. I don't think there will ever be any problem about canonizing you" (392).[10] Jordan is expressing in biblical terms his concern about Pablo's corruption and his inability to improve or evolve as a man,[11] but organized religion is not the issue in this narrative. By phrasing his observation of Pablo in this way, however, Jordan highlights his own secular conversion, the richer existence that his experience with Maria has granted him.

The idea of a void in consciousness signaling an intersection at which the Hemingway protagonist must triumph anew or be vanquished is never compressed more evocatively into a single text than in "The Short Happy Life of Francis Macomber," demonstrated by the allusion to rebirth in the title itself.[12] After Macomber's humiliating retreat from a charging lion, his wife of eleven years regards him and the professional hunter Wilson and "looked at both these men as though she had never seen them before" (SS 4). This gesture at Macomber's new, inferior identity persists when he remarks of her displeasure of him with wry irony: "I suppose I rate that for the rest of my life" (6). In his sullenness, he recognizes the limitations of his current existence, admitting to Wilson, "There are lots of things I don't know" (7). Although Macomber is introduced at perhaps the lowest point of his life—certainly his married life—

the narrative becomes a quest to renew. Like other such renewals in Hemingway, the recovery first necessitates a void. "I'd like to clear away that lion business," Macomber tells Wilson, eager to reach a zero point and to distance himself from his unhappy past (11).[13]

Macomber's zero point occurs as he lies alone in bed, aware that his life is not progressing and that he has reached an unsatisfactorily stagnant existence: "it was not all over. It was neither all over nor was it beginning" (11). This unhappy state reveals an obvious lack: "more than shame he felt cold, hollow fear in him. The fear was still there like a cold slimy hollow in all the emptiness where once his confidence had been" (11). This hollowness and the emptiness that remains effectively replicate the way his stomach was "hollow feeling" during his fearful stalking of the wounded lion earlier in the day (18). Macomber is asked twice what is worrying him, and both times he replies: "Nothing," alluding to that internal void (12). Macomber's mental state approximates the momentous bottoming-out known as a "vastation," which William James and his father both experienced. James recalls his "depression of spirits . . . when suddenly there fell upon me, without any warning, just as if it came out of the darkness, a horrible fear of my own existence. . . . I became a mass of quivering fear. After this, the universe was changed for me altogether" (*Varieties* 146). A vastation equates to, writes James's biographer Robert D. Richardson, "a sort of second birth" (18). As can happen to Hemingway's heroes, James's moment of abject fear becomes a turning point, precipitating a conversion.[14]

Macomber's emptiness is replaced by rage over his wife's infidelity—her dalliance with Wilson almost literally right under his nose—and then by "a drunken elation" as he successfully stalks three buffalo the following day. The triumph is crucial: "In his life he had never felt so good" (29). If his pride is described as pivotal, it sustains him through his next trial. One of the three buffalo he has hunted is wounded and hiding in the bush, just as did the lion from the previous day. However, this time Macomber is undaunted: "For the first time in his life he really felt wholly without fear. Instead of fear, he had a feeling of definite elation" (31). Already in his new, short, happy life, Macomber has felt better and less fearful than ever before; the repeated phrase "in his life" clearly refers to his *vita nuova*, not to his biological one, which has lasted thirty-five years. *The Divine Comedy* also takes place during the biblical midpoint of the protagonist's life, age thirty-five. Wilson articulates the difference: "Yesterday . . . he's scared sick and today he's a ruddy fire eater" (31). We are witnessing Macomber's new identity, postconversion.

His wife, Margot, meanwhile, has undergone a reciprocal change. Her former position of dominance has been upended. Following her husband's killing of the buffalo, "Her face was white and she looked ill" (31). The whiteness is her own blankness, a depletion of the qualities that comstituted her former self. To make matters worse for her, in a parallel action from the previous hunt, she again observes the two men, but this time "There was no change in Wilson. . . . But she saw the change in Francis" (33). Margot and Francis undergo inverse conversions, where she descends from power and he ascends into fulfillment.[15]

As with his portrayal of Jake and Frederic, Hemingway's language is similarly unambiguous. If the title did not suggest a conversion, then Macomber's own recognition of his new life certainly does:

> "You know I don't think I'd ever be afraid of anything again," Macomber said to Wilson. "Something happened in me after we first saw the buff and started after him. Like a dam bursting. It was pure excitement. . . . You know something did happen to me . . . I feel absolutely different." (32)

Wilson, hardly a romantic given to effusion about another man's internal victories, responds by quoting Shakespeare; however, the notion that "a man can die but once" is ironically inapplicable in this narrative.[16] Biological death is less important in narrative matters than in real life.

Wilson's erudite literary allusion only serves to highlight the disparity between Macomber's deaths. We witness the death of his former self and then that of his biological self in the span of twenty-four hours, and, for him, as with another of Shakespeare's characters who reconciles with death, the readiness is all. Upon Macomber's successfully killing the final buffalo—the climax of the narrative and the high point of Macomber's life—his wife blindsides him, creating another void: "he felt a sudden[17] white-hot, blinding flash explode inside his head and that was all he ever felt" (36).

In most Hemingway characters, the void leads to conversion or annihilation. In "The Short Happy Life of Francis Macomber," the protagonist experiences both: the conversion engenders the new existence that reconciles him spiritually to permanent destruction.[18] The examination of this subtle technique shows how concerned Hemingway was with character development, as opposed to thoughtless action. By tracking the interiority of his heroes, we understand how Hemingway conveyed emotion and told the internal narrative of the mind to provide the unseen foundation that enhanced the story he was trying to tell.

Notes

Introduction: Ernest Hemingway and the Life of the Mind

1. This document is available as Folder 270A at the John F. Kennedy Presidential Library and Museum (hereafter JFK) in Boston. It was posthumously published in Peter Griffin's 1985 biography of Hemingway's early years, *Along with Youth*. Griffin, however, elected to ignore Hemingway's title, substituting it with "Portrait of the Idealist in Love—A Story," which Hemingway had crossed out. The only critical commentary ever made about this piece is an uncharacteristically speculative reaction from Paul Smith, who asserts, "There is enough evidence in the typescript . . . to argue that, although the brief introduction and conclusion are Hemingway's, the long, maudlin, and lofty vacuities of the idealist's letter are not Hemingway's but were hastily copied and framed as a private joke and then set aside" ("Hemingway's Apprentice Fiction" 579). Smith continues his point in a footnote, arriving at a conclusion that is impossible to disprove but that is nevertheless unconvincing: "The typescript . . . has several of the sort of errors of omission and repetition one makes in a quick copy of another text. Its style is like nothing else Hemingway wrote, nor is it a parody. I suspect it is a rough copy of another person's letter with Hemingway's frame to ridicule its author and his windy idealism" (579, fn. 13). Although Smith's comments seem to be baseless, the story merits examination if only for Hemingway's attention to it. Hemingway uses a similar framing technique in 1933 in "One Reader Writes," from *Winner Take Nothing*, which Carlos Baker reports is a "slightly edited transcript of an actual letter" that Hemingway received ("Empirical Imagination" 100).

2. Another insult in "The Killers" falls along these lines: "Oh, he's a thinker" (SS 281).

3. Reynolds is quoting the 1920 *Bulletin of the Art Institute of Chicago*.

4. In "The Art of the Short Story," Hemingway recollects of "Fifty Grand":

> This story originally started like this:
>
> "'How did you handle Benny so easy, Jack?' Soldier asked him.
>
> "'Benny's an awful smart boxer,' Jack said. 'All the time he's in there, he's thinking. All the time he's thinking, I was hitting him.'" (88–89)

Lillian Ross reports Hemingway telling the story: "'One time I asked Jack, speaking of a fight with Benny Leonard, "How did you handle Benny so easy, Jack?" "Ernie," he said, "Benny is an awfully smart boxer. All the time he's boxing, he's thinking. All the time he was thinking, I was hitting him."' Hemingway gave a hoarse laugh, as though he had heard the story for the first time. . . . He laughed again. 'All the time he was thinking, I was hitting him'" (64).

5. Elsewhere, Hemingway remarks on the mental acuity of fighters just as he evaluates their physical skill: in 1922, Hemingway describes Battling Siki, the challenger to Georges Carpentier, "siki tough slowthinker but mauling style may puzzle carp" (Reynolds, *Paris Years* 73). In his early journalism, Hemingway reports that "Jack Dempsey has an imposing list of knockouts over bums and tramps, who were nothing but big slow-moving, slow-thinking set ups for him" (Reynolds, *Young Hemingway* 192).

6. Nick may actually mean "conscious," since he is referring to instinct versus intentionality. "Conscience," acting from the dictates of some kind of moral imperative, is not what Nick intends to say.

7. Hemingway once advised a young writer: "Always stop while you are going good and don't think about it or worry about it until you start to write the next day. That way your subconscious will work on it all the time. But if you think about it consciously or worry about it you will kill it and your brain will be tired before you start. . . . How can you learn not to worry? . . . By not thinking about it. As soon as you start to think about it stop it. Think about something else. You have to learn that" (BL 216–17).

8. In *The Dangerous Summer*, Hemingway pointedly compares bullfighting to art: "A bullfighter can never see the work of art that he is making. He has no chance to correct it as a painter or a writer has. He cannot hear it as a musician can. . . . All the time he is making his work of art he knows that he must keep within the limits of his skill and his knowledge of the animal" (198). Earlier in *The Dangerous Summer*, Luis Miguel Dominguín is also compared to an artist: "He had the complete and respectful concentration on his work which marks all great artists" (106). In *Death in the Afternoon*, Hemingway argues that the only thing separating bullfighting from traditional artistic media is its impermanence.

9. Burne Holliday in F. Scott Fitzgerald's *This Side of Paradise* neatly sums up the dilemma: "Any person with any imagination is bound to be afraid" (*Novels and Stories* 117), the modernist's equivalent of Hamlet's "conscience doth make cowards of us all"; perhaps consciousness doth make cowards of us all.

10. Pedro Romero is described as possessing a similar prescience: Mike Campbell observes, "He'll never be frightened. . . . He knows too damned much." Jake agrees: "He knew everything when he started. The others can't ever learn what he was born with" (SAR 172).

11. See Scott Donaldson's *By Force of Will* for a similar point (xii).

12. For the article that introduced this comparison, see Clifton Fadiman, "Ernest Hemingway: An American Byron," *The Nation*, 8 January 1933, 63–64.

13. The other entries: Kipling, Cpt. Frederick Marryat, Yeats's *Autobiographies*, George Moore's *Hail and Farewell*, and *Far Away and Long Ago*, by W. H. Hudson. Although Hudson is included in this lofty list, his *The Purple Land* is lampooned in *The Sun Also Rises* as an overly romantic book in which Robert Cohn had placed too much importance.

14. The use of the "mill race" image appears in the published edition of *To Have and Have Not*, albeit in a more literal context: "About four o'clock when we're coming back close in to shore against the Stream; it going like a mill race, us with the sun at our backs" (19). Given the manuscript simile, the "Stream" they are facing might also be the stream of consciousness. During the panic of Catherine's complicated labor in *A Farewell to Arms*, Frederic sums up the fatalism of their love: "Once it started, they were in the mill-race" (320). See Ott on this topic (28–29).

15. Just as James is being referenced obliquely as an emblem of asexuality in *The Sun Also Rises*, in *Under Kilimanjaro* he is used disparagingly as a symbol of a nonparticipant, a man who was a witness and did not immerse himself in the action of life. In an as yet unpublished letter to Lillian Ross in 1950, Hemingway refers to James as "Henrietta James."

16. *The Dangerous Summer* restates *Death in the Afternoon*; *Under Kilimanjaro* echoes *Green Hills of Africa*; the posthumous efforts *The Garden of Eden* and *A Moveable Feast* return to the material of *The Sun Also Rises*, just as *Across the River and into the Trees* extends the themes of *A Farewell to Arms* and certain stories in *In Our Time*. In chapters 2 and 3 of this book, I argue that *The Old Man and the Sea* serves as a disguised sequel to "Big Two-Hearted River."

Chapter 1. The Solitary Consciousness I

1. Likewise, when Hemingway submitted the piece to *This Quarter* in 1925, Christian Gauss and F. Scott Fitzgerald accused Hemingway of "having written a story in which nothing happened" (Baker, *Writer as Artist* 125).

2. The manuscript of *A Farewell to Arms* is even more harrowing. In the description of emerging from general anesthesia, Frederic recalls, "My legs hurt so that I tried to get back into the choked place I had come from but I could not get back in there and threw up again and again and nothing came" (qtd. in Lynn 380). To illustrate further the grave connotations of this word in Hemingway: in "A Way You'll Never Be" Nick recalls his wounding, "the white flash and clublike impact, on his knees, hot-sweet choking, coughing it onto the rock" (SS 414). Also, in one of Hemingway's most memorable adverbial choices, Mrs. Krebs in "Soldier's Home" is described as responding "chokily" when Harold apologizes for saying he does not love her (SS 152).

3. Elizabeth Wells, using her own statistical criterion of "substantive words only" (62), calculates that 72 percent of the words in "Big Two-Hearted River" are monosyllabic and 4 percent contain two syllables (62, 67).

4. In Hemingway's obnoxious essay "The Art of the Short Story," he describes "Big Two-Hearted River" as being "about a boy coming home beat to the wide from a war. Beat to the wide was an earlier and possibly more severe form of beat, since those

who had it were unable to comment on this condition and could not suffer that it be mentioned in their presence. So the war, all mention of the war, anything about the war, is omitted" (88).

5. A. E. Hotchner reports Hemingway's response as "Poor Faulkner. Does he really think big emotions come from big words? He thinks I don't know the ten-dollar words. I know them all right. But there are older and simpler and better words, and those are the ones I use" (69–70). In Lillian Ross's extended piece on Hemingway, she quotes him: "People think I'm an ignorant bastard who doesn't know the ten-dollar words. I know the ten-dollar words. There are older and better words which if you arrange them in the proper combination you make it stick" (61). In a 1953 letter, Hemingway writes, "Actually if a writer needs a dictionary he should not write. He should have read the dictionary at least three times from beginning to end and then have loaned it to someone who needs it" (SL 809).

6. For an even more thorough dramatization of the distinction between "thinking" and "wondering," see Jake Barnes's fascinating self-conscious prayer in *The Sun Also Rises*: "I *wondered* if there was anything else I might pray for, and I *thought* I would like to have some money, so I prayed that I would make a lot of money, and then I started to *think* how I would make it, and *thinking* of making money reminded me of the count, and I started *wondering* about where he was, and regretting I hadn't seen him since that night in Montmartre, and about something funny Brett told me about him, and as all the time I was kneeling with my forehead on the wood in front of me, and was *thinking* of myself as praying, I was a little ashamed, and regretted that I was such a rotten Catholic" (103, emphasis added). More revealing, see an exchange between Frederic Henry and Catherine Barkley in *A Farewell to Arms*: "Sometimes I *wonder* about the front and about people I know but I don't worry. I don't *think* about anything much." "Who do you *wonder* about?" "About Rinaldi and the priest and lots of people I know. But I don't *think* about them much. I don't want to *think* about the war. I'm through with it." "What are you *thinking* about now?" "Nothing." "Yes you were. Tell me." "I was *wondering* whether Rinaldi had the syphilis" (298, emphasis added). Frederic also notes the distinction earlier: "I would eat and stop thinking. I would have to stop. . . . They might call me drowned. I wondered what they would hear in the States. . . . I wondered what had become of the priest at the mess. And Rinaldi" (232–33). In *Islands in the Stream*, a curious meditation by Thomas Hudson is described: "Sometimes he could think about the stars without wondering about them and the ocean without problems and the sunrise without what it would bring" (369). With this articulation, Hudson's "thought" is an almost Zen-like acceptance, as opposed to "wondering," which in this instance expends mental energy, attempting to solve mysteries and perhaps dredge up dormant memories and sensations in a troubled mind.

7. Bergson's description of a mental "jumping from one thing to another"—or "qui saute indéfiniment d'une chose à une autre" in the original (*L'évolution créatrice* 320)—echoes Jake's solitary meditation in *The Sun Also Rises*: "I lay awake thinking and

my mind jumping around. Then I couldn't keep away from it, and I started to think about Brett and all the rest of it went away. I was thinking about Brett and my mind stopped jumping around and started to go in sort of smooth waves" (39).

8. An exchange between Catherine Barkley and Frederic Henry in *A Farewell to Arms* exemplifies the difficulty of "not thinking" when there is no distracter: "Don't think about me when I'm not here." "That's the way I worked it at the front. But there was something to do then" (257). In *Across the River and into the Trees*, Colonel Cantwell tells Renata, "I'm not lonely when I'm working. I have to think too hard to ever be lonely" (99). Shakespeare's *Romeo and Juliet* also has a wonderful example, in an early conversation between Benvolio and a lovesick Romeo: "Be rul'd by me, forget to think of her." "O, teach me how I should forget to think." "By giving liberty unto thine eyes: / Examine other beauties" (1.1.225–28). Like Frederic and Cantwell, Benvolio is distinguishing between the difficulty of "not thinking" and the ease of a pleasant distraction.

9. Maudsley's quote is from page 155 of *The Physiology of Mind* (New York: Appleton, 1887).

10. Robert Jordan has a decidedly more positive reaction when his drink of absinthe spurs an involuntary memory: "one cup of it took the place of the evening papers, of all the old evenings in cafés, of all chestnut trees that would be in bloom now in this month, of the great slow horses of the outer boulevards, of book shops, of kiosques, and of galleries, of the Parc Montsouris, of the Stade Buffalo, and of the Butte Chaumont, of the Guaranty Trust Company and the Ile de la Cité, of Foyot's old hotel, and of being able to read and relax in the evening; of *all the things he had enjoyed and forgotten and that came back to him* when he tasted that opaque, bitter, tongue-numbing, brain-warming, stomach-warming, idea-changing, liquid alchemy" (51, emphasis added). In *Islands in the Stream*, Thomas Hudson has a drink that contains similar powers: "A drink always unlocked his memory that he kept locked so carefully now" (427), with the adverb "carefully" repeated from "Big Two-Hearted River." For another example from that novel, see page 75 of this book, which also describes the transportative qualities of a drink.

11. See "A Clean Well-Lighted Place" for what might be Hemingway's most brilliant objective correlative, following the older waiter's cathartic, nihilistic "*nada*" prayer: "He smiled and stood before a bar with a shining steam pressure coffee machine" (SS 383).

12. See *A Farewell to Arms*, in which Frederic says to the priest: "I never think and yet when I begin to talk I say the things I have found out in my mind without thinking" (179). Hemingway's 1920 poem, "A Modern Version of Polonius' Advice," opens, "Give thy tongue no tho'ts, / Nor ever think before you speak" (Poems 19). See also *The Sun Also Rises* for the cruel game that Harvey Stone plays with Robert Cohn; reminiscent of psychotherapy, Harvey invites Cohn to express without thinking what he would "rather do" if any wish could be granted. Cohn, falling into his trap, confesses that he wishes he could play football again (50–51).

Chapter 2. The Solitary Consciousness II

1. For a counterpoint, see *A Farewell to Arms*, in which the venerable Count Greffi tells Frederic: "No, that is the great fallacy; the wisdom of old men. They do not grow wise. They grow careful" (261). Greffi anticipates T. S. Eliot's "East Coker": "Do not let me hear / Of the wisdom of old men, but rather of their folly, / Their fear of fear and frenzy, their fear of possession, / Of belonging to another, or to others, or to God. / The only wisdom we can hope to acquire / Is the wisdom of humility: humility is endless" (123–24).

2. Izaak Walton (1569–1683) wrote *The Compleat Angler, or, Contemplative man's recreation: being a discourse on rivers, fish-ponds, fish, and fishing.* Hemingway jokes similarly in an earlier article, a 1920 piece for the *Toronto Star Weekly* headlined "The Best Rainbow Trout Fishing," where he describes trout fishing as "a rough, tough, mauling game, lacking in the meditative qualities of the Izaak Walton school of angling" (BL 9–10).

3. See Hemingway's early poem "Captives": "Thinking and hating were finished / Thinking and fighting were finished / Retreating and hoping were finished. / Cures thus a long campaign, / Making death easy" (Poems 26). Hemingway also brings *A Farewell to Arms* to its tragic close with a similar portrait of a lost consciousness: "Everything was gone inside of me. I did not think. I could not think" (330). Young Joaquín, bleeding to death as he dies with the rest of El Sordo's band, is described: "He had known nothing and had no feeling since he had suddenly been in the very heart of the thunder and the breath had been wrenched from his body when the one bomb struck so close" (FWBT 322). *Islands in the Stream*, too, concludes with a similar image of a vacant Thomas Hudson's mental state: "He felt far away now and there were no problems at all" (446). In Marie Morgan's stream-of-consciousness riff that closes *To Have and Have Not*, she, too, reports a loss of consciousness: "That's the only feeling I got. Hate and a hollow feeling. I'm empty like a empty house" (257). Almost certainly, Hemingway's inspiration for Marie's image derives from the country doctor Peabody in Faulkner's *As I Lay Dying*: "I can remember when I was young I believed death to be a phenomenon of the body; now I know it merely to be a function of the mind . . . in reality it is no different than a single tenant or family moving out of a tenement or a town" (43–44).

4. The most riveting single moment of metacognition in Hemingway comes in the final moments of *For Whom the Bell Tolls*, as he readies himself for one final deed before he dies:

> Think about them being away, he said. Think about them going through the timber. Think about them crossing a creek. Think about them riding through the heather. Think about them going up the slope. Think about them O.K. tonight. Think about them travelling, all night. Think about them hiding up tomorrow. Think about them. God damn it, think about them. *That's just as far as I can think about them*, he said.
>
> Think about Montana. *I can't*. Think about Madrid. *I can't*. Think about a cool drink of water. *All right*. That's what it will be like. Like a cool drink of water.

You're a liar. It will just be nothing. That's all it will be. Just nothing. Then do it. *Do it.* Do it now. It's all right to do it now. Go on and do it now. *No, you have to wait.* What for? You know all right. *Then wait.* (470, emphasis in original)

A similar dynamic appears in "The Strange Country," in which one aspect of Roger Davis converses with another: "You really can start it all over now. You really can. *Please don't be silly*, another part of him said. You really can, he said to himself. You can be just as good a guy as she thinks you are and as you are at this moment." This bizarre conversation continues for a paragraph, and the next paragraph illuminates Hemingway's strategy for presenting Roger's thoughts in this way: "You're getting to be an awful moralist, he thought. If you don't watch out you will bore her. *When weren't you a moralist?* At different times. *Don't fool yourself.* Well, at different places then. *Don't fool yourself.* All right, Conscience, he said" (CSS 635, emphasis in original). The internal dialogue continues, with Roger referring to the voice in his head as "Conscience" for the remainder. Elsewhere, Robert Jordan also tellingly addresses himself as another, with a crucial punch line: "I was ashamed enough of you, there for a while. Only I was you. There wasn't any me to judge you. We were all in bad shape. You and me and both of us. Come on now. Quit thinking like a schizophrenic. One at a time, now. You're all right again now" (FWBT 394). Huckleberry Finn also has an exasperated conversation with his own conscience (110–11).

5. C. P. Heaton's article points out the single occurrence of an exclamation point in *The Old Man and the Sea.*

Chapter 3. Memory in *A Farewell to Arms*

1. Hemingway wrote his editor, Maxwell Perkins, of his literary project with *Green Hills of Africa*: "the person that it happens to has to be equipped to make it come true ie to realize it, so that it has all the dimensions[.] You have to *make* the country—not describe it" (Bruccoli, *Only Thing* 216).

2. In *For Whom the Bell Tolls*, too, absinthe is the "liquid alchemy" that affects Robert Jordan's thinking (51).

3. During Frederic and Count Greffi's conversation, they touch on the state of contemporary fiction, including a reference to Wells's 1916 novel *Mr. Britling Sees It Through* (260–61). Wells is also a target in *The Torrents of Spring*: "Mr. H.G. Wells, who has been visiting at our home (we're getting along in the literary game, eh, reader?) asked us the other day if perhaps our reader, that's you, reader—just think of it, H.G. Wells talking about you right in our home" (68–69).

4. Graves writes: "The truth seems to be that genius is capable at some primitive thought-level of thinking in the fourth and fifth dimensions. In the fourth dimension one can explore the interior of a sealed chamber without breaching its walls. In the fifth, one is no longer bound by time but can see things happening in the past and future as easily as, for instance, if seated at ease in an aeroplane flying faster than clock time, one can watch the setting sun slowly rise again above the sea-horizon. One is also, it seems

capable of communing with other minds in the past, present, or future. The creative act of poetry is fifth-dimensional in the sense that a poet catches at the nucleus of a poem, a single half-remembered phrase, and works at it until every line corresponds as nearly as possible with his foreknowledge of how the completed poem would be. Creative genius in dancing or music follows much the same principles" (12).

5. Conspicuous mathematic references appear in *Across the River and into the Trees*: Cantwell determines the site of his World War I wounding "by triangulation" (26); he notices that the wind "sharpened all the outlines of buildings so that they were geometrically clear" (35); and, finally, "But when the Colonel became a general officer again, as he had once been, and thought in terms that were as far beyond him as calculus is distant from a man who has only the knowledge of arithmetic" (64).

6. A similar evocation of the time-space continuum can be found in *Islands in the Stream*: "But the sea was only the blue beyond the far white spread of the town. It was as distant now as all things that were past and he meant to keep it that way, now that the motion was gone, until it was time to go out onto it again" (215).

7. Another architect in Hemingway's canon is Captain Paravicini in "A Way You'll Never Be," also set in Italy during World War I: "The tall one with the small mustache who was an architect and speaks English" (SS 404).

8. In *Islands in the Stream*, Thomas Hudson tells the obnoxious Johnny Goodner, "You sound like a damned interior decorator" (33). In addition to tweaking Johnny's masculinity, Hudson might also be revealing his aesthetic credo as a painter.

9. The manuscript first read, "Nothing that you learn by sensation is of any value" but "remains" would replace "is of any value" (JFK 64). In an excised portion of *The Garden of Eden*, Hemingway writes, "If you live by the senses you will die by them and if you live by your invention and your head you die by that too. All that is left entire in you is your ability to write and that gets better" (qtd. in Burwell 119).

10. This ninety-one-word passage is repeated verbatim in *Death in the Afternoon* (138).

11. This theme is repeated in *For Whom the Bell Tolls*, speaking of Robert Jordan: "once you got rid of your own self, the always ridding of self that you had to do in war. Where there could be no self. Where yourself is only to be lost" (447). David Bourne's wartime experience is similar: "nobody knows about himself when he is really involved. Yourself isn't worth considering. It would be shameful at the time" (GOE 184).

12. In *The Garden of Eden*, Hemingway offers a convoluted restatement of that idea, giving it a creative accent: "And you must always remember the things you believed because if you know them they will be there in the writing and you won't betray them" (166).

13. James is quoting from Ribot's *Les maladies de la memoire* (Paris: Librairie Germer Balliere, 1881). The English translation is *The Diseases of Memory*, trans. J. Fitzgerald (New York: Fitzgerald, 1883).

14. In *The Garden of Eden*, David Bourne "had his father's ability to forget" (147). In Hemingway's manuscript fragment on the war, entitled "A Story to Skip: A Badly Organized Story of No Importance," he writes: "A broken heart means that never can

you remember and not to be able to remember is very different from forgetting" (qtd. in Griffin 115).

15. See *Under Kilimanjaro*, in which Hemingway drinks cider that "tasted like Michigan" (206), a place he recalls warmly from his childhood. The memory of a taste is described in the harrowing "A Way You'll Never Be," as somebody mentions ether, to which Nick Adams responds: "'I can taste that still,' Nick remembered suddenly and completely" (SS 406).

16. In a 1933 letter to Maxwell Perkins, Hemingway wrote, "I'm going to write damned good memoirs when I write them because I'm jealous of no one, have a rat trap memory and the documents" (SL 396), suggesting the value of the text's fidelity to actual experience.

Chapter 4. "The Stream with No Visible Flow"

1. "To me," Rawlings gushed, "you are pre-eminently the artist" (JFK, Incoming Correspondence). Rawlings (1896–1953) is most famous for her 1938 novel, *The Yearling*.

2. For the notion of Jordan being "cold in the head," see earlier in *For Whom the Bell Tolls*, as he remarks about the act of dynamiting: "In this you have to have much head and be very cold in the head" (21). Jordan is forced to kill Kashkin, and his reaction is similar: "It was very strange because he had experienced absolutely no emotion about the shooting of Kashkin. He expected that at some time he might have it. But so far there had been absolutely none" (171). After a quarrel with Pablo, Jordan's "head was clear and cold from the strain of the difficulty" (60). Pilar later praises Jordan behind his back: "The boy is smart . . . Smart and cold. Very cold in the head" (94). Jordan tells Maria, who wants to help him: "No. What I do now I do alone and very coldly in my head" (172). As David Bourne prepares to write, "His coldness had come back as the time for working moved closer" (GOE 194).

3. To rebut Wilson's concern about the precise thoughts and memories that Hudson buries: "But why did I ever leave Tom's mother in the first place? You'd better not think about that, he told himself. That is one thing you had better not think about" (13). Later: "He thought that he would lie down and think about nothing. . . . He knew there was no use thinking of the girl who had been Tom's mother nor all the things they had done and the places they had been nor how they had broken up. There was no use thinking about Tom. He had stopped that as soon as he had heard. There was no use thinking about the others. He had lost them, too, and there was no use thinking about them" (369). When someone in a bar asks Hudson if they should drink to Tom, Hudson responds, "'Shit, no.' . . . He could feel it all coming up; everything he had not thought about; all the grief he had put away and walled out and never even thought of on the trip nor all this morning" (257). In another vivid example, a memory of his son asking Hudson for a kitten: "'Papa, can't we have him?' asked the one of his sons, that he did not think about anymore" (206). Hemingway's middle son, Patrick, calls the first part of *Islands in the Stream* "very much the story of an artist remembering his children" ("*Islands*" 13).

4. In a letter to Scribner on 20 July 1951, Hemingway says the book about the sea is "some 1900 to 2000 pages of Mss" (SL 730). As posthumous publications prove and as the archives of the Hemingway archives in the John F. Kennedy Library confirm, Hemingway wrote an enormous amount of material for his projected magnum opus.

5. During the urgency of battle in *For Whom the Bell Tolls*, Primitivo begins to tell Pilar, "'If a man has a heart and a little imagination,'" before Pilar interrupts: "'He should learn to control them'" (299). This distinction between intuition and self-conscious intellect is also delineated in the epigraph to "Scott Fitzgerald" in *A Moveable Feast*: "*His talent was as natural as the pattern that was made by the dust on a butterfly's wings. At one time he understood it no more than the butterfly did and he did not know when it was brushed or marred. Later he became conscious of his damaged wings and of their construction and he learned to think and could not fly any more because the love of flight was gone and he could only remember when it had been effortless*" (147, emphasis in original).

6. Cf. General Golz, who prefigures this stance of nonthinking: "I never think at all. Why should I? I am *Général Sovietique*. I never think. Do not try to trap me into thinking" (FWBT 8). Golz continues this attitude, as chapter 6 will discuss. In a related vein, Jordan tells Karkov that he has suspended thought until after the war; however, this proves to be a struggle. Before blowing the bridge, Jordan almost sympathizes with the sentry who will be killed, and then he "lay there and watched the road and tried not to think at all" (433), telling himself, "Just do not think at all" (434).

7. As awkward as the term "internal dialogue" is, it is analogous to the "mental conversation" that Hemingway eventually found expendable in the original draft of "Big Two-Hearted River" (SL 133). In "A Clean, Well-Lighted Place," too, the old waiter "continued a conversation with himself" (SS 382), which then leads to a stream-of-consciousness passage, including his famous *nada* prayer.

8. A 1939 essay by Lionel Trilling contains an intriguing point on this issue: "And when we think how quickly 'mind' capitulates in a crisis, how quickly, for example, it accommodated itself to the war and served it and glorified it, revulsion from it and a turning to the life of action—reduced, to be sure, to athleticism: but skilful physical effort is perhaps something intellectuals dismiss as a form of activity—can be the better understood" (66).

9. Ralph Waldo Emerson refers to action as the "preamble of thought, the transition through which it passes from the unconscious to the conscious" (49). Emerson urges the interrelation of thought and action and decries the type of scholar who would be a "mere thinker" (44), the bookworm he scorns.

Chapter 5. Beating Mr. Turgenev

1. Hemingway referred to Turgenev as "the greatest writer there ever was" (SL 179), yet also bragged to William Faulkner that in his "first fight" he had "Beat Turgenieff . . . soundly and for time" (SL 626). He told Lillian Ross, "I started out very quiet and I beat Mr. Turgenev" (48); to Charles Scribner Jr. he claimed: "I tried for Mr.

Turgenieff first and it wasn't too hard" (SL 673). Hemingway titled his 1926 parody *The Torrents of Spring* in eponymous homage to the 1872 Turgenev novella, a tribute he would repeat seven years later with "Fathers and Sons," the final Nick Adams story. Jake Barnes reads Turgenev in the heady Pamplona nighttime, just as his pastoral excursion to Burguete with Bill Gorton recalls *A Sportsman's Sketches*, usually considered Turgenev's masterpiece. In *Green Hills of Africa*, Hemingway cites Turgenev as the model for authentically rendering natural terrain: "through Turgenieff," he writes, "I knew that I had lived there [i.e., Russia in the mid-nineteenth century]" (108). Henry James has an identical observation of reading Turgenev: "His works savour strongly of his native soil, like those of all great novelists, and give one who has read them all a strange sense of having had a prolonged experience of Russia. We seem to have travelled there in dreams, to have dwelt there in another state of being" ("Ivan Turgenev" 974–75). When asked to name his influences, Hemingway listed Turgenev fifth: "Mark Twain, Flaubert, Stendhal, Bach, Turgenev, Tolstoi, Dostoevski, Chekhov" (Plimpton 27).

2. In *Under Kilimanjaro*, Hemingway echoes this point: "This looking and not seeing things was a great sin, I thought, and one that was easy to fall into. It was always the beginning of something bad and I thought that we did not deserve to live in the world if we did not see it" (225). In the introduction to Hemingway's collection of short stories in 1938, he writes that the artist's job consists of "going where you have to go, and doing what you have to do, and seeing what you have to see" (SS vi), still prizing action, performance, and vision.

3. *Demons* (also known as *The Devils* or *The Possessed*) is not listed among Dostoevsky books that Hemingway read, although he did own *Dostoyevsky: A Life*, Avrahm Yarmolinsky's 1934 biography (Reynolds, *Hemingway's Reading* 204), in which Dostoevsky's satire of Turgenev in *Demons* is detailed. Yarmolinsky describes Turgenev as being "crudely and maliciously caricatured" (295).

4. Depending on the account, the criminal's name is spelled Tropman, Troppman, Tropmann, or Traupmann. The surname of the victims has been spelled Kink and Kinck. Likewise, Turgenev's story—originally titled *Kazn' Tropmana*—is given various English titles. Except when quoting other sources directly, I have adhered to David Magarshack's standard translation.

5. Cézanne is an interesting figure in a discussion of the aesthetic of witness: his favorite poem was Baudelaire's "Une Charogne" ("A Carcass") from *The Flowers of Evil*, which describes a couple witnessing a decaying, maggot-infested animal corpse, and in which the speaker of the poem explains that the object of his affection will one day stink and decay, just like the carrion. Rilke stated in 1907 that this Baudelaire poem contains "the key to 'the whole evolution towards objectivity in expression'" (170, fn. 15), delineating the precise debate between Dostoevsky and Turgenev. See McAlmon's anecdote about Hemingway, later in this chapter.

6. In the novel's typescript, the final phrase: "so I saw no more" is added in Hemingway's hand, a rare addition to a version that contains comparatively few late edits (JFK 83).

7. In a mimetic rendering of frustration, Hemingway himself did not witness the actual lynching on which this incident is based but instead fictionalized an experience of his older sister, Marcelline (Baker, "Empirical Imagination" 105).

8. Cf. a similar moment in *Under Kilimanjaro*: "I put my arm around Mary and turned her away so she would not see Charo slip the knife into the sticking place which would make the old bull legal meat for all Mohammedans" (65).

9. Miriam Mandel points out that E.R. actually refers to Elizabeth Hadley Richardson, Hemingway's first wife (151).

Chapter 6. That Supreme Moment of Complete Knowledge

1. In a letter to Ezra Pound on 5 August 1923, Hemingway claims to have "redone the death of Maera altogether different" (SL 91), indicating his pride at his new depiction of Maera's dying moment. As the repeated takes preserved at the JFK Library demonstrate, Hemingway was indeed determined to break through to a more profound level of meaning.

2. The relevant passage from *The Scarlet Letter*: "Reminiscences, the most trifling and immaterial, passages of infancy and school-days, sports, childish quarrels, and the little domestic traits of her maiden years, came swarming back upon her, intermingled with recollections of whatever was gravest in her subsequent life; one picture precisely as vivid as another; as if all were of similar importance, or all alike a play. Possibly, it was an instinctive device of her spirit, to relieve itself, by the exhibition of these phantasmagoric forms, from the cruel weight and hardness of the reality" (125).

3. Cf. chapter V of *In Our Time*, in which the execution of six cabinet ministers is portrayed objectively, although one man's fear is shown through his legs that refuse to function.

4. Hemingway borrowed *The Idiot* from Sylvia Beach's Shakespeare & Co. in 1929 (Reynolds, *Hemingway's Reading* 118).

5. Cf. "A Day's Wait," from *Winner Take Nothing*, in which the boy who believes he is dying "was evidently holding tight onto himself about something" (SS 438). The phrasing is also reminiscent of the description of Nick Adams in "Big Two-Hearted River" as he watches the trout "holding themselves steady in the current with wavering fins" (SS 209)—an obvious and powerful objective correlative.

6. In the manuscript of *A Farewell to Arms*, the same moment is also described provocatively, using similar terms: "Then I floated, hesitated and instead of going on I felt myself *slide* back as though there was a long thin wire through the center of my soul. The me that was gone out *slid* down that wire through nothing and the wind[;] twice it caught and stood still and once it turned completely over on the wire and then it jerked and stopped and I was back" (qtd. in Reynolds, *Hemingway's First War* 30–31, emphasis added).

Chapter 7. Reading Through Hemingway's Void

1. In "The Battler," Bugs knocks Ad Francis unconscious, claiming, "I have to do it to change him when he gets that way" (SS 136).

2. Although Brett Ashley's claims about herself are arguably fatuous, in the heights of her love of Pedro, she tells Jake, "I feel altogether changed," suggesting a conversion of her own (SAR 211).

3. Cf. Hemingway's short story "The Sea Change," in which a man's conversion—in this case his being convinced that his wife's lesbianism is arousing rather than unfaithful—is expressed similarly: "He was not the same-looking man as he had been before he had told her to go. . . . 'I'm a different man, James,' he said to the barman. 'You see in me quite a different man.'. . . As he looked in the glass, he saw he was really quite a different-looking man. . . . The young man saw himself in the mirror behind the bar. 'I said I was a different man, James,' he said. Looking into the mirror he saw that this was quite true" (SS 400–401).

4. In "On Writing": "He wanted to be a great writer. He was pretty sure he would be. He knew it in lots of ways. He would in spite of everything. It was hard, though" (NAS 238).

5. This sentiment recurs in *For Whom the Bell Tolls*, from the Russian journalist Karkov: "I am a journalist. But like all journalists I wish to write literature" (244). Hemingway wrote Maxwell Perkins in 1933: "I am a journalist *and an imaginative writer*" (Bruccoli, *Only Thing* 203, emphasis in original).

6. As further evidence, Hemingway wrote Maxwell Perkins to compliment the image of Jake Barnes on the first cover of *The Sun Also Rises*. The man, Hemingway writes, "looks much as I had imagined Jake Barnes; it looks very much like a writer who had been saddened by the loss or atrophy of certain non replaceable parts. . . . Still it is fine to have at last succeeded in looking like a writer" (SL 223).

7. As mentioned in note 6 of the previous chapter, the same moment of conversion is described vividly in the manuscript of *A Farewell to Arms*.

8. The word "rebirth" is a loaded one in *Across the River and into the Trees*, as Colonel Cantwell muses over Renaissance art, and his love interest is named Renata.

9. T. S. Eliot incorporates Dante's phrase into lines 37–41 of *The Waste Land*: "—Yet when we came back, late, from the Hyacinth garden, / Your arms full, and your hair wet, I could not / Speak, and my eyes failed, I was neither / Living nor dead, and I knew nothing, / Looking into the heart of light, the silence" (38).

10. By "the road to Tarsus," Hemingway refers to Saul of Tarsus whose conversion took place on the road to Damascus. Hemingway used a similar comparison in his 1953 foreword to *Man and Beast in Africa*, a book by François Sommer, in describing the conversion a man undergoes when he becomes a lover of hunting: "In each person the changes come in a different way. There is no sudden thing such as happened to Saint Paul or to Saint Ignatius Loyola for any who care to kill cleanly and never to excess"

(Bruccoli, *Mechanism* 127). In a 1932 letter to John Dos Passos, Hemingway disparages "recent converts" like Malcolm Cowley and Edmund Wilson, of whom he writes: "He is sometimes boreing [*sic*] because, like any convert, he hasn't the necessary elasticity but he is damned good. But what about the other boys who had no kick against the system as long as it functioned. Did they all see a light like Saint Paul or is it the newest and most necessary religion?" (SL 374–75).

11. As Pilar describes Pablo earlier: "But now he is finished. The plug has been drawn and the wine has all run out of the skin" (FWBT 89).

12. Among Hemingway's many considered titles for the story are other possibilities that corroborate this theme: "The Coming Man"; "The New Man"; and "The Short Life of Francis Macomber" (Smith, *Reader's Guide* 329).

13. Cf. *The Sun Also Rises*, in which Romero's bullfighting is described similarly: "The fight with Cohn had not touched his spirit but his face had been smashed and his body hurt. He was wiping all that out now. Each thing that he did with this bull wiped that out a little cleaner" (223).

14. For another example, after David Bourne's manuscripts are destroyed, "He felt completely hollow" (GOE 216) and "empty and dead in his heart" (219); however, like Macomber, he fills the void when he is able to rewrite the material better than it was before and is thus "Bourne" again.

15. In Hemingway's mocking essay "The Art of the Short Story," he writes of Margot: "Now this woman doesn't change. She has been better, but she will never be any better anymore" (93).

16. Wilson quotes the speech as: "By my troth, I care not; a man can die but once; we owe God a death and let it go which way it will he that dies this year is quit for the next" (32). In *2 Henry IV*, Feeble's actual quote to his fellow soldiers is: "By my troth I care not; a man can die but once, we owe God a death. I'll ne'er bear a base mind. And't be my dest'ny so; and't be not so. No man's too good to serve's prince, and let it go which way it will, he that dies this year is quit for the next" (III.ii.234–38). In his introduction to *Men at War*, Hemingway spends time on this point, writing: "I was very ignorant at nineteen and had read little and I remember the sudden happiness and the feeling of having a permanent protecting talisman when a young British officer I met when in the hospital first wrote out for me, so that I could remember them, these lines: '*By my troth, I care not: a man can die but once; we owe God a death . . . and let it go which way it will, he that dies this year is quit for the next.*' That is probably the best thing that is written in this book and, with nothing else, a man can get along all right on that" (xii, emphasis in original). Cf. a relevant exchange between Frederic Henry and Catherine Barkley: "'Nothing ever happens to the brave.' 'They die of course.' 'But only once.' 'I don't know. Who said that?' 'The coward dies a thousand deaths, the brave but one?' 'Of course. Who said it?' 'I don't know.' 'He was probably a coward,' she said. 'He knew a great deal about cowards but nothing about the brave. The brave dies perhaps two thousand deaths if he's intelligent. He simply doesn't mention them'" (FTA 139–40). This exchange also alludes to Shakespeare, from *Julius Caesar*: "Cowards die many times before their deaths, / The valiant

never taste of death but once. / Of all the wonders that I yet have heard. / It seems to me most strange that men should fear, / Seeing that death, a necessary end, / Will come when it will come" (II.ii.32–37).

17. "Suddenness" is a crucial term in conversion studies. Garry Wills notes: "The stories of Paul and Augustine have led to a belief that 'real' conversion is sudden, effected by the incursion of an outside force, and emotionally wrenching" (*Conversion* 3). Wills writes that these two most renowned conversions "seem abrupt, emotionally charged, with a great lightning bolt dividing the lives of Paul and Augustine into two main parts" (14). In Macomber's conversion, Margot acknowledges, "You've gotten awfully brave, awfully suddenly" (SS 34).

18. One reason Arthur Waldhorn links "The Short Happy Life of Francis Macomber" with "The Snows of Kilimanjaro" is that both Francis and Harry "die at the moment of insight" (151).

Works Cited

Aldridge, John. Rev. of *Islands in the Stream*. In *Hemingway: The Critical Heritage*. Edited by Jeffrey Meyers, 548–56. Boston: Routledge & Kegan Paul, 1982.

Alighieri, Dante. *The Divine Comedy: Inferno*. Translated by Charles S. Singleton. Vol. 1. Princeton, NJ: Princeton University Press, 1989.

Allen, Elizabeth Cheresh. *Beyond Realism: Turgenev's Poetics of Secular Salvation*. Stanford: Stanford University Press, 1992.

Anderson, William R., Jr. "*Islands in the Stream*—The Initial Reception." *Fitzgerald/Hemingway Annual* (1971): 326–32.

Andrews, Larry. "'Big Two-Hearted River': The Essential Hemingway." *Missouri English Bulletin* 25 (May 1969): 1–7.

Augustine. *The Confessions*. Translated by Maria Boulding, O.S.B. Vol. 1 of *The Works of Saint Augustine*. 20 vols. Hyde Park, NY: New City Press, 1990.

Baddeley, Alan. "What Is Autobiographical Memory?" In *Theoretical Perspectives on Autobiographical Memory*. Edited by Martin A. Conway et al., 13–29. Boston: Kluwer Academic Publishers, 1992.

Baker, Carlos. *Hemingway: The Writer as Artist*. 4th ed. Princeton, NJ: Princeton University Press, 1972.

———. "Hemingway's Empirical Imagination." In *Individual and Community: Variations on a Theme in American Fiction*. Edited by Kenneth H. Baldwin and David K. Kirby, 94–111. Durham, NC: Duke University Press, 1975.

Baldwin, James. *Nobody Knows My Name*. 1961. New York: Vintage, 1993.

Beegel, Susan F. "Conclusion: The Critical Reputation." In *Cambridge Companion to Hemingway*. Edited by Scott Donaldson, 269–99. Cambridge, UK: Cambridge University Press, 1996.

———. *Hemingway's Craft of Omission: Four Manuscript Examples*. Ann Arbor, MI: UMI Research Press, 1988.

Bergson, Henri. *Creative Evolution*. 1911. Translated by Arthur Mitchell. New York: Dover, 1998.

———. *L'évolution créatrice*. Paris: F. Alcan, 1908.

———. *Matter and Memory*. 1908. Translated by N. M. Paul and W. S. Palmer. New York: Zone Books, 1991.

————. "The Perception of Change." In *The Creative Mind: An Introduction to Metaphysics*. Translated by Mabelle L. Andison, 107–32. Mineola, NY: Dover, 2007.

————. "'Phantasms of the Living' and 'Psychical Research.'" In *Mind-Energy: Lectures and Essays*. Translated by H. Wildon Carr, 75–103. New York: Henry Holt, 1920.

————. *Time and Free Will: An Essay on the Immediate Data of Consciousness*. 1913. Translated by F. L. Pogson. Mineola, NY: Dover, 2001.

Blake, William. *The Complete Poetry and Prose of William Blake*. Berkeley: University of California Press, 1982.

Blotner, Joseph. *Faulkner: A Biography*. 2 vols. New York: Random House, 1974.

Boutroux, Émile. *The Relation Between Thought and Action: From the German and from the Classical Point of View: The Herbert Spencer Lecture, Delivered at Oxford, October 20, 1917*. Oxford: Clarendon Press, 1918.

Brasch, James D., and Joseph Sigman. *Hemingway's Library: A Composite Record*. New York: Garland, 1981.

Breit, Harvey. "The Sun Also Rises in Stockholm." *New York Times Book Review*. 7 November 1954: 1, 44.

————. "Talk with Mr. Hemingway." *New York Times Book Review*. 17 September 1950: 14.

Brewer, William F. "What Is Autobiographical Memory?" *Autobiographical Memory*. Edited by David C. Rubin, 25–49. New York: Cambridge University Press, 1986.

Brian, Denis. *The True Gen: An Intimate Portrait of Hemingway by Those Who Knew Him*. New York: Grove Press, 1988.

Bruccoli, Matthew J., ed. *Hemingway and the Mechanism of Fame*. Columbia: University of South Carolina Press, 2006.

————, ed. *The Only Thing That Counts: The Ernest Hemingway–Maxwell Perkins Correspondence, 1925–1947*. New York: Scribner's, 1996.

Brumfield, William C. "Invitation to a Beheading: Turgenev and Tropmann." *Canadian-American Slavic Studies* 17.1 (Spring 1983): 79–88.

Budgen, Frank. *Myselves When Young*. New York: Oxford University Press, 1970.

Burwell, Rose Marie. *Hemingway: The Postwar Years and the Posthumous Novels*. Cambridge, UK: Cambridge University Press, 1996.

Cain, William E. "Death Sentences: Rereading *The Old Man and the Sea*." *Sewanee Review* 64.1 (Winter 2006): 112–25.

Campbell, Joseph, with Bill Moyers. *The Power of Myth*. Edited by Betty Sue Flowers. New York: Anchor, 1988.

Chopin, Kate. *The Awakening*. 1899. New York: Avon Books, 1972.

Cohn, Dorrit. *Transparent Minds: Narrative Modes for Presenting Consciousness in Fiction*. Princeton, NJ: Princeton University Press, 1978.

Conrad, Joseph. *Heart of Darkness*. 1899. Orchard Park, NY: Broadview, 1996.

Cowley, Malcolm. "A Double Life, Half Told." *The Atlantic* 226 (December 1970): 105–8.

———. "A Portrait of Mister Papa." In *Ernest Hemingway: The Man and His Work.* Edited by John K. M. McCaffrey, 34–56. New York: World Publishing, 1950.

Dawson, L. S. *Memoirs of Hydrography: Part II.* Eastbourne: Keay, 1885.

DeFalco, Joseph M. "Hemingway's Islands and Streams: Minor Tactics for Heavy Pressure." In *Hemingway In Our Time.* Edited by Richard Astro and Jackson J. Benson, 39–51. Corvallis: Oregon State University Press, 1974.

Dennett, Daniel C. *Consciousness Explained.* New York: Little, Brown & Co., 1991.

DeVoto, Bernard. Rev. of *Green Hills of Africa.* In *Hemingway: The Critical Heritage.* Edited by Jeffrey Meyers, 210–13. Boston: Routledge & Kegan Paul, 1982.

———. Rev. of *To Have and Have Not.* In *Hemingway: The Critical Heritage.* Edited by Jeffrey Meyers, 223–26. Boston: Routledge & Kegan Paul, 1982.

Dickinson, Emily. *The Collected Poems of Emily Dickinson.* New York: Barnes & Noble Classics, 2003.

di Prima, Diane. *Pieces of a Song: Selected Poems.* San Francisco: City Lights Books, 1990.

Dolan, Marc. "The Good Writer's Tale: The Fictional Method of Hemingway's 'Scott Fitzgerald.'" *Hemingway Review* 12.2 (Spring 1993): 62–71.

Donaldson, Scott. *By Force of Will: The Life and Art of Ernest Hemingway.* New York: Penguin, 1978.

Dostoevsky, Fyodor. *Demons.* 1872. Translated by Richard Pevear and Larissa Volokhonsky. New York: Vintage, 1995.

———. *The Idiot.* 1869. Translated by Richard Pevear and Larissa Volokhonsky. New York: Knopf, 2002.

———. *Notes from the Underground.* 1864. Translated by Constance Garnett. New York: Dover, 1992.

Doyle, Ann, and Neal B. Houston. "Adriana Ivancich on Death." *Hemingway Review* 4.2 (Spring 1985): 53.

Eby, Carl P. *Hemingway's Fetishism: Psychoanalysis and the Mirror of Manhood.* Albany: SUNY Press, 1999.

Edel, Leon. "The Art of Evasion." In *Hemingway: A Collection of Critical Essays.* Edited by Robert P. Weeks, 169–71. Englewood Cliffs, NJ: Prentice Hall, 1962.

———. *The Psychological Novel, 1900–1950.* Philadelphia: Lippincott, 1955.

Eliot, T.S. *The Complete Poems and Plays, 1909–1950.* New York: Harcourt, Brace & World, 1952.

Emerson, Ralph Waldo. "The American Scholar." In *The Essential Writings of Ralph Waldo Emerson.* Edited by Brooks Atkinson, 43–59. New York: Modern Library, 2000.

Eriksen, Richard. *Consciousness, Life, and the Fourth Dimension.* London: Gylendal, 1923.

Faulkner, William. *As I Lay Dying.* 1930. New York: Vintage, 1990.

———. *Essays, Speeches, and Public Letters.* Edited by James B. Meriwether. New York: Modern Library, 2004.

———. *Light in August.* 1932. New York: Vintage, 1990.

———. *The Sound and the Fury.* 1929. New York: Vintage, 1990.

————. *The Wild Palms [If I Forget Thee, Jerusalem]*. 1939. New York: Vintage, 1995.

Fitch, Noel Riley. *Sylvia Beach and the Lost Generation: A History of Literary Paris in the Twenties and Thirties*. New York: Norton, 1983.

Fitzgerald, F. Scott. *A Life in Letters*. Edited by Matthew J. Bruccoli. New York: Touchstone, 1995.

————. *Novels and Stories, 1920–1922*. New York: Library of America, 2000.

Flaubert, Gustave. *Madame Bovary*. 1857. Translated by Eleanor Marx Aveling and Paul de Man. New York: Norton, 2005.

Frank, Joseph. *Dostoevsky: The Miraculous Years, 1865–1871*. Princeton: Princeton University Press, 1995.

Freccero, John. *Dante: The Poetics of Conversion*. Edited by Rachel Jacoff. Cambridge, MA: Harvard University Press, 1986.

Freehof, Solomon B. "Modern Moods and Modern Quests." *Carnegie Magazine* 27 (February 1953): 44–48.

Freud, Sigmund. *The Complete Psychological Works of Sigmund Freud*. Vol. 14. Translated and edited by James Strachey. London: Hogarth Press, 1957.

————. *The Interpretation of Dreams*. 1900. Translated by A. A. Brill. New York: Modern Library, 1994.

————. *The Psychopathology of Everyday Life*. 1914. Translated by A. A. Brill. Mineola, NY: Dover, 2003.

Ganzel, Dewey. "*A Farewell to Arms*: The Danger of Imagination." *Sewanee Review* 79.4 (Autumn 1971): 576–97.

Gatrell, V. A. C. *The Hanging Tree: Execution and the English People, 1770–1868*. Oxford: Oxford University Press, 1994.

Gibb, Robert. "He Made Him Up: 'Big Two-Hearted River' as Doppleganger." In *Critical Essays on Ernest Hemingway's "In Our Time."* Edited by Michael S. Reynolds. Boston: G. K. Hall, 1983.

Gingrich, Arnold. "Publisher's Page: Notes on *Bimini*." *Esquire*. October 1970: 6, 12.

Gold, Daniel B., and Daniel M. Wegner. "The Origins of Ruminative Thought: Trauma, Incompleteness, Nondisclosure, and Suppression." *Journal of Applied Social Psychology* 25 (1995): 1245–61.

Graves, Robert. *Difficult Questions, Easy Answers*. London: Cassell, 1972.

Grebstein, Sheldon Norman. *Hemingway's Craft*. Carbondale: Southern Illinois University Press, 1973.

Greyson, Bruce, and Ian Stevenson. "The Phenomenology of Near-Death Experiences." *American Journal of Psychiatry* 137.10 (October 1980): 1193–96.

Griffin, Peter. *Along with Youth: Hemingway, the Early Years*. New York: Oxford University Press, 1985.

Hagemann, Meyly Chin. "Hemingway's Secret: Visual to Verbal Art." *Journal of Modern Literature* 7.1 (1979): 87–112.

Hawthorne, Nathaniel. *The Scarlet Letter*. 1850. Edited by John Stephen Martin. Orchard Park, NY: Broadview, 1995.

Hayden, Dolores. *The Power of Place*. Cambridge: MIT Press, 1976.

Hazlitt, Henry. "Take Hemingway." *New York Sun*. 28 September 1929: 38.

Heaton, C. P. "Style in *The Old Man and the Sea*." *Style* 4 (1970): 11–27.

Hemingway, Ernest. *Across the River and into the Trees*. 1950. New York: Scribner's, 1996.

———. "The Art of the Short Story." *Paris Review* 79 (Spring 1981): 85–102.

———. "Because I Think Deeper." Folder 270A. Hemingway Collection. John F. Kennedy Library. Boston, MA.

———. *By-line: Ernest Hemingway: Selected Articles and Dispatches of Four Decades*. Edited by William White. New York: Scribner's, 1967.

———. *Complete Poems*. Edited by Nicholas Gerogiannis. Lincoln: University of Nebraska Press, 1992.

———. *The Complete Short Stories of Ernest Hemingway: The Finca Vigía Edition*. New York: Scribner's, 2003.

———. *The Dangerous Summer*. 1960. New York: Scribner's, 2004.

———. *Death in the Afternoon*. 1932. New York: Scribner's, 1960.

———. *A Farewell to Arms*. 1929. New York: Scribner's, 1995.

———. Unpublished Manuscript of *A Farewell to Arms*. Folder 64. Hemingway Collection. John F. Kennedy Library. Boston, MA.

———. *The Fifth Column and the First Forty-nine Stories*. New York: Scribner's, 1938.

———. *For Whom the Bell Tolls*. 1940. New York: Scribner's, 1995.

———. Unpublished Manuscript of *For Whom the Bell Tolls*. Folder 83. Hemingway Collection. John F. Kennedy Library. Boston, MA.

———. *The Garden of Eden*. 1986. New York: Scribner's, 2003.

———. Unpublished Manuscript of *The Garden of Eden*. Folder 422. Hemingway Collection. John F. Kennedy Library. Boston, MA.

———. *Green Hills of Africa*. 1935. New York: Scribner's, 2003.

———. *Islands in the Stream*. 1970. New York: Scribner's, 2004.

———. Unpublished Manuscript of *Islands in the Stream*. Folders 112–13. Hemingway Collection. John F. Kennedy Library. Boston, MA.

———, ed. *Men at War: The Best War Stories of All Time*. 1942. New York: Crown Publishers, 1955.

———. *A Moveable Feast*. 1964. New York: Touchstone, 1996.

———. *A Moveable Feast: The Restored Edition*. Edited by Seán Hemingway. New York: Scribner's, 2009.

———. *The Nick Adams Stories*. 1972. New York: Scribner's, 1999.

———. *The Old Man and the Sea*. New York: Scribner's, 1952.

———. "Prologue." In *Hemingway: Essays of Reassessment*. Edited by Frank Scafella, 3–5. New York: Oxford University Press, 1991.

———. *Selected Letters, 1917–1961*. Edited by Carlos Baker. New York: Scribner's, 1981.

———. *The Short Stories of Ernest Hemingway*. New York: Scribner's, 2003.

———. *The Sun Also Rises*. 1926. New York: Scribner's, 2003.

———. *The Sun Also Rises: A Facsimile Edition.* 2 vols. Edited by Matthew J. Bruccoli. Detroit: Omnigraphics, 1990.

———. *To Have and Have Not.* 1937. New York: Scribner's, 1996.

———. Unpublished Manuscript of *To Have and Have Not.* Folder 204. Hemingway Collection. John F. Kennedy Library. Boston, MA.

———. *The Torrents of Spring.* 1926. New York: Scribner's, 1998.

———. *Under Kilimanjaro.* Kent, OH: Kent State University Press, 2005.

———. "The Unpublished Opening of *The Sun Also Rises.*" *Antaeus* 33 (1979): 7–14.

———. "The Way Fish Die." Unpublished Manuscript. Folder 812. Hemingway Collection. John F. Kennedy Library. Boston, MA.

Hemingway, Mariel. *Finding My Balance: A Memoir.* New York: Simon & Schuster, 2003.

Hemingway, Patrick. "*Islands in the Stream*: A Son Remembers." In *Ernest Hemingway: The Writer in Context.* Edited by James Nagel, 13–18. Madison: University of Wisconsin Press, 1984.

———. "My Papa, Papa." *Playboy* 15 (December 1968): 197–200, 263–68.

Hotchner, A. E. *Papa Hemingway.* 1955. New York: Carrol & Graf, 1999.

Howe, Irving. "Great Man Going Down." *Harper's* (October 1970): 120–25.

Hughes, Catharine. "Hemingway's Coda." *Progressive* 34 (December 1970): 47–48.

Jackson, Robert Louis. *Dialogues with Dostoevsky: The Overwhelming Questions.* Stanford: Stanford University Press, 1993.

James, Henry. *The Art of the Novel.* New York: Scribner's, 1934.

———. "Ivan Turgenev." 1874. In *French Writers, Other European Writers, the Prefaces to the New York Edition,* 968–99. New York: Library of America, 1984.

———. *The Portrait of a Lady.* 1880–81, 1908. New York: Norton, 1995.

James, William. *The Principles of Psychology.* 2 vols. 1890. New York: Dover, 1950.

———. *A Pluralistic Universe.* In *Writings: 1902–1910,* 625–819. New York: Library of America, 1987.

———. *The Varieties of Religious Experience.* 1902. New York: Barnes & Noble Classics, 2004.

Joyce, James. *A Portrait of the Artist as a Young Man.* 1916. New York: Viking Penguin, 1964.

———. *Ulysses: The Corrected Text.* 1922. Edited by Hans Walter Gabler. New York: Random House, 1996.

Justus, James H. "The Later Fiction: Hemingway and the Aesthetics of Failure." In *Hemingway: New Critical Essays.* Edited by A. Robert Lee, 103–21. Totowa, NJ: Barnes & Noble, 1983.

Kale, Verna. "Hemingway's Poetry and the Paris Apprenticeship." *Hemingway Review* 26.2 (Spring 2007): 58–73.

Kaufmann, Edgar, Jr., and Ben Raeburn, eds. *Frank Lloyd Wright: Writings and Buildings.* New York: Horizon Press, 1960.

Kern, Stephen. *The Culture of Time & Space, 1880–1918.* Cambridge, MA: Harvard University Press, 2003.

Kletti, Roy, and Russell Noyes Jr. (translating Oskar Pfister). "Mental States in Mortal Danger." *Essence* 5.1 (1981): 6–19.

Lawrence, D. H. "*In Our Time*: A Review." In *Hemingway: A Collection of Critical Essays*. Edited by Robert P. Weeks, 93–94. Englewood Cliffs, NJ: Prentice Hall, 1962.

Lewis, Wyndham. "The Dumb Ox: A Study of Ernest Hemingway." In *Hemingway: The Critical Heritage*. Edited by Jeffrey Meyers, 186–209. Boston: Routledge & Kegan Paul, 1982.

———. *Rude Assignment: An Intellectual Autobiography*. 1950. Edited by Toby Foshay. Santa Barbara, CA: Black Sparrow Press, 1984.

Linhares, Alexandre, Eric P. Nichols, and John Paxton. "Why Life Should Flash Before One's Eyes: Episodic Memory and a Hypothesis Arising from the Recognition-Primed Decision Model." Center for Research on Concepts and Cognition: CRCC Technical Report 143. 1–4.

Lodge, David. *Consciousness and the Novel: Connected Essays*. Cambridge, MA: Harvard University Press, 2002.

Lounsberry, Barbara. "*Green Hills of Africa*: Hemingway's Celebration of Memory." *Hemingway Review* 2.2 (1983): 23–31.

Lynn, Kenneth S. *Hemingway*. Cambridge: Harvard University Press, 1995.

Mandel, Miriam B. "Hemingway Confirms the Importance of the Taurine Baptism: Fictional and Historic Case Studies." *Journal of Modern Literature* 23.1 (Fall 1999): 145–57.

Maudsley, Henry. *The Physiology of Mind*. London: Macmillan, 1876.

McAlmon, Robert. *Being Geniuses Together*. Revised with supplementary chapters and an afterword by Kay Boyle. Baltimore: Johns Hopkins University Press, 1997.

McCarthy, Cormac. *The Road*. New York: Vintage, 2006.

McNally, Richard J. *Remembering Trauma*. Cambridge, MA: Belknap Press of Harvard University Press, 2003.

Melville, Herman. *Moby-Dick; or, The Whale*. 1851. New York: Norton, 2002.

Moloney, Michael F. "Ernest Hemingway: The Missing Third Dimension." In *Hemingway and His Critics: An International Anthology*. Edited by Carlos Baker, 180–91. New York: Hill & Wang, 1961.

Moravia, Alberto. Obituary of Hemingway. In *Hemingway: The Critical Heritage*. Edited by Jeffrey Meyers, 437–42. Boston: Routledge & Kegan Paul, 1982.

Nakajima, Kenji. *"Big Two-Hearted River" as the Extreme of Hemingway's Nihilism*. Tokyo: Eichosha Publishing, 1979.

Nakjavani, Erik. "Hemingway on Nonthinking." *North Dakota Quarterly* 57.3 (Summer 1989): 173–98.

———. "Knowledge as Power: Robert Jordan as an Intellectual Hero." *Hemingway Review* 7.2 (Spring 1988): 131–46.

New Oxford Annotated Bible. Edited by Herbert G. May and Bruce M. Metzger. New York: Oxford University Press, 1973.

Newport, John Paul. "The Science of Golf Addiction." *Wall Street Journal*. 9 June 2007: 3.

Norris, Faith G. "*A Moveable Feast* and *Remembrance of Things Past*: Two Quests for Lost Time." In *Hemingway In Our Time*. Edited by Richard Astro and Jackson J. Benson, 99–111. Corvallis: Oregon State University Press, 1974.

Oates, Joyce Carol. "Dangling Men." *New York Review of Books*. 3 November 2005: 36–37, 40.

O'Brien, Richard Michael. "The Thematic Interrelation of the Concepts of Time and Thought in the Works of Ernest Hemingway." Ph.D. diss. New York University, 1969.

Oldsey, Bernard. *Hemingway's Hidden Craft: The Writing of "A Farewell to Arms."* University Park: Pennsylvania State University Press, 1979.

Ott, Mark P. *Sea of Change*. Kent, OH: Kent State University Press, 2008.

Ouspensky, P. D. *In Search of the Miraculous*. New York: Harcourt, Brace, 1949.

Pearsall, Robert Brainard. *The Life and Writings of Ernest Hemingway*. Amsterdam: Rodopi NV, 1973.

Pennebaker, James W. "Traumatic Experience and Psychosomatic Disease: Exploring the Roles of Behavioural Inhibition, Obsession, and Confiding." *Canadian Psychology* 26.2 (1985): 82–95.

Plimpton, George. "An Interview with Ernest Hemingway." In *Hemingway and His Critics*. Edited by Carlos Baker, 19–37. New York: Hill & Wang, 1961.

Poulet, Georges. "Bergson: The Theme of the Panoramic Vision of the Dying and Juxtaposition." Translated by Mark Cirino and William J. Hemminger. *PMLA* 126.2 (March 2011): 487–99.

———. *Proustian Space*. Translated by Elliot Coleman. Baltimore: Johns Hopkins University Press, 1977.

———. *Studies in Human Time*. Translated by Elliott Coleman. New York: Harper, 1959.

———. "Timelessness and Romanticism." *Journal of the History of Ideas* 15.1 (January 1954): 3–22.

Proust, Marcel. *Swann's Way*. 1913. Translated by C. K. Scott Moncrieff et al. New York: Modern Library, 2004.

Rahv, Philip. "The Social Muse and the Great Kudu." *Partisan Review* 4.1 (December 1937): 62–64.

Reynolds, Michael S. "False Dawn: *The Sun Also Rises* Manuscript." In *A Fair Day in the Affections: Literary Essays in Honor of Robert B. White, Jr.* Edited by Jack D. Durant and M. Thomas Hester, 171–86. Raleigh, NC: Winston Press, 1980.

———. *Hemingway: The 1930s*. New York: Norton, 1998.

———. *Hemingway: The Final Years*. New York: Norton, 2000.

———. *Hemingway: The Paris Years*. Cambridge, MA: Basil Blackwell, 1989.

———. *Hemingway's First War: The Making of "A Farewell to Arms."* Princeton, NJ: Princeton University Press, 1976.

———. *Hemingway's Reading, 1901–1940: An Inventory*. Princeton, NJ: Princeton University Press, 1981.

————. *The Young Hemingway.* New York: Norton, 1998.

Richardson, Robert D. *William James: In the Maelstrom of American Modernism.* Boston: Houghton Mifflin, 2006.

Ricks, Christopher. "At Sea with Ernest Hemingway." *New York Review of Books.* 8 October 1970: 17–19.

Ricoeur, Paul. *Memory, History, Forgetting.* Translated by Kathleen Blamey and David Pellauer. Chicago: University of Chicago Press, 2004.

Rilke, Rainer Maria. *The Notebooks of Malte Laurids Briggs.* 1910. Translated by Michael Hulse. New York: Penguin, 2009.

Rimbaud, Arthur. *Illuminations.* Translated by Louise Varèse. New York: New Directions, 1947.

Ross, Lillian. *Portrait of Hemingway.* New York: Simon & Schuster, 1961.

Savage, D. S. *The Withered Branch: Six Studies in the Modern Novel.* Great Neck, NY: Cora Collection Books, 1978.

Schacter, Daniel L. *The Seven Sins of Memory: How the Mind Forgets and Remembers.* New York: Houghton Mifflin, 2001.

Shakespeare, William. *The Riverside Shakespeare.* 2 vols. Boston: Houghton Mifflin, 1974.

Smith, Paul. "Hemingway's Apprentice Fiction: 1919–1921." *American Literature* 58.4 (December 1986): 574–88.

————. *A Reader's Guide to the Short Stories of Ernest Hemingway.* Boston: G. K. Hall, 1989.

Spilka, Mark. *Hemingway's Quarrel with Androgyny.* Lincoln: University of Nebraska Press, 1990.

————. "The Death of Love in *The Sun Also Rises.*" In *Hemingway and His Critics.* Edited by Carlos Baker, 80–92. New York: Hill & Wang, 1961.

Stein, Gertrude. "*Three Stories and Ten Poems* Reviewed." In *The Left Bank Revisited: Selections from the Paris Tribune, 1917–1934.* Compiled by Hugh D. Ford, 257. University Park: Pennsylvania State University Press, 1972.

Stewart, Matthew. *Modernism and Tradition in Ernest Hemingway's "In Our Time": A Guide for Students and Readers.* Rochester, NY: Camden House, 2001.

Stone, Robert. "American Dreamers: Melville and Kerouac." *New York Times Book Review.* 7 December 1997: 18, 84.

Strychacz, Thomas. *Hemingway's Theaters of Masculinity.* Baton Rouge: Louisiana State University Press, 2003.

Svoboda, Frederic Joseph. *Ernest Hemingway and "The Sun Also Rises": The Crafting of a Style.* Lawrence: University Press of Kansas, 1983.

Tanner, Tony. *The Reign of Wonder: Naivety and Reality in American Literature.* Cambridge, UK: Cambridge University Press, 1965.

————. Rev. of *A Moveable Feast.* In *Hemingway: The Critical Heritage.* Edited by Jeffrey Meyers, 476–82. Boston: Routledge & Kegan Paul, 1982.

"Traupmann and His Crimes." *The New York Times.* 20 January 1870: 4.

Trilling, Lionel. "Hemingway and His Critics." In *Hemingway and His Critics: An International Anthology.* Edited by Carlos Baker, 61–70. New York: Hill & Wang, 1961.

Turgenev, Ivan. "The Execution of Tropmann." 1870. In *Turgenev's Literary Reminiscences and Autobiographical Fragments*. Translated by David Magarshack, 244–70. New York: Farrar, Straus & Cudahy, 1958.

———. "Poems in Prose." In *The Essential Turgenev*. Edited by Elizabeth Cheresh Allen, 873–83. Evanston, IL: Northwestern University Press, 1994.

Twain, Mark. *Adventures of Huckleberry Finn*. 1884. Edited by Thomas Cooley. New York: Norton, 1999.

Updike, John. "Papa's Sad Testament." *New Statesman*. 16 October 1970: 489.

Wagner, Linda W. "The Poem of Santiago and Manolin." *Modern Fiction Studies* 19.4 (Winter 1973): 517–29.

Wagner-Martin, Linda, ed. *A Historical Guide to Ernest Hemingway*. New York: Oxford University Press, 2000.

Wain, John. "Ernest Hemingway: Aim and Achievement: Heroes with Wounds." *Observer* 9 (July 1961): 21.

Waites, Elizabeth A. *Memory Quest: Trauma and the Search for Personal History*. New York: Norton, 1997.

Waldhorn, Arthur. *A Reader's Guide to Ernest Hemingway*. New York: Farrar, Straus & Giroux, 1972.

Wegner, Daniel M. *White Bears and Other Unwanted Thoughts: Suppression, Obsession, and the Psychology of Mental Control*. New York: Guilford Press, 1994.

———. "You Can't Always Think What You Want: Problems in the Suppression of Unwanted Thoughts." In *Advances in Experimental Social Psychology*. Vol. 25. Edited by Mark Zanna, 193–225. San Diego: Academic Press, 1992.

Wegner, Daniel M., and James W. Pennebaker, eds. *Handbook of Mental Control*. Englewood Cliffs, NJ: Prentice Hall, 1993.

Wegner, Daniel M., Joann W. Shortt, Anne W. Blaker, and Michelle S. Page. "The Suppression of Exciting Thoughts." *Journal of Personality and Social Psychology* 58.3 (1990): 409–18.

Wells, Elizabeth. "A Comparative Statistical Analysis of the Prose Styles of F. Scott Fitzgerald and Ernest Hemingway." *Fitzgerald/Hemingway Annual* (1969): 47–67.

Wells, H. G. *The Time Machine*. 1895. Jefferson, NC: McFarland & Co., 1996.

Williams, William Carlos. *Selected Letters of William Carlos Williams*. Edited by John C. Thirlwall. New York: McDowell, Obolensky, 1957.

Wills, Garry. *Saint Augustine's Conversion*. New York: Viking, 2004.

———. *Saint Augustine's Memory*. New York: Viking, 2002.

Wilson, Edmund. "An Effort at Self-Revelation." *New Yorker*. 2 January 1971: 59–62.

———. "Mr. Hemingway's Dry Points." *Dial* 77 (October 1924): 340–41.

Wood, James. "Red Planet." *New Yorker*. 25 July 2005: 88–93.

Wyrick, Green D. "Hemingway and Bergson: The *Élan Vital*." *Modern Fiction Studies* 1.3 (August 1955): 17–19.

Yarmolinksy, Avrahm. *Dostoyevsky: A Life*. New York: Harcourt, Brace, 1934.

Young, Philip. *Ernest Hemingway: A Reconsideration*. University Park: Pennsylvania State University Press, 1966.

Index

175

Cosmopolitanism and Solidarity: Studies in Ethnoracial, Religious, and
  Professional Affiliation in the United States
David A. Hollinger

Thoreau's Democratic Withdrawal: Alienation, Participation, and Modernity
Shannon L. Mariotti

Seaway to the Future: American Social Visions and the Construction
  of the Panama Canal
Alexander Missal

Imaginary Friends: Representing Quakers in American Culture, 1650–1950
James Emmett Ryan

Countercultural Conservatives: American Evangelism from the Postwar Revival
  to the New Christian Right
Axel R. Schäfer

The Trashing of Margaret Mead: Anatomy of an Anthropological Controversy
Paul Shankman

The Presidents We Imagine: Two Centuries of White House Fictions on the Page,
  on the Stage, Onscreen, and Online
Jeff Smith

Unsafe for Democracy: World War I and the U.S. Justice Department's Covert Campaign
  to Suppress Dissent
William H. Thomas Jr.